The Simon Sainsbury Bequest
to Tate and the National Gallery

THE SIMON SAINSBURY BEQUEST TO TATE AND THE NATIONAL GALLERY

Edited by Andrew Wilson

With contributions by Lucy Askew, Tabitha Barber, Tim Batchelor, Matthew Gale, Christopher Gibbs, Neil MacGregor, Christopher Riopelle and Chris Stephens

Tate Publishing

First published 2008 by order of the Tate Trustees
by Tate Publishing, a division of Tate Enterprises Ltd,
Millbank, London SW1P 4RG

www.tate.org.uk/publishing

In association with National Gallery Company, London

© Tate 2008
Text by Christopher Riopelle © The Trustees of the National Gallery

On the occasion of the exhibition *The Simon Sainsbury Bequest to Tate
and the National Gallery*, Tate Britain, London, 8 July – 5 October 2008

British Library Cataloguing in Publication Data
A catalogue record for this book is available from the British Library

ISBN 978-1-85437-790-6

Library of Congress Cataloging in Publication Data
Library of Congress Control Number: 2008930168

Designed and typeset in Adobe Arno by Dalrymple
Colour reproduction by DL Interactive, London
Printed by Grafos SA, Barcelona

Front cover: Lucian Freud, *Girl with a Kitten* 1947 (cat.16)
Frontispiece: Simon Sainsbury. Photograph by Lord Snowdon, 1958

Measurements of artworks are given in centimetres,
height before width

CONTRIBUTORS
LA   Lucy Askew
TEB   Tabitha Barber
TJB   Tim Batchelor
MG   Matthew Gale
CR   Christopher Riopelle
CS   Chris Stephens
AW   Andrew Wilson

Foreword

This display celebrates the bequest of eighteen paintings made
by Simon Sainsbury to the National Gallery and Tate. Simon
had a rare discernment and a remarkable eye and over a period
of forty years built a magnificent and very personal collection of
art, furniture, antiquities and the decorative arts. Ten years ago he
approached the two institutions offering the group of major paintings that has now become one of the most generous and significant
bequests of recent years.

Simon's collection was distinguished, not only for its breadth,
but also for its very English sensibility. Christopher Gibbs gives us
an insight into the course of Simon's collecting since the 1960s and
explains how collecting – emphasising its privacy – was very much
a part of creating a home and an expression of his passions and
enthusiasms in life. A large part of his collection has now been sold
to benefit The Monument Trust (the trust through which Simon
gave so generously over a forty-year period to a wide range of chari-
ties). Simon believed that, just as he had relished living with his
collection, so should others also have the opportunity to encounter a similar enjoyment through the dispersal of his collection.
However, he also recognised that there were a number of works
in his collection that could have a transformative effect on the
national collections, and this is palpably the case with each of the
eighteen paintings that make up Simon's bequest. For the National
Gallery, the selection of works by Claude Monet, Paul Gauguin,
Henri Rousseau and Edgar Degas dovetail with and will greatly
enrich its collection of Impressionist and Post-Impressionist art;
the paintings by John Wootton, Thomas Gainsborough, Johan

Zoffany, Pierre Bonnard, Victor Pasmore, Balthus, Francis Bacon and Lucian Freud will have a similar impact at Tate.

As this bequest makes clear, Simon was one of Britain's most thoughtful and generous philanthropists. However, most of his donations were made under the cover of The Monument Trust rather than in his own name and it was only through the creation of the Sainsbury Wing at the National Gallery, following the magnificent gift made in 1987 by Simon and his brothers, John and Tim, that Simon's name became more widely known; this is discussed here by Neil MacGregor. Simon's donation and his close involvement with every detail of the Sainsbury Wing was, however, only a small part of his charitable activities over some forty years, and other interests which gained his attention included prison reform, the preservation of historic buildings, social regeneration and research into HIV/Aids. His giving was marked, as were all other areas of his life, by modesty, self-effacement and a desire for privacy that underscored his absolute commitment to the causes he believed in.

NICHOLAS PENNY
Director, The National Gallery

NICHOLAS SEROTA
Director, Tate

Acknowledgements

I would like to express my gratitude to all those who have contributed to this publication. Both to Christopher Gibbs and Neil MacGregor, for their sensitive introductions, as well as to my colleagues here at Tate and at the National Gallery who have written the analytical entries on each painting: Tabitha Barber, Tim Batchelor, Christopher Riopelle, Matthew Gale, Chris Stephens and Lucy Askew.

A publication such as this is necessarily a team effort, and I would like to thank Kate Bell, Robert Dalrymple, Tim Holton, Louise Rice, Mary Richards, Anna Ridley and Claire Young, as well as all of my colleagues working in the many different departments at Tate and the National Gallery, without whose invaluable assistance its production would not have been possible. I would also especially like to thank the following people for their generosity, hospitality and thoughtfulness in responding to my many and varied queries: Kate Austin (Marlborough Fine Art); Mary Buckmaster; Richard Calvocoressi, Charles Cator (Christie's, London); David Dawson; Jean Edmonson (Acquavella Galleries); Richard Gault (Redfern Gallery); Abigail Jones and Thomas Gibson (Thomas Gibson Fine Art); Stewart Grimshaw; James Kirkman; Catherine Lampert; Sarah Hovil and Judith Portrait; Diana Rawstron.

ANDREW WILSON
Curator, Tate

A Search for Beauty

CHRISTOPHER GIBBS

Simon Sainsbury, whose splendid gift to the nation is here celebrated, was a scion of the family of J. Sainsbury & Sons, Grocers. Born in 1930, second of the three sons of Alan, later Lord Sainsbury and his first wife Doreen Adams, he was thus the nephew of Sir Robert, trustee of the Tate Gallery, patron of Francis Bacon, connoisseur, collector and benefactor. After Eton, where he was president of Pop and is still a legend for the dazzling hundred runs that saved the Eton and Harrow cricket match of 1947 at Lords, and Cambridge, where he took a degree in history at Trinity College, he did his military service in the Life Guards as sports officer. He trained as a chartered accountant and then worked in the family business for more than twenty-five years, latterly as deputy chairman and finance director, engineering its public flotation on the London Stock Exchange in 1973.

The next thirty years of his life were spent as an imaginative and thoughtful philanthropist, five of them spent masterminding the wing of the National Gallery that bears his family's name. He served for two terms as a trustee of the National Gallery, chaired the Wallace Collection and gave much of his time to The Monument Trust, the charitable foundation he formed in 1965. He also farmed, rode, enjoyed his racing life and yet still found time to create remarkable collections of French and British paintings, splendid English furniture and English Delft. Almost everything that one might imagine in the home of a fastidious and subtle Englishman came his way, but the collection was constantly refined and ruthlessly edited. Beauty, quality and history were his guiding lights. He was a stranger to vulgarity and the second-rate – a man of innate modesty who yet enjoyed his riches and the sharing of them – his houses, his horses, his garden and his capacity to further (almost invariably invisibly) the causes he cared about.

Fig.1 | Lucian Freud, *Red-Haired Man with Glasses* 1987–8
Oil on canvas, 50.5 × 40.2, private collection

He fitted his collecting activities seamlessly and quietly into a busy life. Never a frantic rifler though catalogues, he made time to see the exhibitions that interested him and visited a wide spectrum of dealers in London, and latterly in New York. There were periods when he bought little and ignored what was on the market; I sometimes wondered whether the rhythms of his shopping sprees owed something to planetary influences – or to surges of enthusiasm for racing, farming or the National Gallery.

Inevitably, the pattern was shaped by space available to house what he bought, and by a certain frugality and an inborn dislike of display. As the years went by and the firm prospered, especially after its public issue, his acquisitions became grander and more frequent. Simon and his companion, Stewart Grimshaw, had their charming house, Woolbeding, beneath the Sussex Downs and their elegant baroque home in Cheyne Walk, Chelsea, where Dante Gabriel Rossetti and Paul Getty had been predecessors. Filling their houses with what pleased and delighted them was an enjoyable ingredient in a busy and useful life, never life's purpose.

In the early 1960s when I first knew him, Simon had a pleasant flat in Chesham Place, Belgravia; second floor, walk up, stuccoed and shuttered. It was furnished with elegant simplicity and hung with modern British and American paintings – Prunella Clough, Milton Avery – in quiet harmony. His friend Bruce Chatwin, then a young porter at Sotheby's, would urge him to empty it all and buy an Assyrian relief and a Jacob sofa. He was not yet ready for such radical stuff. His Uncle Robert lent him a grand Bacon, which he hung for two years and then returned because he couldn't own it. At this time he began to guide the family firm in its corporate collecting, adding works by Bridget Riley and the young Howard Hodgkin.

A thirst for beauty, a lively intelligence and the means to acquire were allied to fruitful relationships, some very long lasting, with dealers in the fields he explored. Thus, in twentieth-century British painting, the young Anthony d'Offay, and Caryl Hubbard and Madeleine Ponsonby at the New Art Centre, and for great paintings both by the French Impressionists and the modern British masters, James Kirkman and Thomas Gibson in London, and Bill Acquavella and Peter Findlay in New York. Of his earlier works, through Leger he bought both the Thomas Gainsborough *Mr and Mrs Carter* (cat.2) and the Johan Zoffany *Colonel Blair with his Family and an Indian Ayah* (cat.3), and some early British pictures and a few Pre-Raphaelites through me. His forty-year partnership with Stewart Grimshaw stimulated and enriched his eye, sharpening his focus on twentieth-century painting and on the decorative arts of the nineteenth and twentieth centuries. Every six months, after Simon had retired from the firm, they would make a visit to New York, stay in the Carlyle, look at exhibitions at MOMA and the Whitney, and buy something remarkable, usually through Bill Acquavella with whom both felt at ease. Towards the end of his life Simon also discovered the antiquities dealer, Joseph Coplin, rekindling a lifelong enthusiasm that had begun with John Hewitt (the most erudite of London dealers over three decades in antiquities, carpets and ethnographical material) and Bruce Chatwin. Their acquisition continually added resonance and depth to his houses, delighting him in the process.

Simon's collecting was wide ranging. Paintings and drawings were at the heart of it, but he also made superb collections of English furniture, the finest London clocks of the late seventeenth-century, English Delft, oriental carpets and antiquities. His taste in furniture, though almost entirely for the English, was eclectic. He bought seventeenth-century oak, eighteenth-century mahogany and walnut, lacquer and gilt wood, but also nineteenth-and twentieth-century pieces, from Gillow to Ernest Gimson. Much of the case furniture was sober, but lit up by wild wonders like the grey painted Chippendale mirror crowned with the high-hatted heads of Siamese twins, and exotic cabinets with inlays of pearl and ivory. He liked things in undisturbed but good condition, but would sometimes re-upholster seat furniture with surprising boldness. His homes were comfortable and harmonious, sometimes unexpected, fascinating foils to the constantly changing procession of flat art. He eschewed the pretty and the dainty, so a Regency folio cabinet beneath an Henri Fantin-Latour of hydrangeas and wallflowers is covered in porphyry vessels from Roman Egypt, and then balanced by a curvaceous and stripy yew wood commode, garnished with a Degas nude teasing her bronze curls beneath the Paul Gauguin still life.

Ceramics, almost entirely English Delft from London and Bristol in the seventeenth and early eighteenth century, glimmered in tall glazed bookcases of oak and mahogany. He bought from Jonathan Horne, Alistair Sampson and Tristram Jellinek, and in the saleroom, where his chief rival in earlier days was known as hissing Sid. When he moved to Sussex in the 1970s he bought a collection of rugs from Peter Hinwood, both Persian and Anatolian, many with Kufic borders, and followed this with regular visits to C. John and to David Franses, adding carpets to rugs, culminating thirty years later in the great Braganza carpet, a miraculously preserved Indo-Inspahan carpet on which the kings of Portugal were crowned. This entirely covered his riverside drawing room. He took me to David Franses to embolden him. When I discreetly whispered how much was being asked, he responded, 'As much as a good Matisse drawing, a very, very good one'. As years went by, flowers from Turkey, Persia and India glowed underfoot in all his houses.

He moved to Thurloe Street in 1964, a light and airy house close to the square, decorated in black and white chic with the help of his friend David Bishop. I remember a dining room with a great grey horse, ascribed hopefully to Jacob Cuyp. There was soon a Bacon, bought from Erica Brausen at the Hanover Gallery, works by Prunella Clough from the New Art Centre, later sold, and in 1969 the lyrical Victor Pasmore, *Hanging Gardens of Hammersmith, No. 1* (cat.11). Here also hung paintings by William Roberts, Edward Wadsworth, Wyndham Lewis, C.R.W. Nevinson and David Bomberg, all bought from Anthony d'Offay, and the first of a series of small but exquisite William Nicholsons bought from Browse and Darby. The furniture was distinguished by form and scale, rather than wilful ornament, and included a tall double domed oak cabinet, from the reign of William and Mary, bought from Sam Wolsey, which was later to house the flower of his Delft collection. With Stewart Grimshaw, in 1965 he had also taken a lease from the National Trust of The Monument, a Gothick tower marking the western limits of the park at Petworth. Furnished with fresh and spare elegance – white-painted eighteenth-century chairs, grey Queen Anne pier glasses, no pictures – it was a stepping stone to Sussex life and the move to Woolbeding, another National Trust property, in 1974.

Simon was by now deputy chairman of J. Sainsbury and the spectacular success of the 1973 flotation made him a richer man. He moved to a bigger London house in Moore Street, Chelsea, with the South Kensington tube rumbling underneath, and then to Egerton Terrace, a quiet haven shaded by a huge tree of heaven. For Woolbeding he bought the grand John Wootton (cat.1) from Ballynatray on the river Blackwater, Co. Waterford. It fitted to within a centimetre or two above the rebuilt stairs in the hall. Philip Jebb had recast the house for him and was a stimulating architectural co-conspirator over many years. About this time, on a visit to New York, he bought from Acquavella the early (1875) *Snow Scene at Argenteuil* by Claude Monet (cat.5) and shortly after, the much later Monet, *Water-Lilies, Setting Sun*, of about 1907 (cat.6). He also bought the George Stubbs of Lord Clarendon's keeper with a dying stag that had belonged to Henry McIlhenny, and from James Kirkman the tender portrait by Lucian Freud *The Painter's Mother IV* (cat.18); the first, smallest and most dazzling of the long series of Freuds, *Boy Smoking* (cat.17) having been acquired from

Marlborough Gallery a few years earlier. In 1978 he bought, also from Acquavella, the splendid Toulouse-Lautrec *Two Women Waltzing* of 1884. This was a time of intense activity. He was still deputy chairman of a thriving business, steering the Monument Trust's charitable giving, working on two houses, including Woolbeding, a project that took two or three years to achieve and which proved a sound initiation for his role ten years on in the creation of the National Gallery's Sainsbury Wing.

In this next decade, in the calm of Sussex, he discovered the rural pursuits that were to remain a life-long delight. He made a memorable garden and farmed the downs above. He took up racing and had more than a hundred winners from the jumpers trained for him by Tim Forster. He hacked over the downs, surveying and tending his kingdom, and was moved by the Paul Nash painting of rimy flints from these same downs, *Encounter in the Afternoon* 1938, originally made for Edward James. He also bought the lovely Paul Signac of boats, the *Harbour at Collioure* in 1981, the charming *Elephant Walk* by Jacques-Emile Blanche that had belonged to Paul Wallraf in 1982, and a group of shelter drawings by Henry Moore. In 1983 came works by John Minton, John Craxton, Paul Nash, Matthew Smith, Harold Gilman, the 1936–8 Pierre Bonnard *The Yellow Boat* (cat.10), two Picasso paintings and three drawings from his daughter Marina. In 1984 came an early Degas portrait of a man, to be followed in 1985 by drawings by Bomberg and Giacometti, three Degas bronzes and a bronze torso by Henry Moore. The next year, from Acquavella, he bought Henri Matisse's *Seated Woman with Greek Torso* and a Balthus still life with apples, as well as the warm glorious Gauguin still life of 1890 (cat.8). He also sold an Odilon Redon (a contribution to the price of the Gauguin) and bought another little Nicholson, *Still Life with Goblet*. In 1987 he bought several watercolours by John Piper. He acquired another Freud, *Annabel Sleeping* 1987–8, and sat to the artist over many hours, with more talk about racing than painting, for his own disturbing portrait *Red-Haired Man with Glasses* (fig.1), which captures aspects of the sitter that elevate it far beyond representation. He also bought for his new house in London a big Walter Sickert of *St Mark's in Venice* and the next year, a Eugène Delacroix watercolour of a Moroccan man that had belonged to Degas from Stephen Mazor in New York, and from James Kirkman the 1946 Freud of the caged *Birds of Olivier Larronde*.

In these closing years of the 1980s and first year of the 1990s Simon's greatest gift to the nation was made – his chairing and orchestrating of the memorably complex National Gallery Sainsbury Wing design by Robert Venturi and Denise Scott Brown.

It involved not only the £12 million or so which he and his brothers, John and Timothy, each gave, but hundreds of committee meetings requiring stringent stewardship and endless diplomacy over nearly five years, a contribution given selflessly. 'John's running the business, Tim's running the country, it had to be me', said Simon. 'Thank God for Simon', said the Venturis.

His last move in 1990 was to a fine early eighteenth-century house in Cheyne Walk, big enough for Stewart to be independently installed upstairs and with tall panelled rooms overlooking the river, where larger scale works could hang and noble eighteenth-century furniture look at home. It took a little while to rearrange the house and garden to his satisfaction, but to make sure it sang, he bought some of his greatest things. The Henri Rousseau portrait of the collector Joseph Brummer (cat.7) was positioned over the fireplace, and at the end of the room, over a marble topped George II console, hung the grand disquieting Balthus, *The Golden Fruit* 1956 (cat.14), which had belonged to Henri Samuel. At the other end was a splendid bookcase from Herriard Park, as architectural as the house itself, filled with Delft chargers, heraldic pill slabs and silver-mounted Elizabethan bellarmines. George II seat furniture, carved mahogany again, clad in old rosy velvet, furnished the room – agonising debates about new upholstery, happily resolved with fresh checked covers, and finally, the Braganza carpet knit all together. Antiquities of granite, marble and terracotta kept coming and between the four windows hung a Picasso head of 1906 and a sublime portrait of a Tahitian girl drawn by Gauguin.

At the top of the Lutyens stair was the big green Simon Bussy portrait of Lytton Strachey's sister Dorothy, a tall William and Mary mirror by John Gumley, water-colours of Box Hill by John Martin and the *Desert of Gizeh* by William Holman Hunt. Downstairs in the library that looked on to the garden was nineteenth-century furniture by Augustus Pugin, Edward William Godwin, Robert Lorimer and William Morris. The room was hung with British nineteenth- and twentieth-century paintings: a Bomberg over the fireplace, a moonlit John Craxton, an Augustus John of Dorelia, a lovely Sickert of a girl in pink, a big Rossetti drawing of firm-jawed Jane Morris and a canal scene by Edward Wadsworth. William De Morgan lustre glimmered and a fine bracket clock by Edward East in a little ebony building shone beneath a big water-colour by Arthur Melville. Books and music were everywhere.

In his business room downstairs, always in wondrous order, hung a Picasso – Janus-faced Dora Maar of 1938 – and a series of Freuds, from the early *Scillonian Beachscape*

1945–6 to the vulnerable blue-clad *Annabel Sleeping* and a very late purchase of autumnal *Buddleia*. Over the fireplace hung a big Bacon and opposite it his early screaming head, the *Study for a Portrait* 1952 (cat.15), bought in 1995 from Thomas Gibson, in a seventeenth-century auricular frame. Across the hall, the small dining room had Morris curtains, a Gimson sideboard and rather earlier British pictures: Henry Lamb's portrait of Lytton Strachey, Dora Carrington's painting of the mill which she shared with Strachey and Ralph Partridge, Stanley Spencer's bold portrait of his housekeeper, Mrs Mundy, a Robert Bevan of horses and carts called *Old Crocks*, and a port scene by Christopher Wood.

His beautiful possessions gave him, and the many who shared them, great pleasure. It was an accumulation that was ever changing, bravely culled and boldly augmented. Dealers, to whom he listened, speak of him with rare warmth. He was the collector who knew a lot but always made up his own mind, swift and courteous in business – there was never an unseemly squabble about money – but who could not be deflected from his regular editing of both paintings and furniture. He wanted others to enjoy his treasures; thus, this splendid gift. He wanted, too, for much of his collection to be sold, to delight a new generation, and silently hoped that his example would spur others to go out and do likewise. His houses spoke of the breadth of his enthusiasm but had a settled feel, with furniture from the seventeenth to the twentieth centuries, paintings either French or British, from Elizabethan portraits to the light-burst of the beautiful Frank Auerbach he bought almost last of all. Old carpets were everywhere and clocks that had ticked for him for forty years. There were antiquities from pre-Columbian to Cycladic, from Egypt, Rome and Greece (among them one might discover a Henry Moore greenstone carving of 1946). He loved his last major antiquity, the Egyptian figure (1800 BC) of the law-giver Sesosteris, seated in the bay window, swimming in the river light. Ever ready to champion the causes of beauty in landscape, architecture and the arts, always silently, yet often offering wisdom and time along with money. He weathered first cancer, then Parkinson's disease, with courage, dignity and humour. Least snobbish, most modest; in racing he preferred Plumpton and Fontwell Park to the grander tracks and enjoyed the local betting shop, though no punter. He searched for beauty, found it, relished it and now passes it on to all of us.

Simon Sainsbury: Collector-Patron

NEIL MACGREGOR

As far as we know, Claude Monet never consciously painted a work for a Queen Anne house in Sussex. But looking at *Water-Lilies, Setting Sun* (cat.6) in the cool elegance of Simon Sainsbury's drawing room at Woolbeding, you could be forgiven for imagining that Monet himself would have felt that this was a uniquely felicitous setting for his late masterpiece.

Modest in dimensions, both picture and drawing room shared and explored the mysterious pleasures of light, darkling and glinting. And the maker of Giverny would unquestionably have enjoyed, and I believe envied, the garden beyond the room, created over three decades by Simon with Stewart Grimshaw. Like the drawing room, itself a tranquil fusion of interior and exterior, Monet's painting fulfilled itself here in a very particular way, one aspect of its achievement privileged and set off, as it could be nowhere else.

Other aspects of *Water-Lilies* will emerge to delight the infinitely more numerous visitors who will see it in the National Gallery. There it will necessarily be a different picture, for it will hang, along with Simon's other Monet, the *Snow Scene* of nearly thirty years earlier (cat.5), in the context of the Gallery's collection of paintings from every period of the artist's life, allowing the range of Monet's work to be shown at last in the same kind of depth as the Gallery can tell the stories of Titian and Rembrandt, Poussin and Claude. For Simon, Monet was one of the supreme artists of the European tradition. Thanks to his generosity, that will now be apparent in Trafalgar Square as never before.

If most of us would have hesitated to guess at Simon's emotions (so admirably were they kept under control), I think it can nonetheless be said with confidence that he loved the National Gallery. It was a love expressed not just through repeated acts of generosity, but through decades of disciplined work and unwavering commitment.

Fig.2 | Simon Sainsbury. Photograph by Tessa Traeger, 2006

For nearly ten years, he was a trustee. Although attentive to all the Gallery's concerns, he most keenly engaged in discussions about acquisitions, vigorously defending the view that this must remain a collection of masterpieces, not become a documentary record of Western painting. Although art history was of course important, the key criterion was aesthetic quality. He was always especially eager to see the collection strengthen its nineteenth-century holdings, but he was, I think, most pleased of all when George Stubbs's *Whistlejacket*, arguably the greatest horse portrait of all time, and certainly the handsomest horse in eighteenth-century England, eventually found its permanent home in Trafalgar Square. Two of Simon's enthusiasms had coincided.

As was evident from Woolbeding or Cheyne Walk, Simon enjoyed the complex game that must always be played in order to make a room of pictures look right. As chairman of the Gallery's Building Committee he oversaw, and in part financed (need I say, very discreetly?) the restoration of the 'old' building, which had to be completely re-hung after the opening of the Sainsbury Wing had changed the chronological sequence of the display. At a cracking pace set by Simon, room after room was restored, re-fabricked and re-lit. The original architectural qualities of the spaces were recovered and enhanced, the overall narrative of the Gallery expanded, and the pictures finally installed under the expert guidance of Michael Wilson. More than anybody I know, Simon had the knack of honouring the intentions of the original architect, while insisting on the proper claims of the pictures now to be displayed as they deserved.

It was this rare combination that enabled him so successfully to steer the building of the Sainsbury Wing, from the appointment of the Venturis as architects in 1986 until its opening by the Queen in 1991.

Five years of meetings. Five years of project managers and quantity surveyors, structural engineers and planning consultants; of sourcing stone from Italy and masons from Portugal, oak from America and glass from Austria; of ensuring that everybody concerned with the project was acknowledged and honoured. But above all, five years of masterful diplomacy. His brothers John and Tim held strong opinions, sometimes vigorously voiced. There were the Trustees to handle – an alarming array of disparate talents, numbering among them Jacob Rothschild and Bridget Riley, and led, as far as the building project was concerned, by Caryl Hubbard, of whose lucid and persistent intelligence Simon was, like all of us, in awe. The budget had constraints. The curators had views. The project had deadlines. On the other hand the architects had their concept and, of course, an unwavering commitment to the artistic integrity of their design.

Every hope, every disgruntlement wound up with Simon and somehow wound up resolved. Robert Venturi and Denise Scott Brown realised that here was a patron of rare sophistication and experience, whose decisions they might sometimes not welcome, but who, throughout the project, consistently commanded their admiration and their respect.

For my colleagues and me, those five years were a master class in how to co-ordinate conflicting demands, while always staying true to one over-riding principle: the primacy of the pictures. There was never any question that the aim of the whole undertaking was to provide the best possible setting for the Gallery's supreme early Renaissance collection. After the opening, Simon's delight in the public's enjoyment of the pictures was profound, and he took special pleasure in the fact that in the first year of the Sainsbury Wing's existence, they were probably seen by more people than had lived in the whole of Italy when Giotto was painting.

Fig.3 | Simon, John and Timothy Sainsbury, The National Gallery, London, 1991

In short, Simon the trustee, Simon the leader of the Sainsbury Wing project was so strikingly successful because he was in everything Simon the collector. The same intransigence, impatience and discerning energy that refined and expanded his own collection drove the creation and construction of the new building on Trafalgar Square, his reshaping of the old galleries and his interventions at the boardroom table.

There is no portrait of Simon in the National Gallery – it is not the habit of the house to honour its benefactors in that way – but it is especially pleasing that among his bequest is Le Douanier Rousseau's portrait of the collector Joseph Brummer (cat.7), which will, in due course, hang in one of the last rooms of the Gallery, near Rousseau's other great picture, *Surprised!* It will strengthen the nineteenth-century holdings and expand the representation of a major artist, and its powerful presence will be noticed and enjoyed by every visitor. Allusively, reticently, it will affirm every-thing Simon sought to achieve for this collection. It is perhaps as much of a public epitaph as he would have wished.

Fig.4 | The National Gallery with view of the Sainsbury Wing

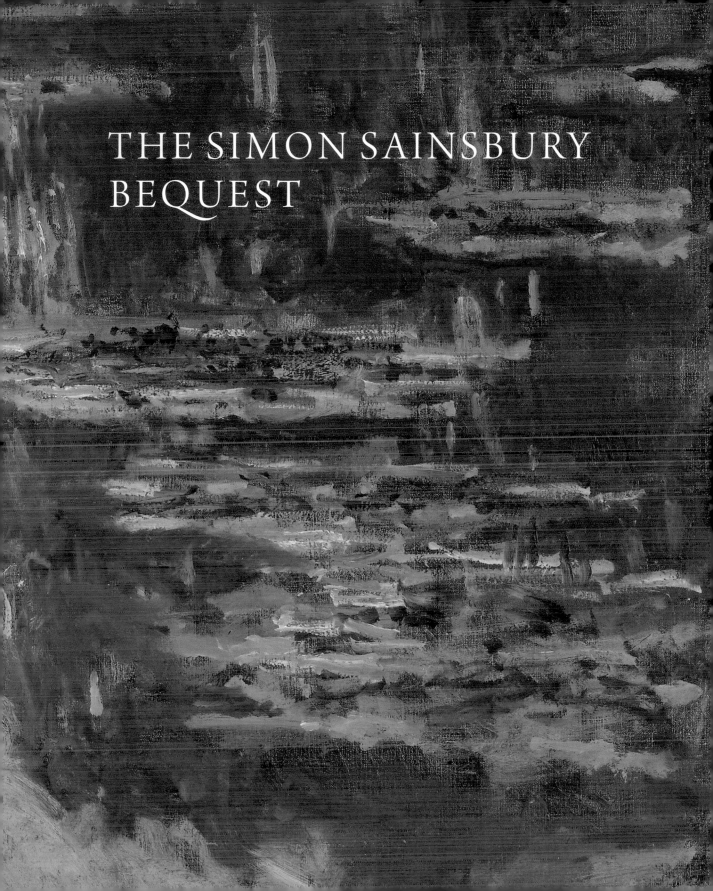

THE SIMON SAINSBURY
BEQUEST

John Wootton 1681/2–1764

1   *Life-Size Horse with a Huntsman Blowing a Horn* 1734

This truly monumental work, both in size and in composition, is one of Wootton's finest single horse paintings. It is signed and dated 1734, on a rock by the side of the stream to the right. This was the period when Wootton, the leading painter of his day for both sporting art as well as landscapes, was creating his tapestry-sized sets of hunting and equestrian scenes for the Great Halls of some of the most important aristocratic houses of England, including Badminton House, Gloucestershire, Althorp, Northamptonshire and Longleat House, Wiltshire.

The Longleat pictures (accepted in lieu of tax and allocated to Tate in 2004, but to remain *in situ* in the Hall at Longleat) were commissioned in the early 1730s by Thomas Thynne, 2nd Viscount Weymouth. Wootton was working on them in 1733–6, and it is therefore not surprising to note compositional parallels with this work. Most striking is the similar hunting horn, silhouetted against the sky, which appears prominently in *Viscount Weymouth's Hunt: Thomas, 2nd Viscount Weymouth, with a Black Page and other Huntsmen at the Kill* (Tate, T11835). The hound, leaping up at the huntsman in anticipation, is also a favourite motif. The subject of Viscount Weymouth's pictures, which form a narrative series, is the hunt, and they are therefore more populated and animated than this single horse portrait. Here, Wootton has created an image of statuesque simplicity, the horse and huntsman standing out starkly against the landscape backdrop. In the 1730s Wootton was arguably at the height of his powers as well as his popularity (a few years earlier, in 1728, he was described as being 'in great Vogue & favour with many persons of ye greatest Quality'),[1] and he was as renowned for his landscapes as he was for his hunting and equestrian pictures. The atmospheric, silvery toned landscape, merging into a subtle sunrise, is a conscious evocation of the classical landscapes of Claude and Nicolas Poussin, lending an elevated mood to the suggested gentleman's estate.[2]

Wootton was creating life-size equestrian images as early as 1711 (for example, the Duke of Rutland's horse, Bonny Black, at Belvoir Castle). They tended to be specific

1

portraits, usually of thoroughbred racehorses but sometimes of hunters, and he also painted hounds, pet dogs and their owners and grooms. This equestrian image is surely a specific portrait too, intended for a dominant position in a stately hunting hall, which brings into question its early provenance. Inherited by descent in the Smyth family of Ballynatray, Glendine, Co. Waterford, it was published in 1992 as depicting a racehorse, the property of Richard Smyth (although Wootton clearly depicts a hunter). The Ballynatray estate, occupying a beautiful position on the Blackwater estuary, was originally owned by Sir Walter Raleigh. Raleigh sold it to Richard Boyle, 1st Earl of Cork, from whom it passed to the Smyth family, Boyle's sister Mary having married Sir Richard Smyth.[3] The owner of Ballynatray House in the 1730s was certainly Richard Smyth, Sir Richard Smyth's grandson, but, so far, there is no evidence of when this picture entered the Ballynatray collection. Smyth never settled in England and Wootton is not known to have travelled to Ireland. It seems, therefore, that Wootton produced this majestic portrait with no first-hand knowledge of the horse's actual appearance. TEB

1 *Life-Size Horse with a Huntsman Blowing a Horn* 1734

Oil on canvas 227.3 × 353
Signed and dated lower right
Tate. Bequeathed by Simon Sainsbury 2006
T12608

PROVENANCE
The Smyth family of Ballynatray, Glendine, Co. Waterford, Ireland, and by descent; Henry Ponsonby 1984; Sotheby's, London, 13 March 1985 (lot 122); Leger Galleries, London; Simon Sainsbury, London, 20 May 1985.

LITERATURE
Mark Bence-Jones, *A Guide to Irish Country Houses*, London 1988, p.27 (photograph of the picture *in situ* in the Hall at Ballynatray)
Leger 1892–1992: A Century of Art Dealing, London 1992, pp.64–5

Thomas Gainsborough 1727–1788

2 *Mr and Mrs Carter* c.1747–8

One of Gainsborough's earliest works, this portrait of Mr and Mrs Carter of Ballingdon-cum-Brundon, just outside Sudbury on the Essex/Suffolk border, first came to public attention when it appeared on the art market in 1983. Never before exhibited, it was first recorded in 1904 in the collection of Canon J.B. Andrews.[1] According to family tradition, the sitters are identifiable as William Carter and his wife Frances, the parents of Frances Andrews (b.1731) who sits genteelly alongside her husband Robert (baptised 1726) in Gainsborough's celebrated *Mr and Mrs Andrews* c.1750 (National Gallery, London; fig.5). In the latter painting, spreading into the distance behind the young married couple is the harvest landscape of their Essex estate, Auberies, in Bulmer, and beyond it is the adjoining parish of Ballingdon, the childhood home of Frances Andrews. The church tower just visible behind the trees is probably All Saints, Sudbury, where Frances was baptised and where the couple were married. Robert Andrews's father had purchased the avowson of the Rectory of Bulmer (the right to appoint the parson).[2] He was buried in the local church, St Andrews, as was William Carter, who directed in his will that he should be placed in a lead coffin 'in a deep Grave in the Chancel without any pall-bearers'.[3]

Fig.5 | Thomas Gainsborough, *Mr and Mrs Andrews* c.1750
Oil on canvas 69.8 × 119.4
The National Gallery, London, NG 6301

2

Bulmer and its surroundings thus had deep personal associations for both families, and Gainsborough's portrait of the Carters is also said to have been painted at Auberies. Unlike *Mr and Mrs Andrews*, however, there is nothing in the landscape background of their picture that specifically links it to Essex, although, as in his daughter and son-in-law's picture, Carter and his wife sit elegantly out of doors, their surroundings and demeanour suggestive of gentlemanly rural living.

The picture's provenance, by direct descent in the Andrews family until 1920, when Canon Andrews sold it to his relatives, the Revd Edgar and Gertrude Stevenson,[4] suggests that the identification of the sitters is correct.[5] William Carter was a merchant and substantial landowner in and around Ballingdon, Bulmer and Sudbury, but also further afield. His date of birth has not been established (the usually-given 1694 baptism at Earls Colne, Essex, son of William Carter and his wife Elizabeth, is a misidentification), but initial research has revealed that his father was George Carter, clerk, of nearby Pentlow.[6] From his father he had inherited freehold land in Foxearth, and in 1730 he consolidated his holdings with land conveyed from his brother George, worth £750.[7] Throughout the rest of his life he gradually accumulated an inheritable estate. The terms of his pre-nuptial settlement of 13 May 1723 had contracted him to purchase £2,000 worth of property, £1,000 for this purpose being provided out of his wife's dowry. A property in Ballingdon, on Ballingdon Street, purchased in 1722, was his principal residence, to which he added further plots of adjoining land, including gardens, orchards and a coach house. He acquired more land and property in Ballingdon, messuages (dwelling-houses with outbuildings and land) in Bures St Mary, Suffolk, leasehold properties in Sudbury and substantial landholdings in Glemsford, which are itemised in his post-nuptial settlement of 20 June 1733.[8] Carter regarded all of the above as his main estate, to be inherited by his eldest son, William. In his will, however, he made further bequests: to his brother George 75 acres in Halstead; to his sister Mary Bridges around 70 acres of Essex farmland; to his son Claude further farmland in Essex, as well as land and tenements in Little and Great Cornard, Suffolk; and to his youngest son Jonathan went over 185 acres of Suffolk and Essex farmland, his freehold and copyhold house and lands in Felixstowe, the avowson of the parish churches of Flempton and Hengrave, as well as part of a freehold property on Gracechurch Street, London, known as The Case of Knives.[9]

Carter was therefore a figure of some substance in the locality and in 1729 had also been appointed one of the Receiver-Generals for Suffolk, a position that entitled him to style himself 'esquire'. The precise nature of his business is unknown, but he is believed to have been a cloth merchant and his marriage to Frances Jamineau (b.1703), the daughter of Claude Jamineau, a wealthy Huguenot merchant of London, was no doubt advantageous to his business.[10] Exactly when Gainsborough painted the Carters is unknown. The portrait is usually dated c.1747–8, making it one of Gainsborough's earliest conversation pieces, executed when he was living in Hatton Garden, London. It is presumed that he made regular trips to his hometown of Sudbury, probably in the summer months, so the Carters could have sat to him on one of these visits. Gainsborough, whose own father had been a prosperous cloth merchant, would have known Carter and they worshipped at the same church, All Saints, Sudbury, where Gainsborough's family is buried.[11] Carter's presumed burial on 27 November 1748 has hitherto provided the latest possible date for the portrait, but this can now be extended a further two years on the discovery of his true date of death, 23 November 1750.[12] Thus the picture could have been painted locally, on Gainsborough's permanent return to his native Suffolk in late 1748 or early 1749.[13] The couple's odd disproportion, however, Carter looming large over his petite wife, possibly indicates a naïve and youthful work; similarities in the screen of trees in *Bumper* 1745 (private collection), Gainsborough's earliest dated work, as well as the absence of any middle ground, also seem to support an earlier dating.[14] On the other hand, the sophisticated handling of the landscape background, with the delicate sunlight filtering through the trees, suggests a work of assured competence. Certainly, Ellis Waterhouse was of the opinion that although the couple appeared 'comical', 'it must have been commissioned to look like that'.[15]

Parallels exist between this picture and other early works, painted before or around 1750, although none are precisely dated, making a progressive chronology difficult to establish. A similar blue dress with wide panniers appears in *Portrait of the Artist with his Wife and Daughter* c.1748 (National Gallery, London); the Carters' rococo garden bench foreshadows the more elaborate one on which their daughter and son-in-law sit; and the elegant plinth placed among the trees, supporting a sculpture of a seated female, is the same as that which originally appeared in *Mr and Mrs Kirby* c.1751–2 (National Portrait Gallery, London), but which Gainsborough painted out.[16] Mrs Carter's outfit is typical of a fashionable, but middle-class, lady of the mid-1740s, while her husband's more old-fashioned wig and cravat could well have been worn by middle-aged gentlemen as late as 1750.[17] The woodland setting, falling away to an

open river landscape on the right, is probably fanciful, adding to the possibility of it having been painted before the specific topography of Essex and Suffolk came to dominate Gainsborough's landscape settings, shown to such marked effect in *Mr and Mrs Andrews*.

In his will Carter is said to have bequeathed to his son-in-law Robert Andrews his moiety, or half share, of the Auberies estate, purchased from Mrs Magrath, supposed heir to the Daniel estates in Essex which had included 'the capital messuage of Awberries, alias Overies'.[18] Gainsborough's *Mr and Mrs Andrews*, therefore, is said not only to celebrate the young couple's marriage of 10 November 1748, but also the unification of the Auberies estate in December 1750, when Carter's will was proved. In fact, the situation does not seem quite so clear-cut. Carter indeed bequeathed freehold land to Andrews that had formerly belonged to Mrs Magrath, but rather than Auberies it was land in Bulmer, Middleton and Little Henny, possibly identifiable as part of Clapps Farm. While the bequest, therefore, would have added to the Andrews's holdings in that area, its importance in relation to Gainsborough's portrait needs further clarification.

What is clear is that both Robert Andrews senior and William Carter shared a determination to establish significant estates in their lifetimes. In his will Carter directs his executors 'as soon as they receive a sum of money that amount to fifty pounds that they put the same immediately out on Land', while Andrews ordered his to 'purchase freehold Lands lying in or as near to Bullmer [*sic*] as may be': Gainsborough's portraits of both the Carters and Robert Andrews's heirs reflect perfectly their success and pride of ownership. *Mr and Mrs Carter* is one of Gainsborough's best-preserved early works, and an important one in the context of Gainsborough's early patronage and his local Sudbury connections. TEB

2 *Mr and Mrs Carter* c.1747–8

Oil on canvas 90.1 × 69.2
Tate. Bequeathed by Simon Sainsbury 2006
T12609

PROVENANCE
Presumed descent in the Andrews family to Canon John Brereton Andrews; his sale Boardman & Oliver, Harlow Vicarage, 18 May 1920; bought by Revd Edgar and Gertrude Stevenson, the latter née Purchas, descendants of Robert Andrews's daughters Harriet and Charlotte respectively; by descent in the Purchas family until sold Christie's, London, 22 April 1983 (lot 93); bought by Leger Galleries, London; Simon Sainsbury, London, 20 May 1985.

EXHIBITED
Realism through Informality, Leger Galleries, London 1983 (no.2; on loan to Gainsborough's House, Sudbury, August 1983)
Young Gainsborough, The National Gallery, London; The Castle Museum, Norwich; The Laing Art Gallery, Newcastle, 1997 (no.26, p.30)

LITERATURE
Sir Walter Armstrong, *Gainsborough and his Place in English Art*, London and New York 1904, p.260
Adrienne Corri, *The Search for Gainsborough*, London 1984, pp.252–8
John Bensusan-Butt, 'The Carters and the Andrews', *Gainsborough's House Review* 1992/3, pp.33–7
Judy Egerton, *National Gallery Catalogues: The British School*, London 1998, p.82

Johan Zoffany 1733–1810

3 *Colonel Blair with his Family and an Indian Ayah* 1786

Zoffany produced this conversation piece showing Colonel Blair (1729–1814)
with his family and an Indian girl during the middle of his period in India (1783–9).
The German-born artist arrived in England in 1760 to great success and received the
patronage of King George III, but by the early 1780s Zoffany had fallen from favour and
decided to seek his fortune from rich members of British society stationed in Bengal.
On 8 March 1783 he enrolled as midshipman on the *Lord Macartney* and sailed from
Portsmouth, arriving in Kolkata (Calcutta) via Chennai (Madras) on 15 September. He
soon received commissions from the most important British figures there including
Sir Elijah Impey, Chief Justice of the Supreme Court of Judicature at Fort William, and
Warren Hastings, Governor-General of Bengal.[1] In 1785 Zoffany travelled to Lucknow,
and it was there in February 1786 that Colonel Blair and his family met the artist. Ozias
Humphrey recorded in his notebook on 19 February the Blair family arriving, 'with a
large suite from Cawnpore'.[2] With the figures arranged in the foreground and painted
landscapes hanging on the wall behind, the Blair conversation piece is similar in its
composition to another picture Zoffany produced during his time in Lucknow, *Colonel
Polier with his Friends* 1786,[3] though more modest in its scale and ambition.

    In the centre of the composition is Colonel Blair, shown wearing his uniform as an
officer in the Bengal Army. He was born William Blair in 1729, the son of John Blair of
Balthayock and the grandson of Peter Blair of Fournart, Perthshire. Blair entered the
Bengal Army as a major on 2 September 1768, being promoted to lieutenant colonel
on 26 February 1778.[4] In around 1780 he was appointed Commandant of Chunargarh
Fort (Chunar Fort) in the Mirzapur District of modern-day Uttar Pradesh. During the
summer of 1781 conflict arose between Warren Hastings and Chait Singh, the Raja of
Varanasi (Benares). Hastings and his retinue were forced to retreat to the security of
Chunar Fort, where he stayed with Blair at his house during the uprising. The painter
William Hodges was accompanying Hastings and recorded the events of this episode,
describing how Blair led a detachment to break up a camp of Chait Singh's forces under

3

the walls of Pateeta, 'which was carried into execution with great gallantry, though with considerable loss'.[5] By the end of September the British forces had regained control and Blair was promoted on 10 December 1781 to the brevet rank of colonel for, 'meritorious services in quelling the insurrection'.[6] Shortly after, in about 1782, Colonel Blair was reassigned to Kanpur (Cawnpore) as commandant of the British forces there. He resigned from the Bengal Army on 19 January 1788 having served the best part of twenty years in India and returned to England. He died at his house in Stratford Place, Marylebone, London, on 27 April 1814, aged eighty-four.

In a scene of warmth and intimacy unusual in the work of Zoffany, Colonel Blair takes the hand and looks into the eyes of his wife Jane, third daughter of the Hon. Roderick Mackenzie, son of John, 2nd Earl of Cromartie. They were married at the church of St Martin-in-the-Fields, London, on 3 March 1768, shortly before they must have sailed for India, and she died on 22 January 1808. She is shown wearing a white satin dress with a turquoise-coloured overdress. Mrs Blair looks ahead to their eldest daughter Jane, who was baptised Jane Frances Blair on 18 September 1773 at Danapur (Dinapore) which was at that time the largest military cantonment of the East India Company in Bengal. She would later elope with her cousin Captain Thomas Blair who was also serving with the Bengal Army in India. They are remembered in the will of Colonel Blair and are recorded as living close to him in Marylebone.[7] Jane is shown wearing a pale blue satin dress and a light yellow overdress. She is seated at a square fortepiano, probably manufactured by the makers Pohlman or Zumpe, and is playing Handel sonatas, her right hand in the action of turning the page. Other sheets of unidentified music are shown resting on the piano and the morah stool by her side. Music was an important aspect of entertainment for the British in India and a Harmonic Society had been established in Kolkata by the early 1760s.[8] Musical entertainment is a feature of other works by Zoffany that he produced in India such as *The Morse and Cator Families* c.1784, which shows Robert Morse playing the cello accompanying his sister Anne Frances on the harpsichord.[9] The harpsichord was considered superior to the piano at this time, the instrument in the Blair conversation piece attesting to their lesser wealth and social standing.[10]

Looking out at the viewer to the right of the composition is the second daughter Maria, wearing a white dress with rose-coloured sash and red shoes. She would later marry William Bodycott Davis, ADC (Aide-de-Camp) to Arthur Wellesley (later 1st Duke of Wellington) in India. The marriage took place in England on 23 May 1803, five days after Davis had retired from the army with the rank of lieutenant colonel. Maria and her husband are also remembered in the will of Colonel Blair and are recorded as living in Nottingham Place, Marylebone, London, close to the residences of her sister and father. Maria is shown as a young girl leaning against her mother's chair and feeding a biscuit to a black and white cat held by an Indian girl of a similar age. To the far right is a King Charles spaniel. The unknown Indian girl wears a kurta (a thin silk or cotton dress) decorated with a striped pattern and the traditional loose-fitting salwar trousers with bare feet. Covering her head and hanging over her shoulders and arms she wears a red hijab of a quality material, possibly cashmere, with a golden trim and lining. She has traditionally been described as an ayah, the old term for a domestic servant combining the functions of maid and nanny. However, the quality of her clothing and the intimate relationship with Maria Blair suggest that she may not fit this role.[11]

At first glance the setting of the composition seems to be outside the Blair house on the veranda. Bright daylight illuminates the family and to the left a column with an ornate capital frames a view to the garden with trees. The ground has the appearance of compacted earth. However, to the right is a view to the inside of the house, and the hanging of the paintings on the wall gives the illusion of an interior room. The overall effect is the impression of a strange conglomeration of both the outside and inside, or the family on the cusp of the two. To the right a curtain is held back to reveal a view of the hall, with a green pier table and rococo gilt-wood pier glass dating from the 1760s. Beyond this is a screen or trellis. The furniture on display is a haphazard mixture which does not seem to fit with the Blair's house and their social position.[12] Colonel Blair sits on a white and gilt armchair with caned seat and back, which looks like the chair used by John Wombell in the Polier group painting. Zoffany may have had a stock of furniture which he used in his paintings, but it is unlikely that he would have taken them on his travels. Alternatively, he may have simply adapted previously painted furniture, or furniture he had encountered in other households, in creating this scene.

Hanging on the wall behind the family are three landscape paintings. All loosely painted, the largest central scene shows a group of Indians encamped with some goats by a river in the foreground. In the middle distance is a procession being led by an elephant with a bullock-cart close behind, passing a bungalow on their way up to a Muslim tomb. The location is probably Sakrigali, a picturesque point on the river Ganges which was painted by other artists in India such as Thomas Daniell.[13] To the right of this scene is a smaller landscape view set on the sandy banks of a river with a palm tree in the distance. It depicts an event of ritual hook-swinging as part of Charak Puja, the popular festival devoted to the deities Shiva and Sakti celebrated in the rural areas of west Bengal. Marked by strict penitence, performers undergo extreme physical pains and stresses in an attempt to reach salvation. The small landscape to the left depicts the ritual scene of sati, the Hindu custom in which the widow is burnt to ashes on her husband's funeral pyre. Here we see the pyre being prepared before the ritual is enacted. It has been suggested that the Blair conversation piece may have been commissioned to celebrate the completion of these landscape paintings by Zoffany and their installation in the Blair household.[14] However, no sketches or records for them are known. It is possible that they were contrived by the artist to fit the scene, the seemingly barbaric rituals of the Indian culture in the background contrasting with the more civilised and compassionate countenance of the British family. TJB

3 *Colonel Blair with his Family and an Indian Ayah* 1786

Oil on canvas 96.5 × 134.6
Tate. Bequeathed by Simon Sainsbury 2006
T12610

PROVENANCE
Commissioned by Colonel William Blair in 1786 (died 1814); Maria Blair, second daughter of the above, who married Colonel William Davis in 1803; Louisa Jane Davis, daughter of the above, who married Edmund Pepys (1806–1878); Captain Arthur Pepys, 4th son of the above (1846–1920); Colonel Christopher Pepys, 3rd son of the above (died 1980); Patricia Pepys, who inherited the painting with her brother, John; sold at auction as the property of the executors of the late J.D.F. Pepys at Sotheby's, London, 18 March 1981 (lot 37); bought by Leger Galleries, London, through whom acquired by Simon Sainsbury, London, 15 July 1985.

EXHIBITED
Royal Academy Winter Exhibition, London 1885 (no.29)
Realism through Informality, Leger Galleries, London 1983 (no.18)

LITERATURE
Victoria Manners and G.C. Williamson, *John Zoffany RA: His Life and Works. 1735–1810*, London 1920, p.111 (repr. as the third image following p.110)
Mildred Archer, *India and British Portraiture 1770–1825*, London 1979, p.157
Richard Leppert, *The Sight of Sound: Music, Representation, and the History of the Body*, Berkeley, CA 1993, pp.114–16
Beth Fowkes Tobin, *Picturing Imperial Power: Colonial Subjects in Eighteenth-Century British Painting*, Durham, North Carolina 1999, pp.123–5

Edgar Degas 1834–1917

4 *After the Bath* 1896

A constant theme of Edgar Degas's art in his later years was the female nude observed from the rear. He studied the subject in oil paintings, pastels, drawings, sculptures and, it seems probable, at least one photograph as well. Most often he posed his models in the studio as if they had just emerged from the bath and were in the act of drying themselves. It is as if the viewer has stumbled upon a scene of intimacy in the moment before the woman herself becomes aware of an alien presence. In the National Gallery's *After the Bath, Woman Drying herself* (fig.6), a pastel of about 1890, the nude is comfortably seated on a low upholstered chair, the yellow slipper on her left foot adding a note of cosy domesticity. Vigorously rubbing her neck with a fleecy white towel, she is oblivious to anything but the sensuous pleasures of the moment, the sense of well-being that infuses her body. In other works, however, Degas positioned his models in more complicated poses, some almost painfully contorted. One such is the present painting. A naked woman sprawls awkwardly on a chaise longue, her body draped along it, one knee raised, the other bent behind her. Her head is all but invisible in the shadows that gather in the

Fig.6 | Edgar Degas, *After the Bath, Woman Drying herself c.*1890–5
Pastel on wove paper laid on millboard 103.5 × 98.5
The National Gallery, London. Purchased 1959
NG 6295

4

corner of the room. The pose has suggested to more than one commentator an unsettling fusion of eroticism and anguish, as if the scene is fraught with swirling, contradictory psychological tensions. Uncomfortable though it may be, the beauty of the pose is unde-niable: the light falling sharply over her arched body accentuates the shadows as they play along her back and catch in the folds of the thick white towel beneath her.

When Degas found a pose that interested him, he often made several variations on the theme, playing with different colour combinations, densities of paint, levels of detail and spatial configurations. (For pastels during these years, he often worked on tracing paper, flipping the sheet in order to work on the figure in reverse as well.) This painting is one of three related oils all titled *After the Bath* executed in about 1896. The genesis of the series is unclear. Two pastel drawings also of about 1896, one more heavily worked than the other,[1] establish the pose of all three oil paintings, but so too does a gelatin silver print photograph that has been convincingly attributed to Degas himself (J. Paul Getty Museum, Los Angeles).[2] Whether the artist's thinking began with the drawing, in imitation of which he then posed the photo, or vice versa, the paintings that followed on from them show a range of responses to the initial configuration. The present work is the smallest of the three but it is also the most complex spatially and the most heavily worked. Flowery paper covers the two walls that meet directly behind the tub. In the foreground a still-life grouping of sponge, basin and ewer stands on a pale blue countertop angled away from the picture plane. It intervenes between the viewer and the nude, the rounded and weighty forms of the objects on it echoing the body of the woman herself. The ewer and basin are monumental presences in the painting, with dark under-layers of blue paint showing through a top layer of dry pink pigment. Such details anticipate some of Picasso's most monumental 'neo-classical' still-life paintings of the post-war era a generation later.

The second version (private collection) – although the actual sequence is conjectural – is in a vertical format unusual for Degas. Here, the bathtub, empty and gaping in the foreground, intervenes between viewer and nude. The canvas as a whole is particularly subtle in colouration, especially in the gradations of tone along the woman's back and buttocks. By contrast, in the largest version (Philadelphia Museum of Art) the woman is more immediately accessible physically, as no objects come between viewer and nude. The canvas is also far sparer, much more thinly painted and of an almost monochromatic red hue. The Philadelphia painting, as well as the National Gallery's own *Combing the Hair c.*1896 (NG 4865), another fiery red composition related to it, have been adduced as evidence of Degas's failing eyesight late in life and his need to use stronger and simpler colours. But all three works date from the same moment, which suggests on the contrary that Degas sometimes painted in monochrome, other times opting for more complicated compositions and colour schemes, but that these were primarily aesthetic choices not having much to do with physiological constraints.

The National Gallery holds a rich collection of eleven paintings and pastels by Degas. Along with a further four on long-term loan, they trace the artist's career from its beginnings. Indeed, along with Monet, Degas is the nineteenth-century painter the Gallery is able to show in greatest depth. This radiant, complex bathing scene, at once intimate and bold, signally strengthens the representation of his later works, however, paintings of a startling modernity and intensity of expression. Degas's works of the 1890s and beyond constitute one of the great 'late period' renewals of artistic energy and imagination in the western tradition. A comparison with Titian in his final, ferociously creative decades comes to mind. *After the Bath* is also a major addition, carrying it to the brink of the twentieth century, to the National Gallery's collection of works on a theme central to the European painting tradition, the female nude. CR

4 *After the Bath* 1896

Après le Bain

Oil on canvas 77 × 83 · Unsigned
The National Gallery, London. Bequeathed by Simon Sainsbury 2006

PROVENANCE
Ambroise Vollard, Paris; Tryggve Sagen, Kristiania (now Oslo), Norway; Alphonse Kann, Saint-Germain-en-Laye and London, by 1937; bequeathed by Kann to Michael Stewart, England, 1948; acquired from Stewart by Arthur Tooth and Sons, October 1953; acquired from Tooth by Sir Alexander Korda, 3 November 1953; Mrs David Metcalfe (Korda's widow); her sale, Sotheby's, London, 14 June 1962 (lot 20), bought by Rosenberg and Stiebel, New York; Henry Ford II, Grosse Pointe, Michigan; his sale, Christie's, New York, 13 May 1980 (lot 8), bought by Wendell Cherry; Wendell Cherry sale, Sotheby's, New York, 13 May 1998 (lot 11), bought by

Acquavella Galleries, New York; acquired from Acquavella Galleries by Simon Sainsbury, London, November 1999.

EXHIBITED
Cinquante ans de Peinture Française, Musée des Arts Decoratifs, Paris 1925 (no.32)
Degas, Musée de l'Orangerie, Paris 1937 (no.52)
Recent Acquisitions VIII, Arthur Tooth and Sons, London 1953 (no.21)

LITERATURE
Degas, ed. A. Vollard, Paris 1914, pl.68
J. Meier-Graefe, *Degas*, Munich 1920, pl.70
P.A. Lemoisne, *Degas: son art, son oeuvre*, Paris 1946, vol.III, no.1233
R. Gordon and A. Forge, *Degas*, New York 1988, repr. p.222
J.S. Boggs, *Degas*, exh. cat., Galeries Nationales du Grand Palais, Paris; National Gallery of Canada, Ottawa; Metropolitan Museum of Art, New York, 1988–9, pp.548, 549

Claude Monet 1840–1926

Monet was pre-eminently a painter of place. As his experience of a location deepened, so too did his desire to explore it through his paintings and to assemble a visual survey of its many facets. Among the earliest sites he intensively studied in this way was Argenteuil, a town along the river Seine to the west of Paris where he moved with his family in 1871. Initially, they lived at 2 rue Pierre Guienne, near the newly-constructed iron railway bridge spanning the Seine, which figures in many of his paintings. In 1874 they relocated around the corner to 5 boulevard Saint-Denis, a larger and more expensive house – Monet's income was improving during these years – remaining there until January 1878. Just fifteen minutes by train from Paris, Argenteuil was a popular destination for Sunday outings and pleasure boating. At a critical moment in his career, it provided Monet with the charms of country life and the amenities of a rapidly growing suburb of the capital. It also presented him with a variety of motifs, old and modern, natural and man-made, all of them changing with the times of day, the weather and the seasons. Monet painted some 200 landscapes of the town and its environs during his stay, and it was there that he perfected his Impressionist technique.

December 1874 saw record snowfall in the region. Although January 1875 was wet, more snow fell in February. Monet had long enjoyed painting winter landscapes and that season he executed no fewer than eighteen views of Argenteuil in the snow, many in the vicinity of his boulevard Saint-Denis home.[1] The present painting shows the boulevard looking towards its junction with the rue de la Voie-des-Bans, with the Seine beyond. The local railway station would have been directly behind Monet as he worked. Of the eighteen snow scenes, this one is by some considerable margin the largest. Canvas size is always a matter of significance with Monet. When he chose to work on a larger scale, he was often hoping to achieve more generalised and atmospheric effects and was willing to sacrifice individual detail in pursuit of this goal. While many of the smaller snow scenes are more richly detailed – some almost anecdotal in their depiction of the to and fro of a small town in wintertime – here the

painting is an almost monochromatic study in closely-valued blues and greys, although shot through with quick accents of colour here and there. The paint along the road in the foreground is markedly thicker than elsewhere on the canvas, as if Monet were attempting to achieve a painterly approximation of the physical presence of thick snow. The canvas is suffused with the ambient mood of a moist and overcast winter's afternoon as the light slowly begins to fade from the sky.

Monet's remarkable skills in suggesting an encompassing atmospheric envelope in such paintings – what he and his contemporaries called an 'effect' – were particularly admired by his fellow Impressionist artists. Indeed, *Snow Scene at Argenteuil* elicited high praise from Edouard Manet himself. He saw the painting when it was in the collection of its first owner, the art critic and connoisseur Théodore Duret. As Duret recounts, the older painter 'considered [Monet] a complete master in his sphere. One winter he [Manet] wanted to paint an effect of snow; I owned one of Monet's which he came to see; he said after examining it: "It is perfect; I would not know how to do better."'[2] At the National Gallery it joins eleven other works by the artist, as well as paintings on long-term loan, of which the first to enter the collection, during the artist's lifetime in 1917, was another winter scene, *Lavacourt under Snow* of about 1878–81 (fig.7), while a more recent acquisition, *The Petit Bras of the Seine* 1872 (NG 6395) shows a stretch of the river immediately adjacent to Argenteuil during the time Monet lived there.

The Argenteuil snow scenes of 1874–5, variations on a wintry theme, anticipate Monet's later series paintings where he depicted the same or very similar motifs over

Fig.7 | Claude Monet,
Lavacourt under Snow c.1878–81
Oil on canvas 59.7 × 80.6
The National Gallery, London.
Bequest of Sir Hugh Lane, 1917
NG 3262

and over again in different conditions of light and atmosphere. Among them, perhaps the most famous series, and certainly the one that occupied Monet for the longest time and produced the largest number of canvasses, was that executed in and around the water-lily pond in the lower of the artist's two gardens at Giverny in Normandy, where he passed the final decades of his long life. *Water-Lilies, Setting Sun c.*1907 is from that series. A richly atmospheric, even melancholic, work – and a spatially complex one as well – it shows pink and yellow rays of the setting sun reflected in the still waters of the lily pond. Also reflected, upside down, its tendrils seeming to float upwards, is a weeping willow on the opposite bank, although, ambiguously, the actual tree is not depicted. Lily pads drift across the water's surface, the depth of which is intimated by vertical strokes of pink in the upper right quadrant of the painting. Tall reeds spring from the water at lower left, almost calligraphic accents dancing across the canvas. The viewer senses that the light will have entirely ebbed away in another fifteen minutes and night have descended on the paradise Monet created for himself, and for his art, at Giverny.

The date of the painting has been the subject of conjecture. A closely related work is illegibly dated either 1907 or 1917.[3] (The painting was stolen in 1972. Thus the interpretation of the date is based on old photographs.) Daniel Wildenstein tentatively opted for the earlier date. Among his reasons, Monet often painted canvasses of this more-or-less square format at that time, but fewer in later years. The artist still had the canvas with him at Giverny in 1923, however, when he sold a group of paintings to the dealer Bernheim-Jeune, including five *Water-Lilies* of which *Water-Lilies, Setting Sun* was one. A brief letter Monet wrote to Bernheim-Jeune at the time of the sale on 16 July 1923 provides salient kernels of information relating to the painting.[4]

Monet first informs the dealer that he had affixed his signature to the paintings he was selling that had not been signed previously, the day before. Thus, the bright red signature at the lower left here may date from as late as 1923. He then goes on to begin to arrange for the dealer to pick up the works, but adds 'as for *Water-Lilies, Setting Sun*, allow me to keep it'. Although he does not specifically connect the request to hold on to the painting to what follows, in the next sentence Monet informs Bernheim-Jeune that in two days' time he will have an operation; the dealer will be informed of the results. Monet's operation in July 1923 was the third of three cataract procedures he underwent that year in the hope of improving his eyesight. Thus, as he is about to undergo treatment on his eyes he asks to keep back a painting, ensuring that it will be at hand upon his recovery. Did he wish to re-study the work when his eyesight improved? Did he

want to re-consider its notable spatial and colouristic complexity? Did he perhaps even intend to return to the canvas, brush in hand, after the operation? It is impossible to say, but a letter of 12 September of that same year informs Bernheim-Jeune that the picture had been picked up for delivery to the dealer that morning.[5]

Water-Lilies, Setting Sun, along with four other *Water-Lilies* sold to Bernheim-Jeune in July 1923, was intended for one of the most passionate collectors of Monet's late works, the wealthy Parisian pharmacist Henri Cannone. Enthusiastically jumping into the market in about 1920, Cannone formed a collection of some forty paintings by the artist, of which seventeen were *Water-Lilies*. He was buying at the same time as Monet was at work on his monumental cycle of water-lily pond images, known as the *Grandes Décorations,* which were intended for public display in the Musée de l'Orangerie in Paris. They remain there to this day, a final statement of Monet's grand landscape vision. Cannone, for his part, shared the conviction of discerning contemporaries like the French prime minister, Georges Clemenceau, who had commissioned the *Grandes Décorations* for the state, that the late, large and remarkably free landscape improvisations Monet was creating at Giverny represented an astonishing renewal of artistic genius in old age. If subsequent generations did not share this appreciation, the reputation of Monet's late works declining immediately upon his death, recent decades have witnessed a resurgence of admiration for them. Today, the late paintings are again

Fig.8 | Claude Monet, *Irises c.*1914–17
Oil on canvas 200.7 × 149.9
The National Gallery, London. Purchased 1967
NG 6383

widely considered to be among the most audacious and innovative manifestations of 'pure' painting in the twentieth century. At the National Gallery, the work joins a *Water-Lilies* dating from approximately 1916, monumental in scale at more than 425 cm long (NG 6343). (It hangs on long-term loan at Tate Modern.) Two further paintings show aspects of the Giverny water garden. An 1899 painting titled *Water-Lily Pond* shows the Japanese bridge that arches over the pond (NG 4240). Another shows *Irises* near the pond and may have been painted by Monet looking down on them from the Japanese bridge (fig.8). A much later *Japanese Bridge* (1919–42) in which form all but dissolves in the scintillating play of paint, is on loan from a private collector.[6] Together with works spanning Monet's entire career, they ensure that the National Gallery offers the finest survey of the artist's achievement to be seen in the United Kingdom. CR

5 *Snow Scene at Argenteuil* 1875	6 *Water-Lilies, Setting Sun* c.1907
Rue sous la neige, Argenteuil	*Nymphéas, soleil couchant*

5 *Snow Scene at Argenteuil* 1875

Rue sous la neige, Argenteuil

Oil on canvas 71 × 91.5
Signed at lower right: *Claude Monet*
The National Gallery, London. Bequeathed by
Simon Sainsbury 2006
NG 6607

PROVENANCE
Acquired from the artist by Théodore Duret,
December 1879; with Boussod, Valadon et Cie,
Paris, 1892; acquired by Harris Whittemore,
Naugatuck, CT, 1893; private collection, USA;
Acquavella Galleries, New York, early 1970s; [...];
Simon Sainsbury, London.

EXHIBITED
London's Monets, K. Adler and J. Leighton, The
National Gallery, London 1997 (no.10, repr.)

LITERATURE
Théodore Duret, *Histoire d'Ed. Manet et de son
oeuvre*, Paris 1902, p.100
Daniel Wildenstein, *Claude Monet: Biographie et
Catalogue Raisonné*, Paris 1974, vol.I, no.352, repr.
Daniel Wildenstein, *Monet: Catalogue Raisonné*,
Cologne 1996, vol.II, no.352, repr.

6 *Water-Lilies, Setting Sun* c.1907

Nymphéas, soleil couchant

Oil on canvas 73 × 92
Signed at lower left: *Claude Monet*
The National Gallery, London. Bequeathed by
Simon Sainsbury 2006
NG 6608

PROVENANCE
Sold by Monet to Bernheim-Jeune, Paris, August
1923; Henri Cannone, Paris, January 1924; Durand-
Ruel, Paris; anonymous sale, Palais Galliera, Paris,
2 June 1971 (lot 92); anonymous sale, Christie's,
London, 2 December 1975 (lot 25); Simon
Sainsbury, London.

EXHIBITED
London's Monets, K. Adler and J. Leighton, The
National Gallery, London, 1997 (no.21, repr.)

LITERATURE
Arsene Alexandre, *La Collection Cannone*, Paris
1930, pp.37, 40, 41, repr.
Daniel Wildenstein, *Claude Monet: Biographie
et Catalogue Raisonné*, Paris 1974, vol.IV, no.1719,
letter nos.2525, 2537, 2532
Daniel Wildenstein, *Monet: Catalogue Raisonné*,
Cologne 1996, vol.IV, no.1719, repr.

Henri Rousseau, called Le Douanier 1844–1910

7 *Portrait of Joseph Brummer (Portrait Landscape)* 1909

The eccentric customs clerk and self-taught artist Henri Rousseau, though he lived and died largely in poverty, nonetheless in his final years attracted a coterie of enthusiastic supporters. They were drawn to the naïve power and originality of his paintings and promoted him among fellow artists, critics and collectors, making him for a time something of a darling of the Parisian avant-garde. One such enthusiast was Pablo Picasso (1881–1973) who collected Rousseau's works and in autumn 1908 held a somewhat tongue-in-cheek banquet in his honour in his (Picasso's) studio at the Bateau-Lavoir, an event that now enjoys renown in the annals of bohemian Montmartre.[1] Gertrude Stein in her best-selling book *The Autobiography of Alice B. Toklas* (1933) penned a famous account of the evening. One other early enthusiast was the American painter Max Weber (1881–1962) who bruited Rousseau's achievement on both sides of the Atlantic and, perhaps as important, introduced him to Joseph Brummer (1883–1947) who would also quickly become a champion, and then a patron, of the older painter.

Brummer had arrived in Paris from his native Hungary in 1906 intending to become a sculptor. Among many odd jobs he took to make ends meet he shaped marbles for Rodin, and for a time he and Weber both studied with Henri Matisse. He also embarked on art dealing, in Japanese prints and African sculpture – the latter itself an enthusiasm of the moment among the avant-garde – at which he quickly demonstrated an intuitive talent; by October 1909 he could afford to open a gallery on the boulevard Raspail.[2] In the spring of 1908, Brummer made Rousseau's acquaintance, thanks to Weber, and fell under the painter's strange spell. He immediately began promoting Rousseau's work among his clients and buying them for his own collection. The following year, he commissioned the artist to paint his portrait on a monumental scale. As Rousseau worked on the painting, on 28 April 1909 he reported in a letter to Guillaume Apollinaire that he was very short of money 'and this evening I have only 15 centimes for supper'.[3] The 300 francs the increasingly flush Brummer paid him for the portrait would have seemed like a fortune, and a godsend, to Rousseau.

The painting is a masterpiece of early twentieth-century portraiture and the only full-length, seated portrait in the artist's oeuvre. Rousseau had Brummer pose in a large wicker chair gazing resolutely out at the viewer. The symmetrical composition confers on him exceptional poise and *gravitas*, imbuing him with the authority and hieratic intensity of a king on a throne. Rousseau paid particular attention to Brummer's features, all but carving out the volumes and planes of his face with his brush. Only the lit cigarette, an unorthodox sceptre lightly held between the young man's fingers, softens the austerity of the image, endowing it with an air of nonchalance. As in many of his portraits, the sitter is depicted in a landscape; Rousseau called such works 'portrait landscapes', the background being intended as a 'commentary' on the sitter's character. Here, Brummer is framed by jungle-like trees and bushes, an allusion, perhaps, to his foreignness and fascination with things African. He is also placed slightly off-centre in the composition, an old artists' trick to confer a hint of spontaneity to a composition.

Rousseau held the traditions of French academic painting in high regard. He felt that he worked in the manner of a Jean-Léon Gérôme or Ernest Meissonier, or indeed of the great Ingres himself, all technical perfectionists. Aspects of the Brummer portrait hark back to Ingres, whose *Napoleon Enthroned* of 1806 (Musée de l'Armée, Paris) and *Portrait of Monsieur Bertin* of 1832 (Musée du Louvre, Paris) share with it monumentality, hieratic frontality and seated poses. Cézanne's seated *Portrait of Achille Empéraire* of 1870 (Musée d'Orsay, Paris), which Rousseau almost certainly saw when it was exhibited at the 1907 Salon d'Automne, has also been adduced as a source. Of course, by 1909 Rousseau was on intimate terms with Picasso. He thought the younger artist's praise to be entirely justified, returning the compliment, not unenigmatically, by declaring Picasso to be the greatest painter working in the 'Egyptian' style.[4] He surely would have known too that Picasso's most important portrait to date, of his patron – just as Brummer was Rousseau's – a painting moreover deeply indebted to the precedent of Ingres's *Monsieur Bertin*, also shows a looming seated figure; the *Portrait of Gertrude Stein* of 1906 (Metropolitan Museum of Art, New York). Indeed, is it not possible to see in the facets and planes of Brummer's face, the pyramidal eyebrows, a response to the 'African' and proto-Cubist features of the Stein portrait.

Joseph Brummer quickly became one of Rousseau's most famous paintings, capturing the attention of Picasso and Fernand Léger, entering the collection of the pioneering German art critic Wilhelm Uhde, author of the first monograph on Rousseau, and hanging on loan for long periods of time between 1939 and 1990 amid seminal works of twentieth-century art in such institutions as the Museum of Modern Art, New York, the Kunsthalle Hamburg and the Kunsthalle Basel. At the National Gallery it joins one other Rousseau masterpiece, *Surprised!* of 1891 (fig.9), the earliest and most painstakingly executed of Rousseau's imaginary jungle scenes. With their luxuriant backdrops of vegetation, both pictures illustrate Rousseau's delight in the exotic, inspired not by foreign travel but by trips to the zoo and the Jardin des Plantes in Paris, by avid reading of illustrated tales of adventure set in foreign climes, and by an unfettered, ingenuous imagination. It also takes its rightful place at the Gallery in the long European portrait tradition, from Jan van Eyck's *Arnolfini Portrait* to Hans Holbein's *Ambassadors,* Thomas Gainsborough's *Morning Walk* to Ingres's *Madame Moitessier,* ceding nothing to them in its air of monumental self-assurance. CR

Fig.9 | Henri Rousseau, *Surprised!* 1891 · Oil on canvas 129.8 × 161.9
The National Gallery, London, NG 6421

7 Portrait of Joseph Brummer (Portrait Landscape) 1909

Portrait de Joseph Brummer (Portrait paysage)

Oil on canvas 116 × 89
Signed and dated at lower left: *H. Rousseau / 1909*
The National Gallery, London. Bequeathed by
Simon Sainsbury 2006

PROVENANCE
Commissioned from the artist by Joseph Brummer,
Paris, 1909; Wilhelm Uhde, Paris, 1912; confiscated
by the French Government as enemy (German)
property, 1914; sale of the sequestered property
of Wilhelm Uhde, Hôtel Drouot (expert Léonce
Rosenberg), Paris, 20 May 1921 (lot 56); bought
by Oscar Mietschaninoff (1886–1956); Oscar
Mietschaninoff sale, Hôtel Drouot (experts
Hessel and Bignou), Paris, 16 December 1927
(lot 21); bought by Fukushima Shigetaro ('Baron
Fukushima'), Paris, until 1933; Galerie Raphaël
Gérard, Paris, by 1936; Dr Franz Meyer, Zurich,
bought through Henry Bing, 1936, and thence by
descent; anonymous sale, Christie's, London, 29
November 1993 (lot 12); Simon Sainsbury, London.

EXHIBITED
XXVème Salon de la Société des Artistes Indépendants,
Paris, Les Grandes Serres de l'Orangerie 1909
(no.1386 as *Portrait (paysage)*)
Henri Rousseau: Exposition Posthume, Galerie Paul
Rosenberg, Paris 1910 (no.8)
Henri Rousseau, Marie Harriman Gallery, New York
1931 (no.5)
Fifty Years of Portraits, The Leicester Galleries,
London 1935 (no.121)
Les Maîtres populaires de la Réalité, Salle Royale,
Paris; Kunsthaus, Zurich, 1937 (no.9)
On loan to the Museum of Modern Art, New York
1939–62
Henri Rousseau, The Art Institute of Chicago; The
Museum of Modern Art, New York, 1942
6 Post-Impressionists, Wildenstein & Co., New York
1942 (no.42)

Henri Rousseau, Sidney Janis Gallery, New York
1951 (no.22)
*Henri Rousseau, 1844–1910: Exposition de son
cinquantenaire*, Galerie Charpentier, Paris 1961
(no.66)
Das naive Bild der Welt, Staatliche Kunsthalle,
Baden-Baden 1961 (no.169)
On loan to the Museum of Fine Arts, Houston
1962–5
Le Monde des Naïfs, Musée National d'Art
Moderne, Paris 1964 (no.24)
The Heroic Years, Paris 1908–1911, Museum of Fine
Arts, Houston 1965
On loan to the Kunsthalle, Hamburg 1965–9
On loan to the Kunsthalle, Basel 1969–90
Die Kunst der Naiven, Kunsthaus Zurich 1975 (no.
H75)
Le Douanier Rousseau, Galeries Nationales du
Grand Palais, Paris; Museum of Modern Art, New
York, 1984–5 (no.56, repr. p.233)

LITERATURE
Les Soirées de Paris, Paris, 15 January 1914, pp.50–2
Wilhelm Uhde, *Henri Rousseau*, Dresden 1921, p.88
Daniel Catton Rich, *Henri Rousseau*, New York
1942, pp.52, 55, 58, repr. p. 59
Roger Shattuck, *The Banquet Years*, New York 1958,
pp.65, 69, 75, 283, no.50, repr. pl.5
Jean Bouret, *Henri Rousseau*, Neuchâtel 1961, repr.
col. pl.46
Dora Vallier, *Henri Rousseau*, Paris 1961, no.134,
repr.
André Salmon, *H. Rousseau*, Paris 1962, repr. col.
p.73
Dora Vallier, *L'Opera Completa di Rousseau il
Doganiere*, Milan 1969, pp.108–9, no.224, repr. col.
pl.LI
Yann Le Pichon, *Le Monde du Douanier Rousseau*,
Paris 1981, repr. col., p.79
Frances Morris et al., *Jungles in Paris*, exh. cat., Tate
Modern, London; Galeries Nationales du Grand
Palais, Paris; National Gallery of Art, Washington
DC, 2005–6, pp.22, 23, repr.

Paul Gauguin 1848–1903

8 *Bowl of Fruit and a Tankard before a Window* probably 1890

While he was a prosperous Paris stockbroker and amateur artist, in the years around 1880, Paul Gauguin acquired six paintings by Paul Cézanne. Of these his greatest admiration seems to have been reserved for *Still Life with Fruit Dish* 1879–80 (fig.10). In 1883 he left behind much of his collection in Copenhagen when he split up with his Danish-born wife and returned to Paris to take up art full time, but appears to have brought back the still life with him. He refused to sell it in 1888 although desperate for funds. In 1890 it accompanied him to Brittany where he included it in the background of his *Portrait of a Woman* (Art Institute of Chicago) painted at about that time. He also used it as a kind of talisman to teach fellow artists gathered around him in Brittany about the artist at work in distant Provence who, he had come to believe, was showing the way forward to a new, more monumental mode of painting.

It was probably in 1890 as well that Gauguin painted this still life combining many of the elements – fruit, pottery and a rumpled linen tablecloth in which the objects

Fig.10 | Paul Cézanne
1839–1906, *Still Life with Fruit Dish* 1879–80
Oil on canvas 46.4 × 54.6
The Museum of Modern Art, New York, Fractional Gift of Mr and Mrs David Rockefeller

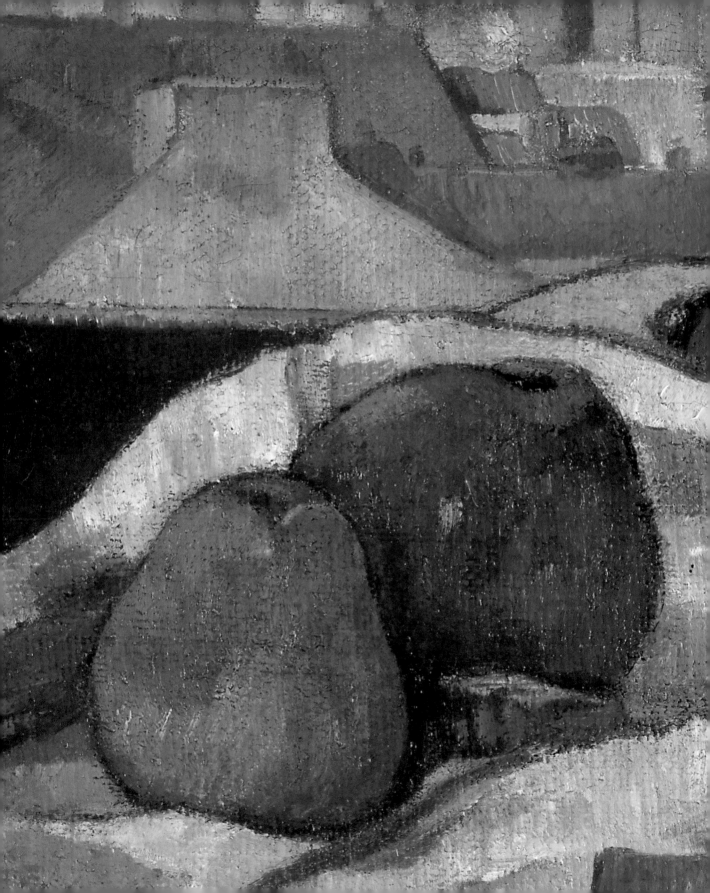

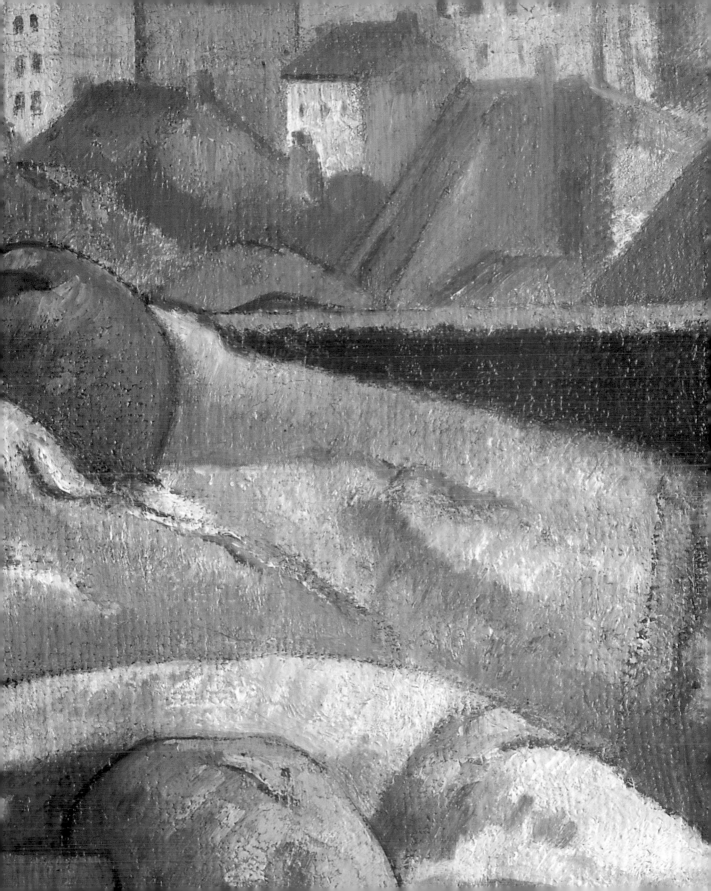

nestle – that Cézanne had employed in his work a decade earlier; the angled knife at lower right in Gauguin's painting is very close to being a quotation from Cézanne's canvas, which might have hung nearby as he worked. The painting is in part an act of homage to Cézanne, by one of his most impassioned admirers. It is also precious evidence of the role Cézanne was coming to play as an exemplar for a handful of French avant-garde artists led by Gauguin, at a time when, isolated in the South of France, he remained virtually unknown to the wider world. Writing about the painting in 1925 the critic Waldemar George noted Gauguin's extensive debt to Cézanne, 'from whom he borrowed his technique, his sense of colour, his vision'.[1]

More than that, the painting is a statement of what Gauguin himself was hoping to achieve in painting at a vital turning point in his career. Like Cézanne, he wished to move beyond Impressionism to an art less reliant on the recording of optical phenomena but aspiring to greater visual complexity and structural rigour. This work combines urgency and directness in the depiction of foodstuffs and objects. The broad weave of the canvas underscores the sense of primitive authenticity. The tankard, humble but solid, surely alludes to the peasants and fishermen among whom Gauguin, searching for a deeper resonance in his art, had settled in Brittany. (The specific source for what probably represents a work of indigenous Breton pottery has not yet been identified.) No less humble is the bowl with a semi-circular indentation along its rim which holds the fruit; it would appear to be a utilitarian man's shaving bowl rather than fine tableware.

At the same time, the painting shows Gauguin's increasing interest in the decorative patterning of forms, the use of bright colours and in collapsing together near and distant spaces. The narrow strip along the upper edge of the painting, for example, shows a view through a window to a town beyond. It is like a second still life composed of roofs and chimneys. So abbreviated is this detail that it registers at first almost as abstract patterning. It may be based on a photograph; Gauguin was a leader among his contemporaries in making wide use of photographic sources in his art. Such decorative tendencies, which Gauguin began exploring in Brittany, came to play an increasing role in the monumental works he executed when he relocated soon afterwards to the South Seas in search of even more primitive and authentic societies.

No explanation has been proposed for why the artist's distinctive signature at the lower left, *P. Go.*, which he began to use at about this time, should have been painted upside down. Such a signature is not unique in his work, however, as a chronologically related painting, *Bathers on the Beach* was signed more fully, *P. Gauguin 90*, but also upside down.[2] Perhaps by doing so here, Gauguin intended to turn the signature into part of the painting's overall decorative patterning, like initials carved with a flourish into the tabletop.

The painting contrasts tellingly with the National Gallery's only other work by Gauguin, also a still life, the brilliantly coloured Tahitian-period *Vase of Flowers* of 1896, a work acquired in 1918 from the collection of Edgar Degas, where the artist's exploration of the decorative is carried even further. It also complements Cézanne's unfinished *Still Life with Water Jug*, on long-term loan to the National Gallery from Tate, and suggests something of the complex dialogue between the works of these two artists in the years around 1890. CR

8 *Bowl of Fruit and a Tankard before a Window* probably 1890

Coupe de fruits et pichet devant la fenêtre

Oil on canvas 50 × 61
Signed at lower left (upside down): *P. Go*
The National Gallery, London. Bequeathed by
Simon Sainsbury 2006
NG 6609

PROVENANCE
Dr Georges Viau (1855–1939), by 1925; M.M. Wildenstein, New York, by 1936; private collection, Buenos Aires, by 1972; J.T. Dorrance, Philadelphia; Acquavella Galleries, New York 1986; Simon Sainsbury, London, November 1986.

EXHIBITED
Paul Gauguin, Kunsthalle, Basel 1928 (no.53)
Paul Gauguin, Galerien Thannhauser, Berlin 1928 (no.47)
Paul Gauguin 1848–1903: A Retrospective Loan Exhibition for the Benefit of les Amis de Gauguin and the Penn Normal Industrial and Agricultural School, Wildenstein & Co., New York 1936 (no.28)
Paul Gauguin, The Fogg Art Museum, Harvard University, Cambridge, MA 1936 (no.26)
Paul Gauguin: A Retrospective Exhibition of his

Paintings, Baltimore Museum of Art 1936 (no.16)
La Vie ardente de Paul Gauguin, Gazette des Beaux-Arts, Paris 1936 (no.75)

LITERATURE
Waldemar George, 'La Collection Viau I: La peinture moderne', *L'Amour de l'Art*, September 1925, p.374, repr. p.373
G. Wildenstein, *Gauguin: Catalogue Raisonné*, Paris 1964, no.402 repr. (as '*Coupe de Fruits et Pichet devant la Fenêtre*')
G.M. Sugana, *L'Opera Completa di Gauguin*, Milan 1972, no.214 repr. (as '*Natura Morta con Frutta e Boccale davanti alla Finestra*')

Pierre Bonnard 1867–1947

9 *Nude in the Bath* 1925

10 *The Yellow Boat* c.1936–8

Nude in the Bath is one of the most remarkable of Pierre Bonnard's compositions, described by one observer as a 'disturbing and erotic image'.[1] Painted in the mid-1920s, it is typically rich in its chromatic range, setting fleshy pinks, cooled with lilac, against light yellows, in a balance of complementary colours hardly disturbed by other elements. The red and yellow rug provides, together with an unidentified item of clothing on the table, a denser concentration of colour, which anchors the space in depth. Bonnard used this chromatic balance to hold in check the extraordinary inversion of the bather. In an act of anonymity, extreme even for his repertoire of stolen glimpses, the body is cut off at the waist, bringing focus to the sex and accompanying hand, but, above all, to the legs: the left leg slightly lifted with the support of the water, the right wedged by its heel against the end of the tub. The pearly enamelled lip of the bath divides the canvas vertically, forming a border between these wet and dry zones, the coolly suffused water, to the right, and the warmly lit floor, to the left. The source of this light, which moulds the shoulder of the bath, is the thinly draped window. Below is a table piled with clothes, its two robustly turned legs mimicking, with a hint of cruel humour, the naked legs stretched out languorously in the water. Matching this echo, the pedestal foot of the bath sits on the same line of the rug as the slippered foot of the accompanying figure at the left margin. Hardly apprehended, this figure is partial and one-handed like the bather, cut along its height and at the chest by the painting's edges, with the dappled clothes (presumably a dressing gown) serving as camouflage.

Though truncated, the figures in this domestic scene are familiar from other works as Marthe (Maria Boursin), the painter's companion and model since 1893, and Bonnard himself.[2] After early, more explicitly sexual paintings, he repeatedly showed her preparing for, immersed in, or emerging from the bath. The viewer is invited to intrude as she twists, turns and stretches in the many stages of washing or drying. There is, inevitably, something photographic in the instantaneity and cropping in such works, and the painter's interest in photography has long been acknowledged.

9

Between 1899 and 1901 Bonnard took photographs of Marthe, posed indoors and outside, which, as one scholar has remarked, served 'to mechanically memorize certain moments'.[3] Although the pose of one of these outdoor images is close (if inverted) to the legs in *Nude in the Bath*,[4] and he may have referred back to such images, he apparently abandoned photography as an active part of his practice in 1916.[5] Instead, the numerous sketches from the later period confirm that he relied upon the swift annotation of momentary glimpses, indeed that maintaining the first impression was crucial to his idea of success.[6] The requirements of Marthe's tubercular laryngitis, alleviated with hydrotherapy,[7] ensured repetition of her daily ablutions and afforded the painter renewed opportunities to catch an instant. At the same time Bonnard imagined her into poses derived from classical statues, so that the figure in Tate's *The Bowl of Milk* 1919 may, for instance, derive from a Greek *kore*.[8] He also consistently imagined Marthe as her youthful self, showing no signs of age in the passage of his inter-war works.

Although Bonnard painted in his studio and not before the motif, the basis of his art lay rooted in reality. This has been demonstrated by the close comparison of his later paintings and their settings at Villa du Bosquet, the house at Le Cannet above Cannes that he bought in February 1926.[9] Renovations over the following year included a modern bathroom installed for Marthe's use.[10] This is recognisable from the staggered iridescent wall tiles and small floor tiles that dominate the 1930s paintings, with the window to the right of the bath. *Nude in the Bath* shows a different room, with the screen-like framed tiling, the red and yellow rug, and the window beyond (and to the left) found

Fig.11 | Pierre Bonnard, *The Bath* 1925, *Baignoire (Le Bain)* Oil on canvas 86 × 120.6 Tate. Presented by Lord Ivor Spencer Churchill through the Contemporary Art Society 1930, N04495

in *Large Nude in the Bathtub* 1924[11] and in Tate's *The Bath* 1925 (fig.11). Whether this earlier bathroom was in their apartment in Paris or, perhaps more likely, in one of 'various villas where the couple had lived (Arcachon, Deauville etc.)' is uncertain.[12] What is clear is that *The Bath* and *Nude in the Bath* show these details and a common handling of paint which secure them both to 1925, despite early inclinations to place the latter in the 1930s.[13] The two paintings crucially share an exploration of the distorting lens created by the water. The way in which it flattens the body towards the surface is demonstrated in *Nude in the Bath* and helps to underline the planar structure of the composition generated by the elevated viewpoint. It is seen even more explicitly in *The Bath* in the play between Marthe's body and the realisation of her protruding head. The theme allowed, therefore, a sophisticated experiment with perception through the very simple and familiar means of water.[14]

The composition of *Nude in the Bath* sets it apart from both its 1925 companion and the later sequence of three paintings made in 1936–46 which reprise the specific pose of *The Bath*.[15] The presence of the self-portrait lends it a different psychological charge. Though physically close within a small space, each figure is in its element in a way that, as Jacqueline Munck has noted, directly recalls the nudes divided by the dark folded screen in the much earlier painting of the couple, *Man and Woman* 1900 (Musée d'Orsay, Paris).[16] From the physical and psychological insight of the bilateral division of male and female zones, it is possible to read *Nude in the Bath* as the unflinching communication of a long co-existence. As a Proustian artist of memory,[17] it seems likely that Bonnard would have been particularly inclined to reflect on their long relationship in 1925, the year in which he and Marthe finally married. It is notable that David Sylvester saw the depictions of the bathing Marthe, in contrast to Botticelli's *Birth of Venus*, as symbols of 'apartness' as the 'nude enclosed in her shell is love's denial'.[18] In place of their post-coital nudity in *Man and Woman* (in which she is already 'going into her shell' in Sylvester's view),[19] the opposition in orientation between the figures is marked. Precedents for the inverted figure would be among those who have 'fallen', both literally and metaphorically, with the overthrowing of the rational order and, often, morality, made manifest. Figures such as these traditionally show their legs as they fall into Hell, or descend on the Wheel of Fortune to compensate for one on the rise. 'The unlikely', Bonnard is said to have remarked, 'is often the truth.'[20]

While the intimacy and colouristic warmth might tend to count against Bonnard's allusion to such fatalistic interpretations, a number of recent scholars have overturned

the comfortable sense of the 'dreamlike resemblance to Monet's wisterias' in these works,[21] to recognise their disconcerting atmosphere. Comparing the two 1925 paintings, Sarah Whitfield has remarked on how 'the body, or what can be seen of it, is made to look so relaxed that it is almost lifeless'.[22] She alludes to the sense of the 'recumbent figure on the tomb', taking up Linda Nochlin's recognition of 'the tomb-like isolation of the tub'. Nochlin, indeed, saw the luminosity of paint as melting the flesh and, tellingly, confessed that admiration for these works was combined with repulsion 'by so much transformation of woman into thing ... into the molten object of desire of the male painter'.[23] Following this line, Suzanne Pagé wrote of the 'discomfort created by the rather brutal composition of a "subject" as a drowned figure' in *Nude in the Bath*.[24] For his part, Timothy Hyman saw a symbiosis in 'the exchange between self and other' in the bathtub works, and in relation to the 'polarized and reversed opposites' of *Nude in the Bath*, in particular, he raised the question whether 'out of these two headless fragmentary persons, a whole can somehow be made?'[25]

Bonnard kept *Nude in the Bath* until his death in 1947. This might be taken as a sign of its charge, as well as its unusualness, were it not for the fact that this was the case with many paintings, including *The Yellow Boat* of c.1936 8. Within months of his death, an exhibition in Copenhagen included some of these works (the latter, among them), but legal actions around the estate that followed then kept them 'sequestered and stored in a Paris bank for the next sixteen years'.[26] While this long period of limbo hindered Bonnard's post-war reputation, the emergence of these paintings once agreement was reached on 26 February 1963 underpinned the major exhibitions of 1964–6 in New York, London, Paris and elsewhere; both of these paintings were seen in the major retrospective at the Royal Academy, London in 1966.

Landscape had long been a counterpoint in Bonnard's art to the cocooned world of the portrayals of Marthe. This is seen in the conjunction of his domestic sketches and the annotations about the weather on the pages of his pocket diaries. The source in nature ensured that preconceived structures were seasoned with variety, even if they were bent to his perception. 'When one deforms nature,' Bonnard noted, 'it always remains as a basis, as distinct from the purely imaginative work.' He added: 'The mistake is to cut out a portion of nature and to copy it.'[27] Extending this idea further, the painter Patrick Heron wrote of the 'abstract music of interactive form-colour' in Bonnard's work. 'If it is abstract, it is nonetheless saturated with the quality of things; even of particular things.'[28]

This relation between particularity and abstraction can be seen in the carefully structured composition of *The Yellow Boat*, most obviously in the (almost Mondrianesque) cruciform relationship of the orange and lilac boat deck to the near-vertical burnt orange mast. A secondary structure develops with the distant shore (blue with a strip of yellow, below the green hill and lilac sky) that also crosses the mast, while the furled sail and the white hull with bowsprit in the foreground set up further horizontals. Bonnard transformed the particularity of place – the bay also seen in the earlier *Landing-stage at Cannes* 1928–34 (private collection)[29] – through saturated colour. The sea is predominantly white bobbled with green, suggesting the blinding gleam of the waves that has bleached the further side of the eponymous yellow boat. The boat itself leaches yellow across its corner of the canvas, pouring out onto the ground and dyeing the discrete figure turned outwards to the unseen continuum to the right.

That Bonnard could achieve this structural and chromatic balance while working on unstretched canvas pinned to his wall shows his remarkable ability to isolate a section of reality and reconcile it in his own terms. He famously adjusted works even after they were sold insisting, for instance, on calling back an earlier seascape, the portrait of his patrons the Hahnlosers in *The Sailing Excursion* 1924–5 (private collection).[30] Without altering the composition, he heightened 'the intensity of the colour', concluding that 'the effect of colour alters the proportions completely'.[31] Though concentrated in the right corner, yellow sets the temperature for *The Yellow Boat* and, presumably, helped to determine the extent of the canvas as Bonnard resolved it. The colour, of which he is said to have remarked 'you can't have too much yellow',[32] flickers across the sky interwoven with a complementary and intensifying lilac. Of this ability to control such intense colour Timothy Hyman has observed:

> *For Bonnard, as for Van Gogh, yellow is felt as the true Primary – the colour of the sun, of pollen, of life itself. But in the late work it can also carry a more complex invocation – of the golden light of anarchism; of a yearning for a lost state of well-being, as well as a rediscovery in the sudden illumination of visionary consciousness.*[33]

MG

9 *Nude in the Bath* 1925

Nu dans la baignoire

Oil on canvas 103 × 64
Estate stamp: 'Bonnard', bottom left
Tate. Bequeathed by Simon Sainsbury 2006
T12611

PROVENANCE
Artist's estate on his death, 23 January 1947 (estate
no.717); Succession Bonnard, resolved 1963; Renée
Terrasse (the artist's niece), France, by 1965; Mr
and Mrs Walter Annenberg, Wynnewood, Penn.,
by 1969; Wildenstein & Co, New York; sold
Sotheby's, London, 28 June 1988 (lot 32, repr.);
Lefevre Gallery, London; acquired by Thomas
Gibson Fine Art, London on behalf of Simon
Sainsbury, London, 31 March 1993.

EXHIBITED
Pierre Bonnard, Royal Academy, London 1966
(no.238, repr. p.100 as '*Nu à la Baignoire* 1938–41,
private collection, USA')
The Annenberg Collection, Tate Gallery, London
1969 (no.2)
Bonnard: The Late Paintings, Centre Georges
Pompidou, Musée National d'Art Moderne,
Paris; Phillips Collection, Washington DC; Dallas
Museum of Art, 1984 (no.30, repr. p.167)
Bonnard, Tate Gallery, London; Museum of
Modern Art, New York, 1998 (no.47, repr. p.147,
'London only')
Bonnard: Early and Late, Phillips Collection,
Washington DC, 2002–3 (no.107, repr. p.205 as
'1925, priv. coll.')
Bonnard: The Work of Art: Suspending Time, Musée
d'Art Moderne de la Ville de Paris, 2006 (no.72,
repr. p.221)

LITERATURE
Annette Vaillant, *Bonnard ou le Bonheur de Voir*,
Neuchâtel 1965, 1981, p.129 repr. (as '1935' and 'coll.
R.T., France')
Sarah Whitfield, 'Bonnard at the RA', *Burlington
Magazine*, February 1966, pp.106–7, repr. p.107,
fig.55
David Sylvester, 'A Nude about the House', *Sunday
Times Magazine*, 6 February 1966, p.26
André Fermigier, *Bonnard*, Paris 1967 and New
York 1969, p.35 repr. (as '1935')
Jean and Henry Dauberville, *Bonnard: Catalogue
Raisonné de l'oeuvre peint; vol.III 1920–1939*, Paris
1973, no.1332 repr.

10 *The Yellow Boat* c.1936–8

Le Bateau jaune

Oil on canvas 57.8 × 75.8
Estate stamp 'Bonnard', bottom left
Tate. Bequeathed by Simon Sainsbury 2006
T12612

PROVENANCE

Artist's estate on his death, 23 January 1947 (estate
no.5154); Succession Bonnard, resolved 1963; Mr
and Mrs Charles Zadock, New York, by 1965; at
Acquavella Galleries, New York, Galerie Beyeler,
Basel and Lefevre Galleries, London, 1977–8;
[...]; acquired Simon Sainsbury, London, 1983.

EXHIBITED

Bonnard, Ny Glyptotek, Copenhagen 1947 (no.39)
Bonnard and his Environment, Museum of Modern
Art, New York; Art Institute of Chicago; Los
Angeles County Museum of Art, 1964–5 (no.63,
repr. p.90)
Bonnard, Carnegie Institute, Pittsburg 1965
Pierre Bonnard, Royal Academy, London 1966
(no.232, repr. p.109 as '1936–8, coll. Mr and Mrs
Charles Zadock')
Pierre Bonnard, Haus der Kunst, Munich (1966–7,
no.125), Musée de l'Orangerie, Paris 1967 (no.141)
Bonnard dans sa lumière, Fondation Maeght, Saint
Paul de Vence 1975 (no.58, repr. p.76)
Pierre Bonnard, Acquavella Galleries, New York
1977 (no.22, repr.)
Pierre Bonnard, Galerie Beyeler, Basel 1977 (no.22,
repr.)
Pierre Bonnard, Lefevre Gallery, London 1978
(no.12, repr. p.24)

LITERATURE

'Couleur de Bonnard', *Verve*, vol.5, nos.17–18, 1947,
repr.
Annette Vaillant, *Bonnard ou le Bonheur de voir*,
Neuchâtel 1965, p.210 repr. (as collection 'Mr &
Mrs Charles Zadock, New York')
Annette Vaillant, 'Les Plus Beaux tableau de
Bonnard à l'Orangerie', *Les Nouvelles littéraires,
artistiques et scientifiques*, 12 January 1967, p.9
Antoine Terrasse, *Pierrre Bonnard*, Paris 1967, p.157
repr.
Makoto Ooka, *Bonnard / Matisse: L'Art moderne
du monde*, Tokyo 1972, p.123, repr. p.132
Jean and Henry Dauberville, *Bonnard: Catalogue
Raisonné de l'oeuvre peint; vol.III 1920–1939*, Paris
1973, no.1563 repr.

Victor Pasmore 1908–1998

11 The Hanging Gardens of Hammersmith, No. 1 1944–7

The Second World War and its immediate aftermath threw modern art in Britain into crisis. Avant-garde groups advocating the Freudian-inspired irrationalism of Surrealism, the utopian idealism of Constructivism or the political engagement of socialist realism, had dominated the pre-war decade. The 1940s saw a review of the history of recent art and much of this retrospective survey can be charted in the work of Victor Pasmore, not least his numerous depictions of the river Thames.

In 1937 he had co-founded the Euston Road School which disbanded with the outbreak of war in September 1939. This group was committed to the depiction of objective reality. The principal inspiration was Paul Cézanne, but Pasmore's work also showed his admiration of Pierre Bonnard, Edouard Vuillard and even Henri Matisse. Having been discharged from military service, from late 1942 Pasmore undertook an intensive study of the Old Masters, aided by his close association with Kenneth Clark, then Director of the National Gallery, who paid him a regular stipend. During 1943–4 Pasmore read the writings of the Post-Impressionists, including Cézanne, Vincent van Gogh and Paul Gauguin. He found in some of these texts what seemed like predictions of art more advanced than that of their authors and resolved to pursue their implications.

In 1942 Pasmore moved to west London. He lived first at 2 Riverside, Chiswick Mall, and then at 16 Hammersmith Terrace, a row of Georgian houses on Chiswick Mall with gardens running down to the Thames. From there he produced a considerable number of paintings based on the outlook towards the river, of varying degrees of abstraction and of several different views. *The Hanging Gardens of Hammersmith, No. 1* 1944–7 shows the view looking south-east from an upstairs window. It is based on an earlier rendition of the same view. In fact, it can be seen as the second in a series of three works, though the artist's relaxed attitude to the consistent titling of his works confuses the sequence. The first of the series is *The Gardens of Hammersmith* 1944.[1] The third, *The Gardens of Hammersmith No. 2* 1949, is in Tate's collection (fig.12).

This sequence was reflected in the numbering of the latter work as 'No. 3' in Pasmore's exhibition catalogues from 1960 to 1980. In the 1980 catalogue raisonné of his work it was designated 'No. 2' while the present painting was 'No. 1'. The artist retained the different main titles – '*The Hanging Gardens of Hammersmith*' and the '*Gardens of Hammersmith*' – to distinguish the two. The sequential titling is further confused by the retrospective designation of a fourth work as '*The Gardens of Hammersmith No. 3 1947–9*'.[2] This last work is, in fact, of a quite different subject and remained unresolved.

The Gardens of Hammersmith 1944 and *The Hanging Gardens of Hammersmith, No. 1* 1944–7 share the same basic composition and components: the gardens running diagonally up from bottom left, the tall leafless tree on the left-hand side and a sequence of willows running to the right; the pergola at the end of one of the gardens towards the right-hand side of the composition. In *The Hanging Gardens of Hammersmith, No. 1*, however, these details are more abstracted. In *The Gardens of Hammersmith* 1944, the far bank of the river is clearly visible through a soft, Monet-esque light, its trees reflected in the water. The successive fences of the gardens, painted in short Cézanne-like brushstrokes, are discernable and clearly distinguished from the ground of the gardens themselves. In the present work, the further shore is distinguished only by spots of yellow denoting lights which are reflected in the water as van Gogh-like spirals. The garden fences are reduced to a series of diagonal lines while the ends of the gardens are marked by a series of vertical lines, precisely one inch apart, topped by exact circles. A similar device appears in *The Gardens of Hammersmith No. 3 1947–8*, and is clearly a

Fig.12 | Victor Pasmore,
The Gardens of Hammersmith No. 2 1949
Oil on canvas 76.5 × 96.9
Tate, T07033

stylised cast-iron fence. In the present work, the foliage is now reduced to conglomerations of Seurat-like dots in crimson and blue or two shades of green. *The Gardens of Hammersmith No. 2* 1949, is not only further simplified but is, in fact, a mirror image of *The Hanging Gardens of Hammersmith, No. 1*. This observation is supported by the fact that Pasmore recalled that the last work had been made after he had left Hammersmith Terrace and following his famous move into totally abstract art in 1948.

One can see in this series, then, Pasmore's formal progress towards abstraction. The first is a conventional impressionistic representation of the scene; the second is based on the same view but is partly invented; the last is almost entirely a formal invention. This incremental move into formalism is reflected in the artist's use of geometric proportions to compose his paintings. He particularly employed the golden section, though one contemporary recalled that he used the wrong ratio for many years (it should be 1:1.618).[3] In *The Gardens of Hammersmith No. 2* 1949, geometric proportions are used extensively in the placing of each element in the composition and can be matched with markings along the edges of the canvas which measure out ¼, ⅓, ½, the root of two and the golden section. In *The Hanging Gardens of Hammersmith, No. 1*, though such a pattern is harder to discern, marks along the bottom and the right-hand edge indicate that Pasmore did employ such systems. Diagonals between such proportional divisions of the field seem to have affected the distribution of the composition. On the right-hand side, for example, the strong diagonal that marks the end of the gardens crosses the edge of the canvas exactly on the golden section. Similarly, the two converging lines that define the longer sides of the pergola cross the left-hand edge on the golden section and the ¼ mark. Such compositional concerns had been characteristic of the Euston Road painters in the 1930s. The small pencil marks associated especially with William Coldstream and used to formulate a composition can been seen along the horizon towards the left-hand side of the painting. It is typical of Pasmore's approach, however, that he felt free to make small, more intuitive adjustments to his compositions.

In Pasmore's depictions of the Thames and his riverside garden can be charted his progress through the history of modern art. Joseph Mallord William Turner was an artist he greatly admired and the treatment of the sun through mist in the present work recalls such late works as Turner's *Norham Castle, Sunrise* 1845 (Tate N01981). Pasmore's 1943 *Thames at Chiswick* is, however, as much influenced by Jean-Baptiste-Camille Corot as the great English Romantic. Similarly, *The Quiet River* 1943–4 seems Turnerian and Whistlerian in equal measure.[4] In the trilogy of Hammersmith garden paintings his attention seems to pass from Monet, through Cézanne to Seurat. Along with the reduction of the image to its most basic components, the most striking change between *The Gardens of Hammersmith* 1944 and *The Hanging Gardens of Hammersmith, No. 1* is the representation of bushes and foliage using Seurat's Divisionist technique of dots in complementary colours. It has been suggested that the title refers back to Sickert's *Hanging Gardens of Islington c.*1924–6.[5] Sickert's title, however, is somewhat ironic, referring to the hanging of washing in the garden running down to the north London canal. So, it seems more likely that Pasmore's title was suggested by the willow trees that dominate and was intended to add grandeur to this everyday scene.

Pasmore's progress was towards Constructivism, a conversion which the critic Herbert Read described as 'the most revolutionary event in post-war British art'.[6] In 1947 he made a small number of geometrically-divided paintings abstracted from observed subjects and, the following year, he produced works that seemed more fully non-representational. His conversion was announced with his exhibition at the Redfern Gallery in November. It was a while, however, before Pasmore could fully dispense with any external references and it is telling that *The Hanging Gardens of Hammersmith, No. 1* and *The Gardens of Hammersmith No. 2* were made either side of this apparently dramatic change of direction. Already, in *The Hanging Gardens* it is clear that the artist's primary concerns are with form, composition, pattern, and spatial and colour relations. His obvious delight in the dramatic, curling forms of the willow trees would be developed later in a series of semi-abstract works which allude to landscape

Fig.13 | Victor Pasmore, *Spiral Motif in Green, Violet, Blue and Gold: The Coast of the Inland Sea* 1950 Oil on canvas 81.3 × 100.3 Inscribed in red oil paint *'V.P.' b.l.,* Tate. Purchased from the artist through the Redfern Gallery (Cleve Fund) 1953, N06191

and natural forms and which are made up of interlocking spirals. Prime examples of this later development are *Spiral Motif in Green, Violet, Blue and Gold: The Coast of the Inland Sea* 1950 (fig.13), and *Spiral Development: The Snowstorm* 1950–1, which Pasmore made for the Festival of Britain.[7] The spiral that formed the basis for those works was anticipated here in the reflected lights on the water. Pasmore's statement for the catalogue accompanying his first exhibition of abstract work in 1948 articulated the challenges in this shift from representation to abstraction: 'By imitating the objects and effects of nature, the painter is able to acquire endless pictorial forms and combinations of forms, with which to express himself … the abstract painter must … find fresh pictorial forms sufficiently potent to strike the imagination.'[8] In the years 1943–9, the forms along the banks of the Thames at Chiswick provided such potency that it was not until the 1950s that Pasmore finally freed himself completely from references to such external references. CS

11 *The Hanging Gardens of Hammersmith, No. 1* 1944–7

Oil on canvas 76.2 × 101.6
Inscribed: '*VP*' b.r.
Tate. Bequeathed by Simon Sainsbury 2006
T12615

PROVENANCE
Redfern Gallery, London; Pamela Harris, by 1950; Sotheby's, London, 23 April 1969 (lot 198), bought by John Hewitt on behalf of Simon Sainsbury, London.

EXHIBITED
London Group, New Burlington Galleries, London 1945 (no.12, earlier state as '*Moonrise*')
Three Large New Landscapes by Victor Pasmore also English Sports: Coloured Aquatints of the 18th & 19th Centuries, Redfern Gallery, London 1947 (no.3, as '*The Hanging Gardens of Hammersmith: Effect of Moonlight*')
The Private Collector, Tate Gallery, London 1950 (no.195, as '*Hammersmith, Moonlight*')
International Exhibition, Carnegie Institute,

Pittsburgh 1950 (no.225)
Victor Pasmore: Selected Works 1926–54, Arts Council Gallery, Cambridge 1955 (no.18, as '*The Hanging Gardens of Hammersmith 1946–7*')
Three Masters of Modern British Painting, Arts Council tour to Victoria Art Gallery, Bath; Carlisle Art Gallery; Shrewsbury Art Gallery; Bournemouth College of Art; Manchester City Art Gallery; Cheltenham Art Gallery, 1958 (no.27, as '*The Hanging Gardens of Hammersmith 1946–7*')
British Pavilion, Venice Biennale 1960 (Pasmore B, repr. as '*The Gardens of Hammersmith No.2 1946–7*')
Victor Pasmore: Retrospective Exhibition 1925–65, Tate Gallery, London 1965 (no.58, repr. pl.28 as '*The Hanging Gardens of Hammersmith c.1944–7*')
Victor Pasmore, Yale Center for British Art, New Haven; Phillips Collection, Washington DC, 1988–9 (no.10)

LITERATURE
Alan Bowness and Luigi Lambertini, *Victor Pasmore, with a Catalogue Raisonné of the Paintings, Constructions and Graphics 1926–1979*, London 1980, pp.11, 293, repr. p.66, no.106

Balthus (Balthasar Klossowksi de Rola) 1908–2001

12 *Still Life with a Figure* 1940

13 *Nude on a Chaise Longue* 1950

14 *The Golden Fruit* 1956

Tate's collection has until now held just one work by Balthus, the compelling yet modest *Sleeping Girl* (*Dormeuse*) of 1943. The three major paintings included in the Sainsbury bequest will have a transformative effect on the way in which this complex artist can be represented. Together, *Still Life with a Figure, Nude on a Chaise Longue* and *The Golden Fruit* present some of Balthus's most potent and important motifs and subject matter, while showing the diversity of his technique and concern with the materiality of his medium. These works also offer an insight into Balthus's somewhat itinerant, shifting existence, tracing his changing locations from Paris to rural retreats, and documenting the significant role of a few of the models who passed through his life, frequently in the role of muse and companion.

The earliest of the three works, *Still Life with a Figure*, was made in 1940 when Balthus was thirty-two. This painting encapsulates Balthus's ability to compose a scene that may at first sight appear quite conventional, but which on further examination is revealed to be peculiar and unsettling.

After the outbreak of the Second World War in 1939 the artist was conscripted into active service, but injured soon after.[1] This apparently traumatic personal experience was followed swiftly by the German invasion of France in 1940, and in June that year Balthus and his wife Antoinette decided to leave Paris and take refuge in the French countryside. They went to Champrovent, a farmhouse in the hamlet of Vernatel in the Savoie region of eastern France where the artist had spent vacations with Pierre and Betty Leyris during the 1930s. The move to the country had a therapeutic effect on Balthus. In correspondence to the writer Pierre Jean Jouve in July 1940, Balthus explained: 'In an almost miraculous way, the ability to work has been restored to me in the midst of these horrors … we intend to stay, to pass the winter here.'[2] In fact they remained there until early 1942.[3]

Typical of the artist's practice, while residing at Champrovent the location and its inhabitants became the subjects of Balthus's work. *Still Life with a Figure* is one of

around a dozen paintings he made using the Savoie landscape and the interior of the farmhouse. It was first exhibited in 1943 under the title *Nature Morte*, yet the presence of the figure transforms the picture into something more than a still life. According to Sabine Rewald, Balthus's model was Georgette, the thirteen-year-old daughter of Champrovent's farmer, who also sat for a group of works entitled *The Salon* made during the same period.[4] The elaborate fruit bowl and glass that appear in *Still Life with a Figure* feature in two of these paintings, and are key motifs in a further work entitled *The Greedy Child*, also painted in 1940.[5]

In *Still Life with a Figure* the girl draws aside a heavy tapestry and pensively surveys a table covered with a white cloth and adorned with a bowl of apples, wine and bread. Past scholars have commented on the possible religious associations of this altar-like scene, with its suggestion of the Eucharist. However, the presence of the knife and the girl's disconcerted look have also been read as undercutting any implication of religiosity and sacrament, instead engendering a sense of uncertainty and threat. Jean Clair notes that *Still Life with a Figure* is one of a number of works Balthus made between 1937 and 1945 which are 'characterised by the violence and ambiguity of a diffused sense of impending danger'[6] and this may, in part, reflect the turbulent times. The highly staged composition is indeed both strange and enigmatic. The flattened picture plane draws the tabletop uncomfortably towards the viewer, and the hyperreal apples float uncannily above and around, rather than within, the antique-looking metal bowl.

The painting also exhibits a sense of organisation and deliberation on the part of the artist. An underlying structure of vertical, horizontal and diagonal lines enhances a sense of precision and definition; the rhythmic arrangements of lines and angles contrasting with the softened forms of the glass, fruit and girl's hair. The girl's head and right hand form a diagonal that is mirrored in the edge of the table and the slant of the knife, which itself forms a triangle with the shadow cast by the fruit bowl and the front line of the table. Balthus appears to have used specific techniques in order physically to communicate a sense of three-dimensionality in the painting, varying his level of paint application between thick bodies of paint and thinner stains, and using pencil markings to augment outlines, particularly accentuating the stripes of the wallpaper.[7] Yet Balthus also changed his mind about various compositional elements, and made small yet significant alterations. A single apple, originally positioned centrally on the table, between the glass and fruit bowl, is still visible despite

the artist's efforts to over-paint the area. There are also indications of where the handle of the knife initially extended, now hidden beneath the girl's wrist and the corner of the tablecloth.

Still Life with a Figure, like a number of the works the artist made at Champrovent during the same period, is painted on paper rather than canvas. This may have been due to the artist's economic constraints, the fact that supplies were limited in rural, war-torn France, or perhaps a combination of both. Yet, despite this more humble support, there is a depth to Balthus's palette that recalls the richness of Gustave Courbet, Dutch still-life painting and the Old Masters, which Balthus had discovered on visits to the Louvre as a young man.[8] Comparisons can also be made with André Derain's staged classicism: the two met during the mid-1930s and his work had a significant influence on Balthus. Derain, already an established figure in French culture, became something of a mentor to the much younger artist. In Derain's rejection of abstraction and return to nature, Balthus recognised the continuation of the great tradition of French painting to which he aspired. The convention of still-life painting was a key aspect of Derain's oeuvre and *Still Life with a Figure* reflects this concern, albeit inflected with Balthus's unique vocabulary.

The history of *Still Life with a Figure* is partially shared with Tate's existing Balthus painting, *Sleeping Girl*, both works having been exhibited at the artist's solo exhibition at the Galerie Georges Moos, Geneva, in 1943. At a later date the two paintings were acquired by the French playwright and dramatist Henri Bernstein (1876–1953) and subsequently passed to his daughter Mme Georges Gruber, the widow of the French painter Francis Gruber. While the theatrical scenario Balthus presented in *Still Life with a Figure* employs a combination of interior, still life and figure, the painting points to the artist's most prevailing theme, that of the female form. Whether asleep, undressing, lying prone or merely present as an observer, the feminine body emerges as one of Balthus's most complex subjects.

Nude on a Chaise Longue is part of an important series of paintings the artist worked on from the late 1940s until around 1953. Several studies exist that have a direct bearing on the work, and these show the artist's exploration of different arrangements of the figure.[9] The closest compositionally is an ink sketch of 1949, in which Balthus experimented with a headless version of the figure, which is a mirror image of Tate's painting.[10] In other paintings from the same sequence the artist expanded the domestic setting and incorporated further figures such as in *The Week of Four Thursdays* 1949,

or the monumental *The Room* 1952–4 in which one of the artist's signature cats also sits in attendance.[11] In *Nude on a Chaise Longue*, however, the body dominates, lying awkwardly on the stiff piece of furniture, her arms outstretched in a crucifix-like gesture. It is likely that Balthus made *Nude on a Chaise Longue* in Paris, in the studio he kept for some years at the cour de Rohan, close to boulevard Saint-Germain. One visitor noted that the studio had an 'atmosphere of disorder and bleakness that seems almost calculated', an ambience that is palpable in the dark corners of this painting.[12]

The model for its extraordinary figure may have been Laurence Bataille who was Balthus's companion from 1947 until 1951. Although only seventeen when she met the artist, Laurence was very much in the midst of the artistic and intellectual circles in Paris as the daughter of Georges Bataille, niece of André Masson and stepdaughter of Jacques Lacan. She later pursued a career in medicine, specialising in Lacanian psychoanalysis. The combination of the almost pre-adolescent torso, knee-high white socks and red shoes, produces an uncomfortable juxtaposition with the girl's highly charged, provocative pose. As so often with Balthus's direct, confrontational style, the viewer appears to be cast in the role of voyeur. Yet the artist was quick to defend his choice of subject matter:

> Some have claimed that my undressed young girls are erotic. I never painted them
> with that intent, which would have made them anecdotal, mere objects of gossips
> [sic]. I aimed at precisely the opposite, to surround them with a halo of silence and
> depth, as if creating vertigo around them. That's why I think of them as angels, beings
> from elsewhere, whether heaven, or another ideal place that suddenly opened and
> passed through time, leaving traces of wonderment, enchantment, or just as icons.[13]

The vertiginous quality of this painting is further complicated by its thickly painted, highly modulated surface. The unusual texture and disparate brushwork, not obviously related to the composition, led Tate curators and conservators to investigate the possibility that an earlier composition could be hidden beneath. X-rays have confirmed suspicions and unveiled an almost complete half-length portrait of a man, sitting side-on (fig.14).[14] The dark hair parted at one side, pronounced features and slim face all point to Balthus's own distinctive appearance and the author believes this hidden painting to be a self-portrait.

Four self-portrait paintings by Balthus are known to exist: *Cathy* 1933, *The King of Cats* 1935 and two further self-portraits of 1940 and 1949.[15] The rather austere, conventional pose and somewhat unsophisticated handling of the hidden portrait, coupled with the youthful look of the subject, suggest this was an early attempt by Balthus; it has neither the drama of *The King of Cats*, nor the subtle elegance of the 1940 self-portrait in which Balthus presents himself as the mature, melancholic artist holding accoutrements of his trade, a paintbrush and rag.

It is not known when Balthus painted the newly revealed portrait, nor why he retained it in his possession only to paint over it at a later date. However, it may be feasible to suggest that financial problems led Balthus to re-use a canvas in 1950 to create a more profitable painting and that a self-portrait – perhaps one he felt to be less satisfactory – may have been the most suitable candidate for this recycling operation. By 1950 he was reliant on a syndicate of supporters to maintain his basic living costs and it is known that in January 1951 he sold *Nude on a Chaise Longue* to his New York dealer, Pierre Matisse.[16]

At the time of its sale, the painting was referred to as *Nude (Study for the Four Sundays)* and was recorded as such when Matisse sold it on in 1960. While 'the Four Sundays' may recall the four Sundays of Advent in the Christian calendar or perhaps suggest a period of extreme religious ecstasy and devotion, its meaning remains

Fig.14 | Balthus
(Balthasar Klossowksi de Rola),
X-ray of *Nude on a Chaise Longue* 1950
Tate, T12614

cryptic and no other painting of that name by Balthus is known to exist.[17] By the time
the work was first reproduced in 1982, it had acquired the more descriptive title *Nude in
an Armchair*, later revised to *Nude on a Chaise Longue* to identify the piece of furniture
more precisely.

After spending the latter half of the Second World War in Switzerland, Balthus
returned to Paris in 1946, after peace had returned to Europe. However, by 1953 he was
again anxious for rural solitude and left the city to take over the dilapidated Château de
Chassy in the Morvan region of Burgundy, discovered while holidaying with Georges
and Diane Bataille.

Balthus's voluntary exile reinvigorated his work and augured a shift towards a more
delicate palette and technique that recalls that of early Italian fresco painting, indeed,
he is known to have blended his media in order to achieve the particular effects of such
work:[18] 'I admire the early Italian painters' matteness [*sic*], which is both light and
heavy. Their art of rendering transparency without shine, a luminous opacity.'[19] He went
further in aligning this material quality with the notion of temporal transience that had
begun to preoccupy him at this time:

> *Giotto and Masaccio's fresco art simultaneously expresses weight and lightness, fluidity
> and torpor, a certain state of somnolence and fleeing, a bit like Bach's variations and
> fugues, in which fleeting movements allow sublime song – the 'golden fruit' – to break
> through.*[20]

He drew on this as he investigated the dual subjects of the sleeping girl and reverie,
beginning with numerous studies in 1954 and culminating with a major series of
paintings that are compositionally almost identical, of which *The Golden Fruit* 1956
is the third.[21] Parallels have been made between these paintings and Courbet's *The
Awakening (Venus and Psyche)* 1866 in the Kunstmuseum Bern, and with Piero della
Francesca's frescoes *The Legend of the True Cross* c.1452–66 in the Basilica di San
Francesco, Arezzo.[22] Balthus was hugely influenced by the Arezzo frescoes which
he first discovered in reproduction as a teenager and subsequently visited in 1926.[23]
Interestingly, the sequence of tableaux includes an image of a dreaming figure: *The
Dream of Constantine.*

The brittle, heavily textured surface of *The Golden Fruit*, coupled with a palette of
pale and jewel-like tones delicately brings to life the day-dream of a young girl, situated
within the parlour at Chassy:

Balthus often drew or painted young girls asleep, saying they were 'dreamers'; but for the first time he represents in these paintings at once the sleeper and the object of her dream … Furthermore, and this is perhaps his most original contribution to the genre, he places the conjured-up figure amidst the reassuring, familiar context of everyday reality … The different studies show how, borrowing from one or the other, Balthus gradually elaborated and rendered, by contrasting them, the difference of nature between the two figures.[24]

The decorative assemblage of patterns in the ornate rug, upholstered sofa and table-cloth in *The Golden Fruit* is reminiscent of Matisse. However, Balthus's interior has a static quality that heightens the sense of time interrupted. The painting oscillates between the extraordinary and the ordinary; the still life of coffee pots, cup and saucer, and tablecloth are all shifted precariously to the edge of the table, drawing the viewer's eye to the golden globe, held symbolically by the mysterious standing figure. Her yellow and ochre clothes contrast with the rich blue and green in which the sleeping girl is dressed. The depth of these colours helps to isolate her from the rest of the room, making her the centrepoint for the painting, and focusing attention on the notion of dream-driven imagination.

Balthus began *The Golden Fruit* while he was still working on the second painting in the sequence, *The Dream II*. He radically modified the figure that presides over the girl and it has been noted that her 'witch-like' features in *The Golden Fruit* are akin to the artist's own profile.[25] Rather than presenting a flower as in *The Dream I* and *II*, this apparition bears the round fruit of the title, which has been interpreted as the apple of Eden or a magical fruit of fairytale and mythology:

This may represent the apple of temptation and sexual knowledge, or it may refer to the golden apples of the Hesperides in classical mythology. These were the property of the goddess Hera, who received them as her wedding gift. She was the protectress of women; the gold apple bestowed the gift of immortality on its bearer.[26]

Notions of magic and mystery reverberated not only throughout Balthus's oeuvre but also in his life, frequently invoked by the artist himself. His self-imposed distance from the mainstream avant-garde enabled him to invent and perpetuate his own mythology, as master of his own, imagined world. While at Chassy he lived with Frédérique Tison, the stepdaughter of his elder brother, Pierre Klossowski. Frédérique was his muse and principal model from 1954 until around 1962, and posed for the sleeping girl in *The Golden Fruit*. She was part of the mise-en-scène that helped to give life to the artist's fantasies of playing the lord of the manor:

> *At Chassy there were days of intense work almost exclusively devoted to painting, in the development of a canvas; I entered into a communion with the landscape and my niece Frédérique, who little by little took possession of the place, became its little 'lady' in a medieval sense.*[27]

Balthus completed *The Golden Fruit* in 1956 and a well-known Parisian interior designer, Henri Samuel (1900–1993), acquired the painting in exchange for antique furniture.[28] Samuel was part of the syndicate that supported Balthus, established by Henriette Gomès in the early 1950s, and *The Golden Fruit* remained in his possession until his death. LA

12 *Still Life with a Figure* 1940

Also known as *The Snack (Le Goûter)*

Oil on paper mounted on wood panel
Paper: 72.9 × 92.8; support: 74.4 × 93.4
Signed and dated bottom right: *Balthus 1940*
Tate. Bequeathed by Simon Sainsbury 2006
T12613

PROVENANCE

Henri Bernstein, Paris; Mme Georges Gruber;
Galerie Henriette Gomès, Paris; André Gomès,
Paris; Mme André Gomès, Paris; Thomas Gibson
Fine Art, London; Simon Sainsbury, London,
12 April 1995.

EXHIBITED

Balthus, Galerie Georges Moos, Geneva 1943 (no.2
as '*Nature Morte* (fin 1940)')
Balthus: Peintures de 1936 à 1946, Galerie Beaux-
Arts, Paris 1946 (no.10, dated 1941)
Balthus, Musée des Arts Décoratifs, Paris 1966
(no.10, repr. b&w p.24 as 'Collection particulaire,
ancienne Collection Henri Bernstein') and Casino
Communal Gemeentelijk; Knokke-le-Zoute,
Belgium 1966 (no.10, repr. b&w p.24)
Balthus, Arts Council of Great Britain/Tate
Gallery, London 1968 (no.17 as '*A Bite to Eat/Le
goûter*')
Balthus, Musée Cantini, Marseilles 1973 (no.10)
Balthus 1908–2001, Centre Georges Pompidou,
Paris 1983–4 (no.23/63, repr. col. p.152, repr. b&w
p.350)
Balthus 1908–2001, Metropolitan Museum of Art,
New York 1984 (no.23, repr. p.100 as '*Still Life with
a Figure / Le Goûter* 1940, signed and dated (indis-
tinctly, lower right)')
Balthus, Museum of Art, Kyoto 1984 (no.7, repr.
col. p.48)
Balthus dans la Maison de Courbet, Musée Maison
Natale de Gustave Courbet, Ornans 1992 (no.15)
Balthus, Musée Cantonal des Beaux-Arts,
Lausanne 1993 (repr. col. p.48, dated 1942, as
'Collection M. et Mme Gomès')

LITERATURE

Cahiers d'Art, Paris 1945–6, vols.20–1, repr. b&w
p.201 (as '*Nature Morte et jeune fille*')
Jean Clair, 'Balthus ou les métampsycoses', *La
Nouvelle Revue Française*, Paris, July 1966, no.163,
pp.148–53
Jean Leymarie, *Balthus*, Geneva and London 1982,
repr. b&w, p.130 (as '*Tea Time*, 1940'), revised ed.
1990, repr. p.131
Stanislas Klossowski de Rola, *Balthus*, London
1983, 1996, pl.36 (as '*Jeune Fille et nature morte*,
1942')
Koharu Kisaragi, Shûji Takashina and Kunio
Motoe, *Balthus*, Tokyo 1994, pl.16
Xiaosheng Xing, *Balthus*, Shanghai 1995, pl.17
Jean Clair and Virginie Monnier, *Balthus:
Catalogue Raisonné of the Complete Works*, New
York 2000, no.P126, p.138, repr. b&w, p.139 (as '*Le
Goûter*')

13 *Nude on a Chaise Longue* 1950

Nu sur une chaise longue
Previously known as *Nude (Study for the Four Sundays)*

Oil on canvas 72.3 × 91.8
Monogrammed and dated bottom left: *Bs 50*
Tate. Bequeathed by Simon Sainsbury 2006
T12614

PROVENANCE
Pierre Matisse Gallery, New York, acquired from the artist January 1951; William N. Copley, April 1960; André Stassant, Paris; Baron H. Thyssen Bornemisza, Lugano; James Kirkman, London, 1981; Simon Sainsbury, London.

EXHIBITED
Balthus 1908–2001, Centre Georges Pompidou, Paris 1983–4 (p.359, no.115)

LITERATURE
Jean Leymarie, *Balthus*, Geneva and London 1982, repr. b&w p.141 (as '*Nude in an Armchair, 1950*'); revised ed. 1990, p.145
Jean Clair and Virginie Monnier, *Balthus: Catalogue Raisonné of the Complete Works*, New York 2000, no.p201, repr. b&w p.157
Balthus, ed. Jean Clair, London 2001, repr. b&w fig.1, p.306

14 *The Golden Fruit* 1956

Le Fruit d'or

Oil on canvas 159 × 160.5
Tate. Bequeathed by Simon Sainsbury 2006
X00110

PROVENANCE
Acquired from the artist by Henri Samuel, Paris, 1956; acquired from the Estate of Henri Samuel, Paris, by Thomas Gibson Fine Art, London, September 1996, and sold to Simon Sainsbury, London, 20 September 1996.

EXHIBITED
Balthus 1908–2001, exh. cat., Centre Georges Pompidou, Paris 1983–4, (no.49/167, p.278, repr. col. p.191, repr. b&w, pp.279, 367)
Balthus 1908–2001, exh. cat., Metropolitan Museum of Art, New York 1984, (no.41, pp.138-9, repr. p.139)

LITERATURE
Jean Clair, 'Les métamorphoses d'Eros' in Paris 1983–4, p.79
Jean Clair, *Metamorphosen des Eros: Essay über Balthus*, Munich 1984, p.67, fig 53
Jean Leymarie, *Balthus*, Geneva and London 1982, revised ed. 1990, p.137
Balthus, Musée Cantonal des Beaux-Arts, Lausanne 1993, p.80
Koharu Kisaragi, Shûji Takashina and Kunio Motoe, *Balthus*, Tokyo 1994, pl.42
Xiaosheng Xing, *Balthus*, Shanghai 1995, pl.41
Claude Roy, *Balthus*, Paris and Boston 1996, pp.174, 178, 179, repr. col. p.187
Jean Clair and Virginie Monnier, *Balthus: Catalogue Raisonné of the Complete Works*, New York 2000, no. P272, p.177, repr. b&w p.176
Balthus, ed. Jean Clair, London 2001, repr. col., fig.2, p.356
Gilles Neret, *Balthus 1908–2001: The King of Cats*, Bonn 2003, repr. col. p.67

Francis Bacon 1909–1992

15   *Study for a Portrait* 1952

Study for a Portrait is the second of four independent heads executed by Francis Bacon
in 1952. It was probably made in the studio of Rodrigo Moynihan at the Royal College
of Art, which Bacon used for about two years from 1951 to autumn 1953. The painting
displays many of the characteristics most typical of Bacon's work of the early 1950s, not
least the ambiguity of its subject matter, which is reflected in the varying titles applied
in its first decade. The 1995 Christie's catalogue states that they were made during the
summer of that year. It is notable, however, that they were not included in Bacon's one-
man exhibition at the Hanover Gallery, London in December 1952.

The work shows the head and shoulders of a bespectacled man, dressed in jacket,
tie and white shirt, who appears to be screaming. The head is surrounded by a space
frame, as if encased in a transparent box. In fact, the frame has been painted twice –
first in pale pink and then strengthened with red and blue. Unusually, the painting's
palette is dominated by blue. The figure is set against a blue curtain that hangs on rings
from a pink rail which horizontally bisects the composition. Blue strokes of paint
define the undulations of the man's jacket and tie, and his chin is highlighted with three
spots of royal blue paint. While the face is painted with considerable care and detail,
the curtain is rendered with an economy of means, as is the figure's suit, the paint of
which thins as it nears the bottom of the picture. The whole image has been painted
over a thin black ground. While the folds of the curtain were described using simple
vertical strokes of paint, the impact of the colour has been modified by the application
of considerable amounts of sand. Bacon claimed to have used dust as early as 1945 to
give his paint more body. Here, sand or some similarly textured material, such as saw-
dust, was mixed in with the paint to give the face more volume. It is especially promi-
nent around the eyes and under and around the mouth. In contrast, on the curtains
the sand seems not to have been mixed in with the paint but to have been stuck on
top. It thus modifies the strength of the blue colouring as well as adding texture to the
surface of the work.

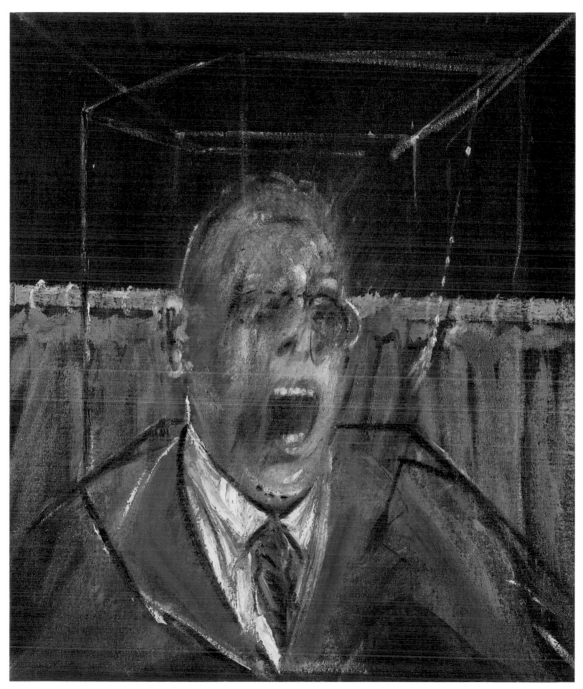

15

In his art, Bacon sought to articulate a view of human existence in a world without God. Drawing on the philosophy of Nietzsche amongst a wealth of other intellectual and literary sources, Bacon saw the human simply as a physical being, just the same as any other animal. The vehicle for this message was almost always the human body, which was generally shown in isolation and either full-length or bust-length, as here. The violence, anguish and loneliness that have often been identified in his work are the inevitable qualities of human behaviour and the human condition. From that harsh reality springs any anxiety, pathos, cruelty or absurdity that may be seen in these works. This remained the basis for his art throughout his mature career. Exactly how the body was represented, however, changed over time. The type and nature of the body varied and the contexts within which it was located changed. Bacon first painted the head in isolation in a series of six works made between 1948 and 1949. In the first two the head is abstracted and the artist has imposed on to it the snarling mouth of an ape, copied from a photograph. By the sixth, the subject is based on the head and shoulders of Velázquez's *Portrait of Pope Innocent X c.*1650 (Galleria Doria Pamphilj, Rome) from which Bacon famously and repeatedly drew inspiration, and the mouth is the wide, gaping void that appears in the present work.

Though quite distinct in appearance, style and handling, the present work reuses several details from those first *Heads*. The head is set in a shallow space, defined by the curtain behind it, as is *Head II* 1948; the mysterious tasselled cord that occurs in a number of works first appeared in *Head I* 1948. The curtain rail is similar to a form suggestive of a brass bedstead that recurs in a number of works including a series

Fig.15 | Still from Sergei Eisenstein's *Battleship Potemkin* 1925, British Film Institute

of *Studies for Portraits*, based on the Velázquez, from 1953. The open mouth had first appeared in precisely the present form in *Figure Study II* 1945–6 and by 1952 was secured as a staple of Bacon's iconography. While Bacon suggested a few possible sources for the image, to which historians have added more, the closest and most commonly cited is a still from Sergei Eisenstein's film *Battleship Potemkin* 1925, showing a nurse who has just been shot in the eye (fig.15). Both the mouth and the broken pince-nez spectacles derive from this source. This wide, gaping mouth that recurs in Bacon's work is most commonly thought to be screaming. The Eisenstein source would suggest so. In discussing Bacon's gaping mouths, Dawn Ades cited George Bataille's proposal that 'it is through the mouth that our most concentrated experiences of agony or ecstasy are physiologically expressed'.[1] As Wieland Schmied put it, Bacon's scream has 'a primal quality: it bears witness to unbearable pain and the yearning for salvation'.[2] Nevertheless, alternative ways of reading the gaping mouth have been proposed and it would be typical of Bacon's approach to representation to make a virtue of ambiguity. In particular, reference has been made to the artist's asthma and the inference drawn that this gaping mouth might be struggling for breath and so a sign of suffocation and desperation.

A comparable instability might be discerned in the subject matter of *Study for a Portrait*, 1952. The 'Study for…' formulation was common in Bacon's work from the 1944 *Three Studies for Figures at the Base of a Crucifixion* to some of his very last paintings. It suggests a degree of contingency, that the work is preparatory and that the artist was not aiming for a definitive representation. Bacon commented that in distorting the image of a person he sought a more accurate representation than a photographic illustration. That ambition is somewhat undermined, perhaps, by the fact – common in Bacon's art of this period – that the sitter is anonymous. The work, the title would suggest, is more a generic portrait than a specific likeness. The varying titles that have been attached to it suggest the different ways in which it has been interpreted. The work that precedes it in the sequence of four heads was based on Velázquez's *Innocent X* and, perhaps because of that, this work has been discussed in relation to the series of pope paintings.[3] The figure's attire would suggest quite clearly that the intended subject was not that. Indeed, the jacket and tie might associate it with a series of works that Bacon started the following year. So called 'Men in Blue', these depict men in suits, apparently businessmen or politicians, against a blue-black ground. The figures are generally set apart from the view, elevated or seated behind a table or a counter, and consequently have both a sense of domination and pathos. This was certainly how John Russell read the work when it was

reproduced in the landmark record of the London art scene, *Private View*, published in 1965. Assuming the image was of some kind of public figure, Russell went on to suggest that the reception of Bacon's work had changed as the world of images had changed to show his early paintings to be prophetic:

> *Life has gone Bacon's way, and Bacon's paintings are by that much the more natural and inevitable. This is true above all of public images like [Study for a Portrait, 1952]. In 1952 the politician on the TV screen was still relatively rare, and Eichmann, on trial in his glass box, had yet to be heard of. People took it for granted, with no warrant from the artist, that the open mouths of Bacon's characters were open in a scream. But a manic hilarity, a mindless good fellowship, or the silence of total breakdown, all are possible alternatives.*[4]

So Russell identified the ambiguity at the heart of Bacon's work. Whether screaming or laughing, in pain or ecstasy, Bacon used such generic portraits to articulate the ambiguities of existence through the distorted representation of the human form. CS

15 *Study for a Portrait* 1952

Oil on canvas 65.9 × 55.9
Tate. Bequeathed by Simon Sainsbury 2006
T12616

PROVENANCE
Leicester Galleries, London from whom acquired by R.D.S. May, London, in 1953; Lord Beaverbrook, London; The Beaverbrook Art Gallery, New Brunswick; Brook Street Gallery, London; Luca Scacchi Gracco, Milan; Marlborough Fine Art, London; private collection from which sold Christie's, London, 29 June 1995 (lot 12) and bought by Thomas Gibson Fine Art, London, on behalf of Simon Sainsbury, London, 5 July 1995.

EXHIBITED
New Year Exhibition, Leicester Galleries, London 1953 (no.97)
The Collection of R.D.S. May: A Recently Formed Collection, Leicester Galleries, London 1953 (no.15, as 'Head')
Collector's Choice, Gimpel Fils, London 1953 (no.10, as 'Head')

Bacon, Sutherland, Hilton, Wynter, Piper, Mackenzie, Davie, Nicholson, Luca Scacchi Gracco, Milan 1961 (no numbers, repr. as '*Businessman 1, 1952*')
Opere Scelte di Tobey, Fautrier, Bacon etc, Associazione Arti Figurative, Turin 1961 (repr.)
L'Incontro di Torino: Pittori d'America Europa e Giappone, Palazzo della Promotrice al Valentino, Turin 1962 (no numbers, repr. as '*Businessman, 1962*')
Panorama di Pittura Contemporanea Straniera, Galleria d'Arte Sianesi, Milan 1962 (no.7, repr.)
Francis Bacon, Solomon R. Guggenheim Museum, New York 1963–4 (no.17, repr.)

LITERATURE
John Rothenstein and Ronald Alley, *Francis Bacon*, London 1964, p.61, no.42 repr. (as '*Study for a Portrait*')
Bryan Robertson, John Russell and Lord Snowdon, *Private View*, London 1965, p.65, repr. p.64
Lorenza Trucchi, *Francis Bacon*, London and New York 1976, no.20 repr.

Lucian Freud born 1922

With the end of the Second World War, Lucian Freud, like many artists in Britain, was keen to visit Paris, but after a failed attempt at stowing away on a Breton fishing boat he went instead with John Craxton to the Scilly Isles. The mixture of gorse, thistle, sea holly and puffins provided both artists with a spiky and otherworldly exoticism that was drenched in the clear Atlantic light, offering a surrogate for the Mediterranean. Freud had been friendly with Craxton since at least 1942 when Peter Watson, the collector and publisher of *Horizon* magazine, provided him with a studio room at 14 Abercorn Place in St John's Wood, London – Freud arrived to find Craxton installed in another room. After a year Freud moved into a flat in Delamere Terrace near Little Venice, yet remained friendly with Craxton. In 1946, with travel options becoming easier, Freud spent July and August in Paris, armed with introductions provided by Watson as well as a weekly advance from the London Gallery (backed by Watson

Fig.16 | Lucian Freud,
Man with a Thistle (Self-Portrait) 1946
Oil on canvas 61 × 50.2
Tate. Purchased 1961, T00422

and the surrealist artist and collector Roland Penrose) and the promise of a solo exhibition once he returned.

In Paris he met the printmaker Javio Vilató, who introduced Freud both to his uncle, Pablo Picasso, and to a printer for Freud's first etchings.[1] While in Paris, Freud heard from Craxton who was in Athens and encouraged him to travel on to Greece. He joined Craxton in Poros where they took lodgings with a Greek family until February 1947. Their living conditions were described by George Millar who visited them at this time. They each had a bedroom where they lived and worked:

> Craxton's was the more untidy of the two rooms. It enjoyed a superb view down the harbour and over the mountain called, from its remarkable outline, The Sleeping Woman. Beside Craxton's bed there hung an unusual set of photographs: one of the strangest showed Freud wearing the football jersey, seated in an armchair and holding in his arms the head of a stuffed zebra; another seemed to represent an actor declaiming, and two more were of young women in expensive and modish clothes. Freud's room, like his painting, was neater, harder, and more self-conscious than Craxton's. Freud was working on a self-portrait. Only the curly chestnut hair, one enraged eye, a long nose, had been minutely and exquisitely painted. Down in a corner of the canvas the outline of a tall Greek thistle had been pencilled in.[2]

Lucian Freud's solo exhibition at the London Gallery in October 1947 was shared with Craxton, and provided evidence of a shift in his art that was captured well, if coincidentally, by Millar. His description of the self-portrait in progress – most likely *Man with a Thistle (Self-Portrait)* 1946 (fig.16) – is echoed by his description of one of Freud's mannerisms, his 'disconcerting habit of glaring at you, and then looking swiftly down in sudden shyness'.[3] Freud's painting had always been driven by an intense and obsessive scrutiny of its subject (he has said how he had hoped that 'if I concentrated enough the intensity of scrutiny alone would force life into the pictures'),[4] however, this was now increasingly allied to a more explicitly stated preference for his paintings to 'appear *factual* not literal'.[5] However, in claiming this for his painting – in one respect a way of expressing his distance from the illustrational caprices of Surrealism as well as the supposed objectivity of the Euston Road school of realism, then prevalent – it also helps to clarify how far removed he has always been from the notion of the artist either as creator of imaginary narrative or as disinterested observer, but rather as somebody intimately involved in the life of his subjects.

Girl with a Kitten marks the point at which, as John Russell identifies, 'he had entered a world of total commitment, in which whimsicality played no part'.[6] From this point Freud's paintings are formed by a commitment to fact and to intimacy. Shortly after returning to London from Greece, Freud fell in love with Kitty Garman, the daughter of Kathleen Garman and Jacob Epstein. With *Girl with a Kitten* and subsequent portraits of Garman, Freud in effect painted the course of his changing relationship with her. Garman is depicted wearing a loose fitting, light blue, long-sleeved blouse. Her head is turned to her left, eyes fixed in that direction. In her right hand, raised up to her chest, she tightly clasps a kitten by its neck; the kitten looks directly out at the viewer. Both sets of eyes – the kitten's and Garman's – carry the reflection of a window frame, the only indication that the portrait has been painted in an interior. By giving no other clues to the setting, the full force of the viewer's attention is drawn towards Garman and the kitten. Yet this dynamic of the exchange of gaze is not quite so easily described. While her eyes are turned from ours, the kitten's, full of curiosity, are not. Given that the kitten is the namesake, and so perhaps pictorial surrogate for Garman, this shifting gaze might describe one aspect of her character near the start of their relationship. However, the painting also sets the tone for what would now become the bedrock of Freud's art. The painter scrutinises the subject, the kitten returns the gaze, but Garman shies away, deflecting scrutiny but at the same time betraying the emotion she feels as the subject of this particular scrutiny.

Freud's scrutiny is directed to all aspects of his subject and the painting. There is an equality of touch and depiction between, for example, the rendering of Garman's hair, her eyes, the texture of the fabric of her blouse and the kitten's fur. Over the whole surface of the painting there is, unnaturally, no loss of focus. This is intensified by the manner in which Freud had prepared his canvas and constructed the painting's composition. The coarse-weave canvas was given two thickly-applied priming layers – the brushstrokes being predominantly in a horizontal orientation. This has contrived to give the paint surface the feel more of a panel than canvas, and enabled the artist to depict skin, fur, hair, textile without having to compensate for the intrusion of the weave of the canvas.[7] This flat surface describes a shallow space, emphasised by the way in which areas of the priming layer stand for the halftones in the flesh paint and also for highlights in the blouse, and the equality of focus over the painting also serves to flatten space as well as form. One effect of both this sense of flatness and precise rendering of details is to suggest Freud's closeness to painters of the Northern Renaissance such as Hans Memling (a correspondence much alluded to then as now). The sense of flatness and shallow space, the delineation of Garman's face, and especially that of her left profile – described by eye, eyebrow line to sweep of nose to mouth – also suggests an equation with late cubist portrayal. In this respect it is perhaps revealing that around 1942 Roland Penrose lent Picasso's *Weeping Woman* 1937 for a private exhibition at his friend Hugh Willoughby's flat in Brighton. Freud travelled by train to Brighton with the unwrapped painting propped up on the seat opposite him and the painting impressed him with its strength of expression: 'I was so amazed that the bright sunlight in no way made it any worse or more garish or weaker or more painty. It seemed it was as powerful and strong as possible.'[8]

Girl with a Kitten joins *Girl with a White Dog* 1950–1, also in Tate Collection (fig.17), and the last in the series of portraits of Garman (that also includes *Girl with Roses* 1947–8, British Council Collection). Here, Garman looks directly out, seated on a mattress on the floor of their home in Clifton Hill, St John's Wood, rather than at Freud's studio. Dressed in a heavy lime-green dressing gown, pulled off her right shoulder, she cradles her exposed right breast in her arm. Her right leg is pulled up on the mattress and a white bull terrier nuzzles her leg and thigh. The relationship of the different textures of skin, fabric and fur, and the psychological charge of the exposed vulnerability of Garman's cradled breast, is echoed in the position of the trusting dog, equally cradled by leg and thigh, forming a striking counterpoint to the relationship between Garman and her kitten each looking in different directions. Here, the details of dog collar and wedding ring are more subtly focused emblems (Freud and Garman were to divorce in 1953). Herbert Read's statement that Freud was 'the Ingres of Existentialism'[9] seems most apposite in paintings such as this; combining a virtuoso classicism with his often-oppressive observation of the essential loneliness of existence, which infused the post-war atmosphere.

Girl with a Kitten is far removed from paintings of two years earlier such as those that charted the ending of his relationship with Lorna Wishart, Garman's aunt, in 1945. A comparison of these paintings with those of Garman is indicative of the changes that could be observed in Freud's painting at his 1947 London Gallery exhibition. However much *Woman with a Daffodil* 1945 (Museum of Modern Art, New York) and *Woman with a Tulip* 1945 (private collection) were derived from a process of a continued observation of Wishart, they had been primarily constructed by Freud as emblems of emotional intensity – just as had, in its own way, *Man with a Thistle (Self-Portrait)*.

In the two portraits of Wishart, there is an inbuilt awkwardness to the way in which the pictures are painted and composed that impresses in terms of the directness of Freud's rendering of expression and mood. Wishart's head and shoulders are depicted behind a shelf on which rests a single tulip head or a cut daffodil. The flowers echo and exemplify Wishart's emotional state: the true love of a tulip coincides with Wishart looking out full face, open eyes full of hope, while the unrequited love and misfortune described by the single daffodil shows her looking mournfully downwards and to one side. The manner of portrayal is as emblematic as the use of the flowers, but the expression of emotion, however true, is delivered here as if a generalised type.

Comparison of Freud's painting with paintings by Craxton, with whom he had shared his exhibition at the London Gallery in October 1947, is similarly instructive. The following month work by both artists was illustrated in *Horizon* magazine – *Girl with a Kitten* being reproduced opposite Craxton's *Portrait of Eleni* of the same year. The flat, stylised nature of Craxton's portrait – the graphic faceting of hair and arms, altogether generic in its effect – is close in type to the portraits by Freud of Wishart and his later Greek self-portrait (also included in the exhibition at the London Gallery), but the portrait of Garman holding a kitten in her right hand is not descriptive of a type of person or emotion, but is solidly alive to the complications of feeling. It was the star of the exhibition and a few years later encouraged David Sylvester to make the observation that while Freud's painting is:

Fig.17 | Lucian Freud,
Girl with a White Dog 1950–1
Oil on canvas 76.2 × 101.6
Tate. Purchased 1952
N06039

... more concerned with psychological than with formal values – it is not illustra-
tive: his pictures are not statements, they are presences ... His pictures suggest that
he has hypnotized the subject, rendering it intensely strange and perverse. Under his
stare the process of existence is slowed down into a hysterical stillness – as if he had
had to bring the world to stop lest the perversity of its inhabitants might be exercised
to provoke a catastrophe: if his girl with a kitten were allowed to move, she would
strangle it; if the same girl with a rose were allowed to breathe, her breath would
wither it. Any slackening in the tension, any concession to life – movement – would
surely bring disaster.[10]

Sylvester's reading of Freud's painting allies it – as Herbert Read did later – to the
existential philosophy of Jean-Paul Sartre, whose works had started to be translated
into English and discussed in magazines, such as *Horizon*, from 1948. Whether or not
such a correspondence is correct (and it is similarly dangerous to wed Freud's painting
directly to psychoanalytic theories), the degree to which watchfulness and scrutiny is a
decisive aspect of the existentialist condition is perhaps instructive. John Rothenstein
had explained how the expression of stillness in Freud's paintings was the result of a
'tension between obscure contending forces apparent to his wide-eyed penetrating
stare'[11] and Sylvester's description of *Girl with a Kitten* suggests how its 'hysterical
stillness' engenders a 'source of acute anxiety'. However, if such a sense of surveil-
lance or scrutiny was one determinant for existential crisis, the extent to which this
crisis was located in the domain of the artist or viewer is one aspect of Freud's manner of painting. That this response exists in the domain of the viewer and artist rather
than the subject, allies it to the phenomenology of Maurice Merleau-Ponty, as David
Mellor has persuasively argued.[12] The condition of the subject of Freud's paintings is
to exist under the artist's gaze, and Freud's paintings depict the embodiment of this
penetrating gaze as one that provokes different forms of depicted anxiety.

What also starts to occur in Freud's painting from 1947 is a change in subject matter.
If the successive portraits of Kitty Garman provoked a shift in his painting, they did
so for two reasons. He had a greater continual intimacy with Garman than he had had
with any other subject of his paintings to date (save for himself) and the success of
these paintings might have suggested to him that the recreation of a similar intimacy in
terms of his response to other subjects could have a similar effect. The second reason,
and it is allied to the first, was his adoption of the portrait as his primary means of

expression. The equation of scrutiny with intimacy implies an autobiographical basis to his painting, which Freud has done little to hide, claiming that his painting is 'about myself and my surroundings. It is an attempt at a record. I work from the people that interest me and that I care about, in rooms that I live in and know. I use the people to invent my pictures with, and I can work more freely when they are there.'[13] On another occasion he has declared that 'everything is autobiographical, and everything is a portrait',[14] enlarging on this comment recently stating that 'a great portrait has to do with the way it is approached … It's to do with the feeling of individuality and the intensity of the regard and the focus on the specific. So I think portraiture is an attitude. Painting things as symbols and rhetoric and so on doesn't interest me.'[15]

If *Girl with a Kitten* stands as an example of his developing maturity as an artist, it also marks the point at which portraiture becomes the major subject of his painting. In the late 1940s and early 1950s this manifested itself, in the main, with a concentration on a head and shoulders composition, where the subject would be isolated from their immediate surroundings – by now almost invariably Freud's studio – dispensing with the earlier whimsy of the emblematic attribute in favour of a clinically close attention to the specific facts of his subjects re-invented in paint. Freud may have admired the way in which Picasso, in his portraiture, 'was so malevolent',[16] yet it would be wrong to impart a similar motivation to Freud. What might, on the surface, appear malevolent is the result of his piercing scrutiny and desire for truth which he has himself understood as both 'revealing and intrusive'.[17] Robert Hughes's description of *Francis Bacon* 1952 as showing a face 'caught in a moment between reflection and self-projection. It is as naked as a hand,'[18] describes one aspect of what is essential about the transaction between painter and subject that is realised in Freud's work after 1947. His subjects both gaze inwards and project their image of themselves out to be met by Freud's scrutiny – a scrutiny that might defeat, if it is not deflected in some way, or met head on.

Arguably, the most revealing of these portraits from the early 1950s are those, like *Boy Smoking* 1950–1, in which the head is cropped by the edges of the support – more often than not a re-used copper etching plate – that is itself of diminutive size. That Freud provides his subjects with no setting or environment with which to interact, the experience of beholding the painting is akin to that of Freud in painting it. Sitting often only inches away from his subject, it is as if he takes possession of their particularities in a way that is exactly 'revealing and intrusive', that projects both physical and psychological closeness. The subject's depicted gaze is, not surprisingly, usually averted

– sidelong or downcast – an attempted defence against Freud's intrusion. His close-cropping of the image also has the effect of denying narrative and identity. For James Hyman, these are not portraits of types but represent the human condition. Despite the sense of closeness and intimacy with his subjects, Freud 'denies all social information, clues as to the person's identity, precise relationship to the artist, class or origins. We can neither define those figures by their clothing, nor by their environment. What we are encouraged to do is consider the person both as someone particular and as something more general and metaphoric.'[19] This avoidance of declaring a subject's identity or clues provided by their surroundings stresses the extent to which they are not so much sitters as subjects for paintings that are invented ('I use the people to invent my pictures with') just as he would like his work 'to appear *factual* not literal'. As he has recently explained 'Many people are inclined to look at portraits not for the art in them but to see how they resemble people. This seems to me a profound misunderstanding.'[20]

The head of the youth in *Boy Smoking* fills the copper panel, cropping the top of his light brown hair, which has been brushed back and upwards in a quiff. A lit cigarette held in the right corner of his mouth droops down, almost touching the bottom left-hand corner of the painting. He faces the source of light that falls on the face from his right, casting shadows that accentuate his left cheekbones and his full bottom lip. The boy looks straight out at Freud, and so at us, with a look that is both menacing and provocative. It is impossible to tell if we are inside or outside. He has been identified as Charlie Lumley, one of two brothers that Freud was friendly with and painted in the early 1950s, and who he first met when he encountered him breaking into his studio. Something of his character comes out in Stephen Spender's description of meeting him in July 1955: 'While we were lunching, Lucian Freud arrived in the restaurant, the Perroquet, with his friend Charlie. They were both dressed like workmen, Charlie almost in rags, without ties. The restaurant was appropriately shocked. I thought: this is part of the war of the bohemians against the bureaucrats.'[21] At this time Freud still had his studio in Delamere Terrace, near Paddington (he had moved there in 1943 but relocated in 1962 to a condemned building nearby in Clarendon Terrace). Scarred by bomb damage, the area was home to a shifting underclass that Catherine Lampert has described as 'people who existed outside regular employment – costermongers, villains and thieves – men who guarded their women and showed drunken, dangerous strength in the weekend street fights.'[22] Such people existed at the furthest boundaries of the law and offered Freud a role that he could slip into. Freed from the pressure of social

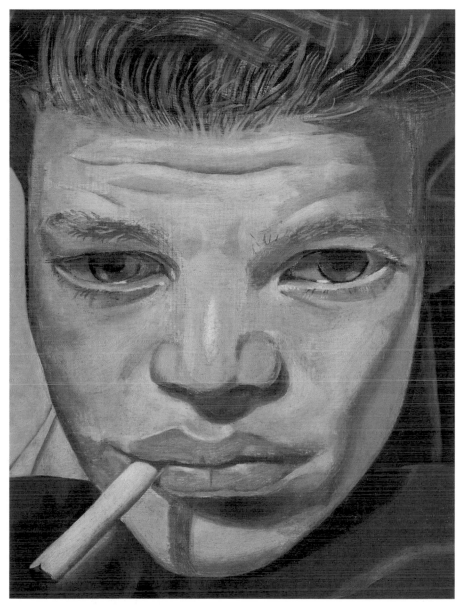

17

convention, this assumed identity of the outsider inhabiting a world of desolation provided him with a viewpoint that coloured the way in which he approached his subjects.

When *Boy Smoking* is compared to the earlier drawing *Narcissus* 1948 (Tate, T11793) and also to the portrait of *Francis Bacon* 1952 (fig.18), the distance Freud has travelled as an artist becomes apparent. The earlier drawing[23] shows a young man looking down, cupping his face in his hands, the lower third of the drawing being a fragmented discontinuous reflection of his chin, mouth and nostrils. The drawing is, in its way, a conceit illustrative of one type of scrutiny: the self-scrutiny of the self-portrait. Yet this is no self-portrait (though it has been often misidentified as such) but an image of self-scrutiny under scrutiny. Its style of drawing is tight and almost scientific, with line and form described in minutest detail by areas of stippling and dotting (akin to aspects of his etching technique at that time). Neither *Boy Smoking* nor *Francis Bacon* is illustrative in this way. Both paintings suggest the beginnings of his move away from a concern with the drawn line to a bolder use of paint, which encompasses a different way of looking at his subjects.

In *Boy Smoking*, the precise painting technique of, for instance, *Girl with a Kitten* has started to free up and the paint is applied to the support in a much looser manner. There is a greater sense of brushstroke – of paint being bodied with individual brushstrokes readily identifiable in the flesh paint, yet even so smoothly blended wet-in-wet;

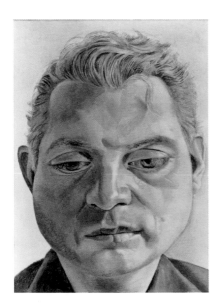

Fig.18 | Lucian Freud, *Francis Bacon* 1952
Oil on metal 17.8 × 12.7
Tate. Purchased 1952, N06040
Present whereabouts unknown

the highlight delineating the nose being the most bodied impasto of the painting. Elsewhere the thinness of the paint layers is underlined by Freud's exposure of areas of the white priming surface for all but the highest highlights. No initial drawing stage can be discerned, which chimes with his feeling that his compulsion for linear accuracy was 'a limited and limiting vehicle … the idea of doing paintings where you're conscious of the drawing and not the paint just irritated me.'[24] There is no longer the wish to capture minute detail such as the reflection of window frame in an eye, but Freud's scrutiny of his subjects remains at high pitch.

What is significant here is the extent to which Freud is creating a language of realism where his capacity for observation is now being conveyed through the painted surface rather than the drawn line. In 1954, coinciding with his inclusion in the Venice Biennale, Freud published 'Some Thoughts on Painting' in *Encounter* magazine, which makes explicit his aims. He describes himself as a 'painter' and locates his object in painting as a quality of obsession with his subject, but where reality is not copied:

> *My object in painting pictures is to try and move the senses by giving an intensification of reality … The painter makes real to others his innermost feelings about all that he cares for … A painter's tastes must grow out of what so obsesses him in life that he never has to ask himself what it is suitable for him to do in art … The painter's obsession with his subject is all that he needs to drive him to work … The subject must be kept under observation: if this is done, day and night, the subject – he, she, or it – will eventually reveal the all … The picture in order to move us must never merely remind us of life, but must acquire a life of its own, precisely in order to reflect life.[25]*

The series of aphoristic statements reveals his closeness to Francis Bacon and his attention to a 'brutality of fact'. They also indicate the moves he was making towards a different kind of painting. Rather than sit down and paint his subjects knee to knee, from around 1954 he would stand up to paint, walking around the studio and the subject as he did so (he has said that 'I often use things I see when I go further round').[26] Where before he had used small sable brushes, in the latter half of the 1950s he started to wield hog-hair brushes. As Lawrence Gowing incisively described, paint is 'driven across the surface with the springy bristles of a hog-hair brush quite unlike the touch of the pliant sable, which had followed the forms with obedient literalness.'[27] Bacon – a close friend since 1944 – was behind Freud's words in *Encounter* and also informed his changes in his manner of working. Bacon talked to Freud about 'the paint itself carrying the form, and imbuing the paint with this sort of life. He talked about packing a lot of things into one single brushstroke, which amused and excited me and I realized that I was a million miles away from anything I ever could or would do: the idea of paint having that power was something which made me feel I ought to get to know it in a different way that wasn't subservient.'[28]

In 1972 Freud's mother Lucie attempted to kill herself, her husband having died two years earlier. As a way of combating her depression Freud painted her in over 1,000 sittings between 1972 and 1984, producing no less than ten paintings, at least five drawings and three etchings (he had started to make etchings again in 1982). This sequence of works has been described by William Feaver as 'perhaps his greatest, certainly his most sustained, achievement. Each one of them, each touching instance, is simply "there on its own", representing in deep reflection "what is there to be seen."'[29] *The Painter's Mother IV* 1973 is the last of the first group of these paintings by Freud, which were exhibited together at his 1974 retrospective at the Hayward Gallery, London. All are fairly small with the head filling the canvas. In the first two from the series Lucie Freud looks straight out, confronting her painter son, her hair cropped at the top edge. This composition is repeated in the final version of the three etchings that Freud made of her ten years later, *The Painter's Mother* 1982 (fig.19). This etching portrays an uncharacteristically fierce and questioning look – in contrast with the direct look in the first two paintings, which seem more quizzical and resigned. In the

Fig.19 | Lucian Freud, *The Painter's Mother* 1982
Intaglio print on paper 17.8 × 15.2
Tate. Purchased 1982, P07783

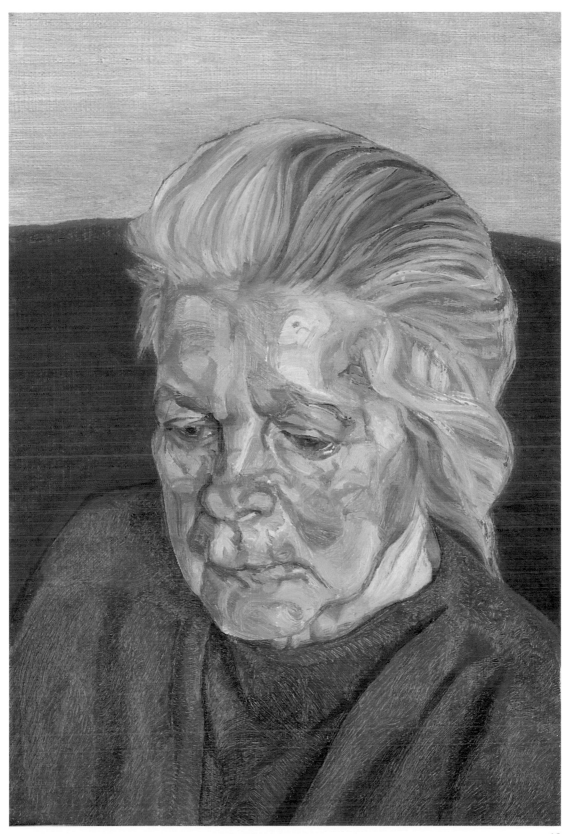

third painting from 1972 she has her head turned slightly to the right, her gaze glancing away, whereas in this, the fourth, although her head is turned slightly away to her right she looks down, self-contained, composed and utterly introspective; in both of these paintings her head is centred within the canvas. Where the first two paintings are relatively thickly painted, the third and fourth in the series are much more controlled in execution and painted more thinly.

In composition *The Painter's Mother IV* relates closely to the manner in which his mother is depicted in *Large Interior, w9* 1973 (Devonshire collection). This large painting shows Lucie seated in the studio armchair. On the floor beside her is a pestle and mortar that Freud used for grinding the charcoal he often mixed in his paint. Lying on a mattress behind her, arms pillowing her head, is a naked woman with a blanket covering her legs that are pulled up to create a pyramidal shape behind Lucie's head. Both seem unaware of each other's presence and indeed both subjects, unusually for Freud, sat separately for this painting. The angle of Freud's mother's head and her introverted gaze, repeats that of *The Painter's Mother IV*, the brown background now recognisable as the chairback in *Large Interior, w9*.[30]

Further paintings from the series continue to depict Freud's mother as self-contained, an aim that is confirmed by the circumstances in which they were painted and Freud's own relationship with his mother. Freud was the middle child of three sons and was his mother's favourite. The youngest brother, Clement, remembered how, 'when she came into the nursery, she nodded to Stephen and me, and sat down with Lucian and whispered. They had secrets.'[31] For his part, Freud rebuffed his mother's attention. In 1972 he had 'started painting her because she'd lost interest in everything, including me. Before then, I always avoided her because she was so intuitive that I felt my privacy was rather threatened by her … From very early on I realised it was important not to be affected by her, not to see her.'[32] For Freud, her new lack of interest in him made her 'a good model'.[33] Self-contained, disinterested, passive, she offers no defence to her son's scrutiny because she has no reserves with which to defend herself – and no need to anyway; her depression at her continued existence is nakedly apparent. Bruce Bernard astutely noted how in these paintings Freud recorded 'his father's widow's vulnerability and what obstinately remained of the girl and child in her, as well as the unarrestable dissolution of a human being when the siege of old age has established its final hold. The pictures show her as being almost naked to the world – though dressed, as always, with a touching neatness and propriety.'[34] The paintings have a contained, almost compressed, emotion about them; they capture Lucie Freud's loneliness and the resulting lack of purpose to her life, but they are also a form of self-portrait that lays bare Freud's complex relationship with his mother. This sense of intense examination allied to the particular relationship these paintings record might suggest something of the action of the analyst's couch. However, it is important to recognise that Freud's painting is not analytical and neither is it diagnostic. Freud's activity is instead that of specifying things and people, as well as the relationships between people, through the action of a scrutiny that creates a painting. This is one key to unlocking the power of Freud's concentration on the portrait, and his reliance on subjects that are in some way 'autobiographical'. If the object of his scrutiny can be identified as the subject that is being painted, and also the painting itself, it is, however, also to be found in the relationship between Freud and his subject, and so ultimately with Freud himself.

Fifty years after he wrote 'Some Thoughts on Painting', Freud re-read it, having been asked if there was anything he felt he had left out. He suggested that 'on re-reading it I find that I left out the vital element without which painting can't exist: PAINT. Paint in relation to a painter's nature. One thing more important than the person in the painting is the picture.'[35] It is this other conundrum that also lies at the heart of Freud's painting. He paints portraits. However, he doesn't copy what he sees but observes his subjects so that he might invent them afresh through the activity of painting them from life. As he admitted to John Richardson, 'Aesthetic and biological truth-telling is what my painting is all about'.[36] What makes everything a portrait is not just the particular way in which he observes his subjects, but that this goes hand in hand with a scrutiny of paint and the act of painting as he prowls around his subjects – both the painted and the painting – brush or palette knife in hand. AW

16 *Girl with a Kitten* 1947

Oil on canvas 41 × 30.7
Signed and dated on reverse: *Septem 47 Lucian Freud*
Tate. Bequeathed by Simon Sainsbury 2006
T12617

PROVENANCE
London Gallery, London; Stephen Freud, London; James Kirkman, London; Simon Sainsbury, London.

EXHIBITED
Lucian Freud and John Craxton, London Gallery, London 1947 (no.42)
London/Paris; New Trends in Painting and Sculpture, ICA, London 1950 (no.45, as '*Girl with Kitten 1947–8*')
Ben Nicholson, Francis Bacon and Lucian Freud, British Pavilion, XXVIII Venice Biennale 1954 (no.45, as '*Girl with cat*')
Lucian Freud, Hayward Gallery, London; City Art Gallery, Bristol; Museum and City Art Gallery, Birmingham; City Museum and Art Gallery, Leeds, 1974 (no.43, repr. p.52)
Artist and the Model, Whitworth Art Gallery, Manchester 1986 (no.10)
Lucian Freud Paintings, Hirshhorn Museum and Sculpture Garden, Smithsonian Institute, Washington DC; Musée National d'Art Moderne, Paris; Hayward Gallery, London; Neue National Galerie, Berlin, 1987–8 (no.3, repr.)
Lucian Freud: dipinti e opere su carta 1940–1991, Palazzo Ruspoli, Rome; Castello Sforzesca, Milan; Tate Gallery, Liverpool; Museum of Fine Arts, Tochigi; Otani Memorial Art Museum, Nishinomiya, 1991–2 (no.6, repr. p.32 and cover)
Lucian Freud, Art Gallery of New South Wales, Sydney; Art Gallery of Western Australia, Perth, 1992–3 (no.3, repr. p.22 and cover)
Lucian Freud: Early Works, Robert Miller Gallery, New York, 1993–4
Lucian Freud, Tate Britain, London; Caixa Forum, Barcelona; Museum of Contemporary Arts, Los Angeles, 2002–3 (no.20, repr.)

LITERATURE
Horizon, ed. Cyril Connolly, November 1947 repr. between pp.244–5 (as '*Portrait*')
Lawrence Gowing, *Lucian Freud*, London 1982, pl.56, repr.
Bruce Bernard, *Lucian Freud*, London 1996, pl.59, repr.
David Alan Mellor, *Interpreting Lucian Freud*, London 2002, pl.2, repr. p.8
William Feaver, *Lucian Freud*, New York 2007, pl.54, repr.
Sebastian Smee, *Lucian Freud*, London 2007, pl.18, repr.

17 *Boy Smoking* 1950–1

Oil on copper 15.5 × 11.5
Tate. Bequeathed by Simon Sainsbury 2006
T12618

PROVENANCE
Hanover Gallery, London; Arthur Jeffress,
London, by 1954; Sotheby's, London, 26 April
1961 (lot 60); bought by 'Jerdine'; [. . .]; Nicholas
Luard, sold to Marlborough Gallery, London,
17 March 1972, and sold to Simon Sainsbury,
London, 10 May 1972.

EXHIBITED
Lucian Freud, Hanover Gallery, London 1950
(no.9)
Lucian Freud, Hanover Gallery, London 1952
(no.12)
Ben Nicholson, Francis Bacon and Lucian Freud,
British Pavilion, XXVIII Venice Biennale 1954
(no.77)

LITERATURE
William Feaver, *Lucian Freud*, New York 2007,
pl.83, repr.

18 *The Painter's Mother IV* 1973

Oil on canvas 27.3 × 18.6
Tate. Bequeathed by Simon Sainsbury 2006
T12619

PROVENANCE
James Kirkman, London; the Hon. Colin Tennant;
Simon Sainsbury, London, after 1978.

EXHIBITED
Lucian Freud, Hayward Gallery, London; City Art
Gallery, Bristol; Museum and City Art Gallery,
Birmingham; City Museum and Art Gallery,
Leeds, 1974 (no.132, repr. as 'The Artist's Mother IV
1973', p.52)
Lucian Freud Recent Paintings, Anthony d'Offay
Gallery, London; Davis & Long Company, New
York, 1978 (no.1, repr. as 'Head of the Painter's
Mother')

LITERATURE
William Feaver, *Lucian Freud*, New York 2007,
pl.143, repr. (as *The Painter's Mother* 1972)

Notes and References

1 · John Wootton

1. *George Vertue Notebooks*, vol.III, *Walpole Society*, vol.22, 1933–4, p.34.

2. For Wootton's study of Claude and Poussin, see Arline Meyer, *John Wootton: Landscapes and Sporting Art in Early Georgian London*, exh. cat., The Iveagh Bequest, Kenwood, London 1984, pp.15–17.

3. For the Smyths of Ballynatray see *Burke's Landed Gentry of Ireland*, 1899; Bence-Jones 1988, pp.26–7; and Deirdre Conroy, 'Ballynatray House Restored', *Irish Arts Review*, vol.20, no.1 (spring 2003), p.102. The current Ballynatray House is a 1795–7 rebuild, which partly incorporates the structure of the former castellated house.

2 · Thomas Gainsborough

1. Armstrong 1904, p.260.

2. Bequeathed in his will (9 November 1734, codicil 31 May 1735, proved 9 February 1737/8) to his son Robert Andrews, The National Archives PROB 11/687.

3. 7 August 1749, proved 4 December 1750, The National Archives, PROB 11/784.

4. Distantly related, but shared descent in the Andrews family, from Robert and Francis Andrews.

5. Adrienne Corri's suggestion that the sitters are Claude Fonnereau, of Christchurch Mansion, Ipswich, and his wife, would demand an extremely early, and unlikely, dating for the picture (Corri 1984, pp.253–6); Ellis Waterhouse initially dismissed the Carter identification 'as the late owner [of the picture] assured me that it was a myth of Armstrong's' – see Ellis Waterhouse's review of John Hayes, *Gainsborough: Paintings and Drawings*, 1975, *Art Bulletin*, vol.58, no.3 (Sept. 1976), p.459.

6. Mentioned in William Carter's post-nuptial settlement, 20 June 1733, Essex Record Office D/DQ 84/49.

7. Essex Record Office D/DQ 84/47.

8. Essex Record Office D/DQ 84/49, in which the terms of his 1723 pre-nuptial settlement are also mentioned.

9. 7 August 1749, proved 4 December 1750, The National Archives, PROB 11/784.

10. Claude Jamineau is possibly identifiable as the London representative of Jamineau & Rousseau, a trading house with operations in Venice. He was most probably related to Daniel Jamineau, one of the Directors of the London Assurance company and a considerable merchant with international connections, importing spices to England and exporting textiles and leather gloves to Europe – see Robin D. Gwynn, *Huguenot Heritage: the history and contribution of the Huguenots in Britain*, London 1985, pp.87, 151.

11. Carter's children were all baptised at All Saints, Sudbury, also the church from where his daughter was married. His burial at St Andrew's, Bulmer marks a shift of allegiance.

12. Cited in an attested copy of conveyance from William Dalton of Great Henny, second husband of Frances, widow of William Carter, to William Carter her eldest son, 11 November 1758, Essex Record Office, D/DQ 84/50.

13. His return was most likely prompted by the death of his father in October 1748, although he continued to rent his Hatton Garden house until spring 1749 – see D. Tyler, 'Thomas Gainsborough's Days in Hatton Garden', *Gainsborough's House Review* 1992/3, p.32 n.24.

14. The latter comments made by Hugh Belsey, to whom I am grateful for discussing the dating of this work.

15. Letter from Ellis Waterhouse to Adrienne Corri, 2 April 1983, in Corri 1984, p.257.

16. Verbal communication with Rica Jones (X-ray of *Mr and Mrs Kirby* held in the Conservation Department, Tate).

17. Notes on costume provided by Vanda Foster: letter to Hugh Belsey, 10 July 1983.

18. See Bensusan-Butt 1993, p.35. The 1717 Registration of Papist estates, however, indicates that ownership of Auberies was split into three parts. Robert Andrews took out a 99-year lease, at the annual rent of £11, from Barbara Daniel (who lived until 1740) in 1703. Precisely when he purchased the estate has not been conclusively established.

3 · Johan Zoffany

I would like to thank Charles Greig for his help and advice in the writing of this entry.

1. *Sir Elijah Impey* 1783, Asia, Pacific and Africa Collections, The British Library; *Mr and Mrs Warren Hastings* 1783–7, Victoria Memorial Hall, Kolkata.

2. Ozias Humphrey, *Notebook*, British Library, London, Photo Euro 043 (photocopy of the original held by Yale University Library).

3. *Colonel Polier with his Friends* 1786, Victoria Memorial Hall, Kolkata.

4. The original papers of Blair's army career do not survive in the Asia, Pacific and Africa Collections at The British Library. Details of his life and career are obtained from V.C.P. Hodson, *List of the Officers of the Bengal Army, 1758–1834*, London 1927, p.161.

5. William Hodges, *Travels in India, During the Years 1780, 1781, 1782 and 1783*, 2nd ed., corrected, London 1794, p.54.

6. *Fort William – India House Correspondence and other contemporary papers relating thereto, Vol.VII, 1771–1781*, ed. Hira Lal Gupta, Delhi 1981, p.18.

Brevet is a promotion without added pay and does not impede promotion of others.

7. Will of William Blair, late Colonel in the Honourable East India Company's Service of St Marylebone, Middlesex, 11 May 1814, Public Records Office, The National Archives, PROB 11/1556.

8. R. Head, 'Corelli in Calcutta: Colonial Music-Making in India during the 17th and 18th Centuries', *Early Music*, vol.13, no.4, November 1985, pp.548–53.

9. *The Morse and Cator Families c.1784*, Aberdeen Art Gallery.

10. Leppert 1993, p.114.

11. Ibid., p.115.

12. Ibid., p.114.

13. Thomas Daniell, *Siccra Gulley on the Ganges* 1788, in 'Oriental Scenery', vol.4, no.9.

14. Mildred Archer, *India and British Portraiture 1770–1825*, London 1979, p.157.

4 · Edgar Degas

1. The first, in a private collection, is Lemoisne 1232, the second, without a Lemoisne number, is on the Paris art market. Both are illustrated in Paris-Ottawa-New York 1988–9, figs.309, 311.

2. On the photograph, see *Edgar Degas photographe*, exh. cat., Bibliothèque Nationale de France, 1999, no.40a, repr.

5 & 6 · Claude Monet

1. The eighteen paintings are Wildenstein 1996, nos.348–63, including 353a and 357a.

2. Duret 1902, p.100.

3. Wildenstein 1996, no.1718.

4. Wildenstein 1974, letter no.2525.

5. Wildenstein 1974, letter no.2532.

6. Wildenstein 1996, no.1922.

7 · Henri Rousseau

1. The date of the banquet has not been recorded but John Richardson believes it was on Saturday 21 November 1908. (*A Life of Picasso: Volume II, 1907–1917*, New York 1996, p.111.)

2. Brummer would decamp for New York in 1917, where he continued to deal in contemporary and medieval art. He died there, a very wealthy man.

3. Quoted in Jean Bouret, *Henri Rousseau*, London 1961, p.42.

4. Richardson 1996, p.113.

8 · Paul Gauguin

1. George 1925, p.374. At the time, the painting was in the collection of Georges Viau who had also owned Cézanne's *Still Life with Fruit Dish*, discussed above. He had sold the latter in 1907 and the two works were not in the collection simultaneously.

2. The painting, formerly in the Matsukata collection, Japan, but now lost, is Wildenstein 1964, no.400.

9 & 10 · Pierre Bonnard

1. Sasha M. Newman, *Bonnard: The Late Paintings*, exh. cat., Phillips Collection, Washington DC; Dallas Museum of Art, 1984, p.166.

2. See Sarah Whitfield in London-New York 1998, p.146.

3. Emmanuelle l'Ecotais, 'Photography', in Paris 2006, p.114; see also Michel Frizot, 'Pierre's Stupefaction: The

Window of Photography', ibid., pp.262–7, and Françoise Heilbrun and Philippe Néagu, *Pierre Bonnard: Photographe*, Musée d'Orsay, Paris 1987.

4. 'Marthe standing in the sun' (Musée d'Orsay), repr. ibid. p.116, pl.17.

5. Nicholas Watkins, *Bonnard: Colour and Light*, London 1998, pp.26–7.

6. Bonnard remarks to Ingrid Rydbeck 1937, discussed by Yve-Alain Bois, 'Bonnard's Passivity', in Paris 2006, pp.61–2.

7. See Whitfield in London-New York 1998, pp.26–8.

8. Ibid., p.122.

9. Thompson and Mann 1994.

10. 'Chronology', London-New York 1998, p.261.

11. *Large Nude in the Bathtub* 1924, private collection, repr. in Paris 2006, p.211. However, Newman (in Washington-Dallas 1984 p.166) took this bathroom to be Villa du Bosquet.

12. Jacqueline Munck, 'The Nudes in the Bathtub' in Paris 2006, p.204.

13. E.g. Vaillant 1965, p.129 as 1935, and London 1966, p.100 as 1938–41.

14. See John Elderfield's discussion of perception in 'Seeing Bonnard' in London-New York 1998, pp.33–52.

15. *Nude in the Bath* 1936–8 (Musée d'Art Moderne de la Ville de Paris), *The Large Bathtub* 1937–9 (private collection) and *Nude in the Bath and Small Dog* 1941–6 (Carnegie Museum of Art, Pittsburgh), repr. in Paris 2006, pp.225, 227, 229.

16. Paris 2006, p.220.

17. See Michel Makarius, 'Bonnard "Du Côté de chez Proust"', ibid., pp.279–81.

18. David Sylvester, *About Modern Art: Critical Essays 1948–96*, London 1996, p.138.

19. Ibid.

20. Newman in Washington-Dallas 1984, p.166.

21. Vaillant 1965, p.135.

22. Whitfield in London-New York 1998, p.28.

23. Linda Nochlin, 'Bonnard's Bathers', *Art in America*, July 1998, pp.63–7, and 'Bonnard's "Bathers"' in Paris 2006, p.205.

24. 'Introduction', ibid., p.26.

25. London-New York 1998, pp.167–8; he dates the work to 1938–41.

26. Whitfield, 'A Question of Belonging' in Paris 2006, p.65.

27. Notes dated 16 Jan. and 22 Jan. 1934, in 'Notes de Bonnard', Paris 1984, p.190.

28. Patrick Heron, 'Pierre Bonnard: Abstraction', February 1947, republished in *Painter as Critic; Patrick Heron: Selected Writings*, ed. Mel Gooding, London 1998, p.21.

29. Repr. in Paris-Washington-Dallas 1984, p.139.

30. Repr. ibid., p.95.

31. Mme Hahnloser's account in Vaillant 1965, p.182.

32. Vaillant 1965, p.146.

33. Hyman in London-New York 1998, p.182.

11 · Victor Pasmore

1. Repr. Clive Bell, *Victor Pasmore*, Harmondsworth 1945, pl.31, col., formerly collection of Hugo Pitman, now private collection, USA.

2. Bowness and Lambertini 1980, no.133, repr. p.80.

3. Terry Frost in conversation with the author, 1998.

4. *Thames at Chiswick* 1943, repr. Bowness and Lambertini 1980, p.59, no.61, collection National Gallery of Canada, Ottawa; *The Quiet River* 1943–4, collection Tate T00197.

5. Repr. Wendy Baron, *Sickert: Paintings and Drawings*, New Haven and London 2006, p.467, no.530.

6. Quoted by Ronald A. Davey, 'Introduction', *Victor Pasmore*, exh. cat., Hatton Gallery, Newcastle upon Tyne, 1960, p.4.

7. *Spiral Development: The Snowstorm*, 1950–1, Arts Council Collection, London, repr. Bowness and Lambertini 1980, p.91, no.158.

8. Victor Pasmore, 'A Note on Abstract Painting' in *Victor Pasmore*, Redfern Gallery, London 1947, p.4.

12, 13 & 14 · Balthus

1. Balthus's accounts of his wartime service and injury have been questioned by some commentators as invented, or at the very least, exaggerated, as part of the artist's tendency to self-mythologise. See discussion in Nicholas Fox Weber, *Balthus: A Biography*, London and New York 1999, pp.402–5.

2. Letter from Balthus to Pierre Jean Jouve (26 July 1940) quoted in Robert Kopp, 'Balthus and Pierre Jean Jouve. Previously Unpublished Documents' in Clair 2001, p.70.

3. Balthus and his wife subsequently left

France for Switzerland; Balthus returned to France after peace had resumed.

4. Sabine Rewald in New York 1984, p.100. Balthus made four paintings on the subject of *The Salon*: two studies (now private collection and collection of Mr and Mrs Roger Berlind) and two finished paintings: *The Salon 1* 1941–3, Minneapolis Institute of Art, and *The Salon II* 1942, Museum of Modern Art, New York, collection Mr and Mrs John Hay Whitney. All reproduced Clair and Monnier 2000, p.140.

5. *The Greedy Child* (*L'Enfant gourmand*) 1940, private collection, see Clair 2001, p.274 and Clair and Monnier 2000, p.138.

6. Clair 2001, p.274.

7. See Structure and Condition Report, Tate Conservation Department 2008. Thanks to Kate Stonor, Tate Painting Conservator.

8. 'After his arrival in Champrovent, the severe atmosphere of his Parisian work is replaced by the more decorative forms and richer colours of the farm. The resulting pictures often have an Old Master character, evident here in the deep claret of the curtain and table covering and in the finely painted apples and Victorian fruit bowl, which forms a still life reminiscent of Caravaggio's fruit baskets.' Rewald in New York 1984, p.100.

9. See Clair and Monnier 2000, p.254, nos.D650, D651 (verso of D652), D652 (verso of D651) and D653.

10. Ibid. D653.

11. *The Week of Four Thursdays* (*La Semaine des quatre jeudis*) 1949, Ploughkeepsie, The Frances Lehman Loeb Art Center, Vassar College,

Katherine Sanford Deutsch collection, see Clair 2001, pp.302–5; and *The Room* (*La Chambre*) 1952–4, private collection, see Clair 2001, pp.128–9.

12. Quoted in Fox Weber 1999, p.315.

13. Balthus, *Vanished Splendors: A Memoir*, New York 2001, p.37.

14. Thanks to Kate Stonor, Tate Painting Conservator and Tate Conservation department for taking this investigation forward.

15. *Cathy* 1933, Musée National d'Art Moderne, Centre Georges Pompidou, Paris; *The King of Cats* 1935, private collection, Switzerland; *Self-portrait* 1940, private collection; and *Self-portrait* 1949, private collection, Geneva. See Clair 2001, p.310, regarding the latter work: 'The 1948 [*sic*] *Autoportrait* is the most austere of the four he did of himself. The background is practically black. The emaciated face is stern, the nose like a sabre blade, and the thick lips remind us of the head of a bird of prey.' Balthus also made self-portrait drawings, for example, a charcoal drawing in 1942 (now lost) and another in 1943 (private collection). See Clair 2001, pp.284–5. The artist appears more relaxed in these drawings than in the painting of 1940.

16. The syndicate was established by Balthus's Parisian dealer, Henriette Gomès who ran the Galerie Beaux-Arts, from the premises of *Gazette des Beaux-Arts*. The group also included Claude Herseint; Balthus's New York dealer, Pierre Matisse; Alix de Rothschild; Marie-Laure de Noailles, who had also been a member of the Zodiac Group that supported Salvador Dalí in the early 1930s; Maurice Rheims; and Henri

Samuel. In return for a basic maintenance allowance, Balthus gave the group paintings from time to time. Pierre Matisse's gallery stock book shows that the painting was purchased from Balthus for $346 in January 1950. It was not sold on by Matisse until 1960 when William N. Copley acquired the work for $5,500 (see papers held Pierre Matisse Gallery Archive, Morgan Library & Museum, New York).

17. My thanks to Andrew Wilson for the second of these possible readings.

18. My thanks to Patricia Smithen, Head of Painting Conservation at Tate for her insights into the artist's working processes.

19. Balthus 2001, p.213.

20. Balthus 2001, p.214.

21. The first two paintings in the series were *The Dream I* (*Le Rêve I*) 1955 and *The Dream II* (*Le Rêve II*) 1956.

22. Clair in Paris 1983–4, pp.277–8. See also *Christie's Impressionist and Modern Art Evening Sale Catalogue*, 6 November 2007, p.275 (entry for *Le Rêve II*, lot 78).

23. See Rewald in New York 1984, p.18 in which she notes that Balthus 'was strongly influenced by Piero's "insistence on representing Scripture in terms of daily experience".'

24. Clair 2001, p.334.

25. *Christie's Impressionist and Modern Art Evening Sale Catalogue*, 6 November 2007, p.276.

26. Ibid.

27. Balthus 2001, p.153–4, quoted in ibid, p.275.

28. I am indebted to Sabine Rewald for

noting Henri Samuel's ownership of *The Golden Fruit*.

15 · Francis Bacon

1. Dawn Ades, 'Web of Images' in London 1985, p.13.

2. Wieland Schmied, *Francis Bacon*, Munich-London-New York 2006, p.21.

3. For example in the catalogue of the sale at Christie's, London, 29 June 1995 (lot 12).

4. London 1965, p.65.

16, 17 & 18 · Lucian Freud

1. *The Bird* and *Chelsea Bun*, both 1946.

2. George Millar, *Isabel and the Sea*, London 1948, pp.357–8. Millar had been a member of the Special Operations Executive towards the end of the Second World War in Southern France where he carried out sabotage operations with the Maquis. After the war, with money earned from two books of wartime reminiscences, he bought a yacht and with his wife, Isabel Paske-Smith, sailed his 30-ton ketch *Truant* through the French canals to the Mediterranean and on to Greece where they met Freud and Craxton. *Isabel and the Sea* relates the story of this journey.

3. Ibid., p.364.

4. Robert Hughes, 'On Lucian Freud' in *Lucian Freud Paintings*, The British Council, 1987, p.14.

5. John Russell, 'Introduction' in London-Bristol-Birmingham-Leeds 1974, p.5.

6. Ibid., p.18.

7. See Structure and Condition Report Tate Conservation Department 2008. My thanks to Kate Stonor, Tate Painting Conservator, for her insights on this painting as well as *Boy Smoking* and *The Painter's Mother IV*.

8. From an interview with William Feaver, broadcast on BBC Radio 3 on 7 February 1992, quoted in William Feaver, 'Beyond Feeling' in Sydney 1992, p.13.

9. Herbert Read, *Contemporary British Art*, Harmondsworth 1964 (revised ed.) p. 35.

10. David Sylvester, 'Two Painters, Stanley Spencer and Lucian Freud', *Britain To-day*, July 1950, pp.38–9.

11. John Rothenstein, 'Lucian Freud' in London 1954.

12. David Alan Mellor, 'Existentialism and Post-War British Art' in *Paris Post War: Art and Existentialism 1945–55*, ed. Frances Morris, Tate Gallery, London 1993, p.59. See also Mellor 2002, pp.53–5.

13. John Russell in London-Bristol-Birmingham-Leeds 1974, p.13.

14. William Feaver, *Lucian Freud*, London 2002, p.27.

15. Sebastian Smee, 'A Late-Night Conversation with Lucian Freud' in *Freud at Work*, London 2006, p.33.

16. William Feaver, 'Beyond Feeling' in Sydney-Perth 1992–3, p.14.

17. Starr Figura, *Lucian Freud· The Painter's Etchings*, exh. cat., Museum of Modern Art, New York 2007, p.13.

18. Hughes 1987, p.7.

19. James Hyman, *The Battle for Realism, Figurative Art in Britain during the Cold War 1945–1960*, London and New Haven 2001, p.147.

20. Smee 2006, p.32.

21. Stephen Spender, *Journals 1939–1983*, London 1985, p.158.

22. Catherine Lampert, *Lucian Freud*, exh. cat., Whitechapel Art Gallery, London 1993, p.15.

23. A similar drawing from the same series was identified by Lincoln Kirstein as a 'Borstal Boy as Hercules' in *Quarry: A Collection in Lieu of Memories*, Pasadena 1986, p.107.

24. Figura 2007, pp.16–17.

25. Lucian Freud, 'Some Thoughts on Painting', *Encounter*, July 1954, p.23.

26. Wiliam Feaver, 'Freud at the Correr: Fifty Years', *Lucian Freud*, Milan 2005, p.33.

27. Gowing 1982, p.118.

28. Feaver 2007, p.321 (from a conversation with Lucian Freud, November 1992).

29. Ibid., p.10.

30. The naked woman in the painting is Jacquetta Eliot, Freud's then girlfriend. She is also the subject of *Naked Portrait 1972–3* (Tate).

31. Cited in William Feaver, 'Betting heavily on yourself', *Spectator*, 27 October 2001.

32. Smee 2006, pp.31–2.

33. Smee in London 2007, p.43.

34. Bernard 1996, p.15.

35. Feaver 2007, p.37.

36. John Richardson, *Sacred Monsters, Sacred Masters*, London 2002, p.331.

Index

Credits

without the calories | comfort food

Justine Pattison

Low-calorie recipes, cheats and ideas
for feel-good favourites

contents

introduction

MY STORY

I struggled with my weight for years. After being a skinny child and teenager, I piled on the weight during my last years of school and went into my twenties feeling fat and frumpy. A career as a cookery writer and food stylist has helped me understand good food but because my kitchen is always overflowing with great things to eat, temptation is never far away. My weight yo-yoed for twenty years and at my heaviest I weighed more than 15 stone.

A few years ago, I worked on the hit TV series *You Are What You Eat* – I put together those groaning tables of bad food. I also had the chance to work with the contributors on the show, guiding them through the dieting process and helping them discover a whole new way of eating and cooking. Having been overweight myself, I became passionate about helping people lose weight.

Since then, I've worked as a food consultant on many of the weight-loss shows you've seen on TV, and written diet plans and recipes for best-selling books, newspapers and magazines. I'm so proud that thousands of people have successfully followed my way of cooking and lost weight.

This book, and the others in the *Without the Calories* series, are ideal for anyone who wants to lose weight while leading a normal life. Cooking my way will help you sustain a happy, healthy weight loss. That's what it's all about: you don't have to be stick thin, but you deserve to feel good about yourself. My *Without the Calories* recipes will help you reach your goal.

ABOUT THIS BOOK

For me, comfort food is all about indulgence; dishes that are rich, full flavoured and satisfying. Think of creamy sauces, golden pastry pies, hearty stews and luscious chocolate puddings. Not surprisingly, comfort food tends to be very high in fat, sugar and starchy carbohydrates – not what you need when you are trying to lose weight!

In this book, I've taken classic comfort food dishes and given them a healthy makeover. I've reworked the ingredients to reduce the number of calories as much as possible, while still keeping all the flavour and appetite appeal, helping you lose weight in the most delicious and simple way possible.

I'm not going to make rash promises about how many pounds my alternative recipes will help you shed, but I do know that when it comes to losing weight, finding foods that give you pleasure and fit into your lifestyle are the key to success. When you eat well without obsessing over rapid weight loss, it's easier to relax and lose what you need to comfortably – and safely.

To help everyone enjoy these reinvented dishes, I've used easy-to-find ingredients and given clear, simple cooking instructions. There's lots of freezer information included, so you know which dishes you can put aside safely for another day.

If you're already following a diet plan, you'll find additional nutritional information at the back of the book that'll help you work my recipes into your week. And, if you're stuck for inspiration and have a few pounds to lose, try my 123 Plan – it couldn't be easier.

USING THE 123 PLAN

If you're not following a diet regime at the moment and want a great kick-start, try my 123 Plan for a few weeks. I've tried to make it really easy, and you don't need to do too much adding up. Just pick one recipe from any section to bring your daily intake to between 900 and 1,200 calories. Add an *essential extra* 300 calories a day and you'll be on your way to a healthy, sustainable weight loss of between 2–3lbs a week.

ONE
up to 300 calories

TWO
300–400 calories

THREE
400–500 calories

YOUR ESSENTIAL EXTRAS

These extra 300 calories can be made up of accompaniments, such as potatoes, rice and pasta, as well as snacks or treats; there are suggestions and serving sizes on page 180. You'll also find recipes that contain under 200 calories a portion, which can be included as part of your essential extras. As long as your extras don't exceed 300 calories a day, you'll be on track.

WHEN TO EAT

The 123 Plan is flexible, so if you find you fancy a **ONE** or **TWO** recipe rather than a **THREE** as your third meal of the day, just add enough calories to bring it into the right range. Don't worry if the calculations aren't absolutely accurate – a difference of 25 or less calories per serving won't affect your weekly allowance.

You don't have to eat your lightest meal for breakfast and the most calorific meal late in the day – in fact, the opposite often works best. I tend to eat my largest meal at lunchtime if I can, and have a lighter meal in the evening, but work with what suits you and your family best.

If you want to add your own favourite meals into the plan, just make sure they are within the recommended calorie boundaries and calculate accordingly. (You may find this useful when planning breakfast especially.)

DON'T RUSH IT

Weight tends to be gained over time, and losing it gradually will make the process easier and help give your body, especially your skin, time to adapt. You're more likely to get into positive, enjoyable long-term cooking and eating habits this way too.

WHAT IS A CALORIE?

Put simply, a calorie is a unit of energy contained within food and drink which our bodies burn as fuel. Different foods contain varying amounts of calories and if more calories are consumed than the body needs, the excess will be stored as fat. To lose weight, we need to eat less or use more energy by increasing our activity – and ideally both!

I've provided the calorie content of a single serving of each dish. In my experience, most people will lose at least 2lbs a week by consuming around 1,200–1,500 calories a day, but it's always best to check with your GP before you start a new regime. Everyone is different and, especially if you have several stones to lose, you'll need some personalised advice. The calories contained in each recipe have been calculated as accurately as possible, but could vary a little depending on your ingredients.

A few wayward calories here and there won't make any difference to your overall weight loss.

If you have a couple of days of eating more than 1,400 calories, try to eat closer to 1,100 for the next few days. Over a week, things will even out.

My recipes strike a balance between eating and cooking well and reducing calories, and I've tried them all as part of my own way of enjoying food without putting on excess weight. Even if you don't need to lose weight, I hope you enjoy cooking from my books simply because you like the recipes.

SECRETS OF SUCCESS

The serving sizes that I've recommended form the basis of the nutritional information on page 182, and if you eat any more, you may find losing weight takes longer. If you're cooking for anyone who doesn't need to watch their calorie intake, simply increase their servings and offer plenty of accompaniments.

The right portion size also holds the key to maintaining your weight loss. Use this opportunity to get used to smaller servings. Work out exactly how much food your body needs to maintain the shape that makes you feel great. That way, even when counting calories feels like a distant memory, you'll remain in control of your eating habits.

Stick to lean protein (which will help you feel fuller for longer) and vegetables and avoid high-fat, high-sugar snacks and confectionery. Be aware that alcohol is packed with empty calories and could weaken your resolve. Starchy carbs such as pasta, rice, potatoes and bread are kept to a minimum because I've found that, combined with eating lots of veg and good protein, this leads to more sustainable weight loss. There's no need to avoid dairy products such as cheese and cream, although they tend to be high in fat and calories. You can swap the high-fat versions for reduced-fat ones, or use less.

Ditch heavily processed foods and you will feel so much better. Switching to more natural ingredients will help your body work with you. If you don't cook often, try a few of my recipes and see how easy they can be.

Most recipes here form the main part of each meal, so there's room to have your plate half-filled with freshly cooked vegetables or a colourful, crunchy salad. This will help fill you up, and boost your intake of vitamins and minerals.

Make sure you drink enough fluids, especially water – around 2 litres is ideal. Staying hydrated will help you lose weight more comfortably, and it's important when you exercise too.

IN THE KITCHEN

Pick up some electronic kitchen scales and a set of measuring spoons if you don't already have them. Both will probably cost less than a takeaway meal for two, and will help ensure good results.

Invest, if you can, in a large, deep non-stick frying pan and a medium non-stick saucepan. The non-stick coating means that you will need less oil to cook, and a frying pan with a wide base and deep sides can double as a wok.

I use oil and butter sparingly, and use a calorie-controlled spray oil for frying. I also keep a jam jar containing a little sunflower oil and a heatproof pastry brush to hand for greasing pans lightly before frying.

STICK WITH IT

Shifting your eating habits and trying to lose weight is not easy, especially if you have been eating the same way for many years. But it isn't too late. You may never have the perfect body, but you can have one that, fuelled by really good food, makes you feel happy and healthy. For more information and menu plans visit www.justinepattison.co.uk.

Enjoy!

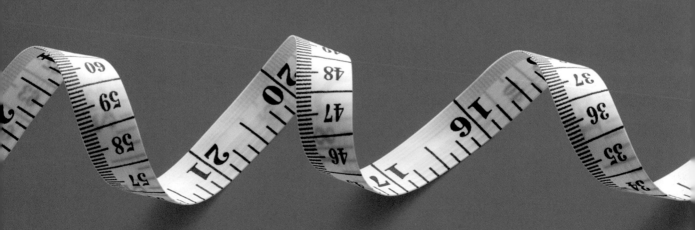

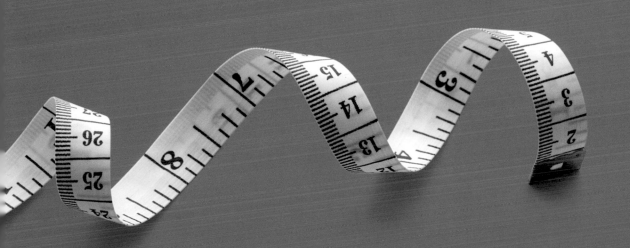

breakfast and brunch

212
CALORIES
PER SERVING

overnight porridge
with juicy berries

SERVES 4
**PREP: 5 MINUTES, PLUS
OVERNIGHT CHILLING TIME**
COOK: 5 MINUTES

200g fresh strawberries,
   hulled and halved,
   or quartered if large
175g fresh raspberries
75g fresh redcurrants,
   blueberries or
   blackberries
1 tbsp caster sugar
120g jumbo porridge oats
500ml semi-skimmed milk
200ml water
1 tbsp soft light brown
   sugar (optional)

I've found that by soaking oats overnight, I can make my porridge taste extra creamy while still keeping the calories fairly low. Mix your fruit the night before and the berries will be lovely and juicy the next day too. Use any combination of berries you like, or thaw frozen mixed berries and sweeten with a touch of sugar.

Put the fruit in a bowl and mix lightly with the caster sugar. Cover and leave in the fridge overnight to macerate. The sugar will help draw out the juices.

Put the porridge oats, milk and water in a bowl and stir well. Cover and leave in the fridge overnight. (You can prepare the porridge right away if you prefer.)

The next day, place the soaked oats and liquid in a large non-stick saucepan over a medium heat. Bring to a gentle simmer and cook for about 5 minutes, stirring frequently until the oats are tender and very creamy.

Pour the porridge into bowls and top with the fruit. Sweeten with a little soft light brown sugar (adding an extra 9 calories) if you like.

188
CALORIES
PER SERVING

bircher muesli

SERVES 4

**PREP: 5 MINUTES,
PLUS SOAKING TIME**

75g jumbo porridge oats
25g flaked toasted almonds
2 eating apples, peeled,
　cored and coarsely grated
100ml pressed apple juice
100ml semi-skimmed milk
150g fat-free natural
　yoghurt
1 tbsp soft light brown
　sugar (optional)
150g fresh blueberries,
　mixed fresh or frozen and
　thawed berries, or clear
　honey, to serve

Tip: I find that brown
sugar goes further than
white – I think it must be
the depth of flavour that
makes it more satisfying.
If you can, use golden
caster sugar too.

A serving of Bircher muesli always makes me feel healthy
inside and out. Soaked overnight, It makes a really quick
breakfast and should fill you up until lunchtime.

Put the oats and almonds in a bowl. Stir the grated apple
and apple juice into the oats.

Add the milk, yoghurt and sugar, if using, and stir until
well mixed. Cover and chill in the fridge for at least 1 hour
or overnight.

Serve the muesli topped with fresh blueberries, mixed
berries or a drizzle of honey.

247
CALORIES
PER SERVING

fluffy fruit pancakes

SERVES 4

PREP: 15 MINUTES

COOK: 20 MINUTES

175g self-raising flour
½ tsp baking powder
275ml semi-skimmed milk
1 eating apple (about 140g), peeled, cored and coarsely grated
2 large egg whites
1 tbsp caster sugar
oil, for spraying or brushing
250g mixed fresh or frozen and thawed berries
2 tbsp maple syrup or clear honey

Open freeze the cooled pancakes. Once solid, place in a large zip-seal bag, label and freeze for up to 1 month. To serve, heat through in a dry non-stick pan over a low heat or microwave for a few seconds until piping hot.

American-style pancakes make a lovely treat for breakfast but can be time-consuming to prepare. For this recipe, I make four large pancakes rather than 12 small ones and serve them topped with lots of berries and a dribble of maple syrup.

Sift the flour and baking powder into a large bowl. Stir the milk slowly and gradually into the flour mixture, then beat hard with a metal whisk to get rid of any lumps. Stir the grated apple into the batter.

Whisk the egg whites in a separate bowl until stiff but not dry. Whisk in the caster sugar. Fold a quarter of the whisked egg whites into the pancake batter with a large metal spoon until evenly combined, then very gently fold in the rest. You want to try to keep as much air in the pancakes as possible, so they are light and fluffy when you cook them.

Spray or brush a medium non-stick frying pan with a little oil and place over a medium-high heat. Ladle a quarter of the mixture into the frying pan.

Cook the pancake for 2½ minutes on one side, or until the surface looks almost dry and you can see small air bubbles rising to the surface. Flip the pancake over and cook on the other side for a further 2½ minutes until puffed up and lightly browned.

Transfer to a plate and keep warm. Cook the three remaining pancakes in exactly the same way. Serve the hot pancakes topped with plenty of fresh fruit and dribbled with maple syrup or honey.

145 CALORIES PER MUFFIN

banana and blueberry muffins

SERVES 12
PREP: 15 MINUTES
COOK: 20 MINUTES

oil, for spraying or brushing
1 very ripe banana (around 100g peeled weight)
250ml semi-skimmed milk
3 tbsp sunflower oil
2 large eggs, beaten
275g self-raising flour
3 tbsp soft light brown sugar
1 tsp bicarbonate of soda
finely grated zest of 1 lemon
150g fresh blueberries

Freeze the cooled muffins in a large freezer bag and freeze for up to 1 month. Thaw at room temperature and heat for a few seconds in the microwave or reheat for 5 minutes in a hot oven before serving for the best results.

These muffins make a light, sweet breakfast or snack. Because they are so low in fat, you may find that when they're hot the mixture sticks a little to the paper cases but the paper should easily peel off when the muffins have cooled.

Preheat the oven to 210°C/Fan 190°C/Gas 6. Line a 12-hole, deep muffin tin with non-stick paper cases or folded squares of baking parchment. Spray or brush the insides of the muffin cases lightly with oil – this will help prevent the muffin batter sticking to the paper.

Mash the banana with a fork until almost smooth and stir in the milk, oil and beaten eggs. Put the flour, sugar, bicarbonate of soda and lemon zest into a large bowl and stir until thoroughly mixed. Make a well in the centre.

Pour the banana mixture onto the flour and mix until lightly combined. Stir in two-thirds of the blueberries. Divide the batter between the muffin cases and top with the remaining blueberries.

Bake for 20 minutes or until well risen, golden brown and firm. Serve warm or leave to cool on a wire rack. Store in an airtight container and eat within 2 days. (Reheat for a few seconds in a microwave oven if you like, but not for too long or the muffins will toughen.)

148
CALORIES
PER SERVING

all-in-one breakfast

SERVES 2
PREP: 5 MINUTES
COOK: 10 MINUTES

oil, for spraying or brushing
4 smoked back
   bacon rashers
2 large portobello or
   field mushrooms,
   stalks trimmed
150g cherry tomatoes
   on the vine
2 eggs
flaked sea salt
ground black pepper

Tip: Add two thin slices
of wholemeal toast for
an extra 138 calories
per serving.

A great weekend fry-up and hardly any washing up. Make sure you use really fresh eggs as they won't spread so far across the pan when broken.

Preheat the oven to 220°C/Fan 200°C/Gas 7. Spray or brush a large baking tray with oil.

Trim any visible fat from the bacon with a pair of kitchen scissors and place the bacon on the tray along with the mushrooms, stalk-side up. Bake for 5 minutes.

Add the cherry tomatoes and crack the eggs directly onto the tray, seasoning with salt and plenty of pepper. Bake for another 5–7 minutes or until the egg yolks are hot but not completely set. Tip away the juice from the mushrooms and divide everything between two plates to serve.

385
CALORIES
PER SERVING

scrambled eggs with smoked salmon

SERVES 2
PREP: 5 MINUTES
COOK: 2–3 MINUTES

4 eggs
1 wholemeal bagel
10g butter, plus 1 tsp,
    softened
4 smoked salmon slices
    (around 75g)
snipped fresh chives,
    to serve (optional)
flaked sea salt
ground black pepper

Wholemeal bagels take the place of thickly buttered toast here. One bagel can serve two people and if you slice it thinly enough, it looks deceptively generous. Use a couple of thin slices of toast from a small wholemeal loaf if you prefer. You can lower the calories even further by reducing the amount of butter.

Beat the eggs in a bowl using a metal whisk until well combined. Season with a pinch of salt and lots of black pepper. Cut the bagel carefully in half horizontally and then each half in half again to give 4 thin slices.

Melt 15g of butter in a medium non-stick saucepan over a low heat. Pour the beaten eggs into the pan and cook very gently for 2 minutes, stirring regularly, until the eggs are softly scrambled. Remove from the heat.

While the eggs are cooking, toast the bagel and spread very thinly with the softened butter. Divide the bagel between two warmed plates, cut side up. Spoon the scrambled eggs over the bagel toasts, add slices of smoked salmon and season with a little more black pepper. Garnish with chives before serving if you like.

320

CALORIES
PER SERVING

eggs benedict

SERVES 4
PREP: 5 MINUTES
COOK: 10 MINUTES

4 fridge-cold eggs
2 English muffins, sliced
    in half
4 slices of lean smoked
    ham (about 120g)
snipped fresh chives,
    to serve (optional)

**FOR THE LOWER-FAT
HOLLANDAISE**
4 tbsp white wine vinegar
1 small bay leaf
4 peppercorns
½ tsp flaked sea salt,
    plus extra to taste
200ml semi-skimmed milk
15g cornflour
20g butter
3 large egg yolks
ground black pepper

Note: This recipe contains
lightly cooked eggs.

My usual recipe for hollandaise sauce contains almost a whole block of butter! This one is much lower in fat because I've thickened the sauce with cornflour rather than making a buttery emulsion.

To make the hollandaise, put the vinegar, bay leaf, peppercorns and salt in a small non-stick saucepan over a medium heat and bring to a simmer. Boil until the liquid has reduced to just 2 tablespoons. Remove from the heat and strain through a fine sieve into a small bowl.

Mix 2 tablespoons of the milk with the cornflour to form a smooth paste. Pour the rest of the milk into a medium non-stick saucepan and add the butter and cornflour mixture. Bring to a gentle simmer, stirring continuously until smooth and thick.

Beat the egg yolks in a bowl until light and pale and add to the cornflour and milk mixture, stirring continuously. Stir in the vinegar reduction and cook very gently over a low heat for a few seconds, stirring continuously. The sauce should have the consistency of custard. Do not allow the mixture to overheat or the eggs will scramble. Take the pan off the heat and adjust the seasoning to taste.

Half fill a medium pan with water and bring to the boil. Reduce the boiling water to a very gentle simmer. Crack the eggs gently into the water and let them drop to the bottom of the pan. Gently stir the water once and cook the eggs for 3 minutes. The water should be gently bubbling and the eggs will rise to the surface when they are nearly ready. While the eggs are cooking, warm the sauce gently, stirring continuously.

Toast the muffin halves and arrange them on warmed plates or a platter. Top with a slice of ham and a poached egg (remove the eggs from the water with a slotted spoon). Spoon over the hollandaise sauce and sprinkle with snipped chives to serve.

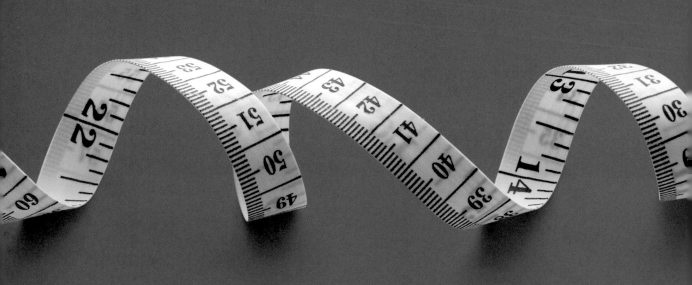

soups

266
CALORIES
PER SERVING

smoked haddock chowder

SERVES 4
PREP: 25 MINUTES
COOK: 20 MINUTES

15g butter
1 tsp sunflower oil
1 small onion, finely
    chopped
2 celery sticks, finely
    chopped
750ml chicken stock (made
    with 1 chicken stock cube)
300g potatoes (ideally
    Maris Piper), peeled and
    cut into 1.5cm cubes
25g cornflour
3 tbsp cold water
1 medium leek, thinly sliced
285g smoked haddock
    (undyed), skinned and cut
    into roughly 3cm chunks
3 tbsp white wine (optional)
400ml semi-skimmed milk
198g can sweetcorn, drained
roughly chopped fresh flat-
    leaf parsley, to garnish
flaked sea salt
ground black pepper

A creamy-tasting, rich and comforting soup that's perfect for a cold day. Serve as a generous lunch or supper dish in deep bowls.

Heat the butter and oil in a large non-stick saucepan. Fry the onion and celery for 5 minutes or until softened and lightly coloured, stirring regularly.

Add the stock and potatoes to the pan, bring to a gentle simmer and cook for about 10 minutes or until the potatoes are tender, stirring occasionally.

Mix the cornflour with 3 tablespoons of cold water and stir the mixture into the soup. Add the leek, haddock, wine (if using), milk and sweetcorn and return to a gentle simmer. Cook for a further 2–3 minutes, stirring gently until the haddock is cooked (it should look creamy white throughout) and the leek is tender.

Season to taste and ladle into deep bowls. Scatter with chopped parsley just before serving.

145

minted pea soup with feta

SERVES 4
PREP: 10 MINUTES
COOK: 10 MINUTES

8 spring onions, thinly sliced
350g frozen peas
2 fresh mint stalks
　(without leaves)
850ml vegetable or chicken
　stock (made with
　½ stock cube)
15g fresh mint, leaves finely
　chopped, plus a few
　leaves to garnish
4 tbsp soured cream or
　half-fat crème fraiche
80g feta cheese, drained
　and crumbled
a few pinches of ground
　nutmeg, to garnish
flaked sea salt
ground black pepper

Freeze the cooled, ungarnished soup by dividing between labelled zip-seal bags. Seal and flat freeze. To serve, warm through gently in a large saucepan until thawed, then simmer until piping hot, stirring regularly. Garnish as above.

A delicious, fresh-tasting soup that only takes a few minutes to knock together and makes a perfect light lunch or supper. Serve with a couple of slices of warmed ciabatta bread for a more substantial meal, but don't forget to add the extra calories.

Place the onions, peas, mint stalks and stock in a medium saucepan and bring to a simmer. Cook for 5 minutes, stirring occasionally. (The mint stalks will add extra flavour to the soup.)

Remove the pan from the heat and blitz with a stick blender until smooth. Alternatively, leave to cool for a few minutes, then blend in a food processor and return to the saucepan.

Stir in the chopped mint leaves and warm the soup through gently for a couple of minutes without boiling. Adjust the seasoning to taste but be careful not to add too much salt as the feta will be salty.

Ladle the soup into warm, deep bowls and top with a little soured cream or crème fraiche, crumbled feta, a pinch of nutmeg and a good grinding of black pepper. Garnish with a few extra mint leaves if you like.

103
CALORIES
PER SERVING

minestrone soup

SERVES 6
PREP: 25 MINUTES
COOK: 20 MINUTES

2 tsp olive oil
1 large onion, finely
    chopped
2 garlic cloves, thinly sliced
2 carrots, peeled and cut
    into roughly 1.5cm dice
400g can chopped
    tomatoes
1.5 litres chicken stock
    (fresh, see page 32, or
    made with 2 chicken
    stock cubes)
50g orzo pasta or dried
    spaghetti, broken into
    short lengths
2 tbsp sun-dried tomato
    purée or tomato purée
2 courgettes, cut into
    roughly 1.5cm dice
100g frozen peas
100g green beans, cut
    into 2cm lengths
100g curly kale or savoy
    cabbage, thinly shredded
flaked sea salt
ground black pepper

Freeze the cooled soup by
dividing into freezer-proof
containers. Cover tightly and
freeze for up to 3 months. To
serve, warm through gently
in a large saucepan until
thawed then simmer until
piping hot throughout,
stirring regularly.

A hearty, low-calorie minestrone packed with fresh
vegetables. This soup tastes wonderful served with a little
basil pesto or freshly grated Parmesan. Two teaspoons of
basil pesto will add around six calories per serving and
two teaspoons of Parmesan an additional four calories.

Heat the oil in a large non-stick saucepan and fry the onion
gently for 5 minutes or until softened but not coloured, stirring
often. Add the garlic and carrots to the pan with the onion.
Stir over a low heat for 2 minutes more.

Stir in the chopped tomatoes, pour over the chicken stock
and bring to the boil. Drop the pasta gently into the pan. Add
the tomato purée and return to the boil. Cook for 8 minutes,
stirring occasionally.

Reduce the heat slightly, add the courgettes, peas, green
beans and the kale or cabbage and simmer for a further
5 minutes more, or until the pasta is just tender.

Season the soup with salt and lots of black pepper. Serve in
warm, deep bowls, topped with pesto or Parmesan if you like.

160
CALORIES
PER SERVING

chicken noodle soup

SERVES 4
PREP: 20 MINUTES
COOK: 15 MINUTES

oil, for spraying or brushing
1 small onion, finely
    chopped
2 celery sticks, thinly sliced
1 large carrot, peeled and
    cut into roughly 1cm dice
1.5 litres fresh chicken stock
    (shop-bought or see
    recipe below)
1 bay leaf
1 tsp fresh thyme leaves
    or ½ tsp dried thyme
100g vermicelli pasta
    or spaghettini
200g cooked, skinless
    chicken breast, torn
    into shreds
1 small leek, thinly sliced
flaked sea salt
ground black pepper

Freeze the cooled soup
by dividing into freezer-
proof containers. Cover
tightly and freeze for up to
3 months. To serve, warm
through gently in a large
saucepan until thawed
then simmer until piping
hot, stirring regularly.

This nourishing soup is made from chicken pieces, noodles
and vegetables simmered in a light broth. It's one of those
recipes that needs a proper chicken stock but you can always
use a ready-made one from the supermarket if you don't
have time to make your own. You'll need to use 2 x 500ml
tubs topped up with 500ml of water.

Spray or brush a large non-stick saucepan with oil and gently
fry the onion, celery and carrot for 5 minutes or until they are
beginning to soften. Stir in the stock, bay leaf and thyme and
bring to a gentle simmer.

Break the pasta into short lengths and drop it into the pan.
Return to a simmer and cook for 5 minutes. Add the chicken
and leek and cook for 4–5 minutes more or until the chicken
is hot and the leek and pasta are tender. Season with salt
and pepper before serving.

Fresh chicken stock: Put 1 skinless roast chicken carcass
(you can use any leftover lean chicken meat for the soup),
1 quartered onion, 1 roughly chopped carrot, 2 roughly chopped
celery sticks, 2 bay leaves, a few fresh thyme sprigs and
½ teaspoon of fine sea salt into a large saucepan, breaking the
chicken carcass up if necessary to help it fit. Pour over 2 litres
cold water and bring to a very gentle simmer. Cover loosely
with a lid and cook for 1 hour without boiling. Strain through
a fine sieve into a wide jug before using. Makes 1.5 litres.
Calories per recipe: under 50

188

CALORIES
PER SERVING

french onion soup

SERVES 6
PREP: 20 MINUTES
COOK: 50–55 MINUTES

2 tsp sunflower oil
6 medium onions,
    thinly sliced
1 tbsp fresh thyme leaves,
    plus extra to garnish
2 tbsp plain flour
1.5 litres hot beef stock
    (made with 2 beef
    stock cubes)
12 thin slices of baguette
    (about 15g per slice),
    cut diagonally
50g Gruyère cheese,
    finely grated
flaked sea salt
ground black pepper

Freeze the cooled soup by
dividing into freezer-proof
containers. Cover tightly and
freeze for up to 3 months.
To serve, warm through
gently in a large saucepan
until thawed then simmer
until piping hot throughout,
stirring regularly.

Freeze the croutons by
toasting the bread and
topping with the cheese,
but do not grill again. Open
freeze the toast until solid
and stack in a freezer-proof
container interleaving with
baking parchment. Grill from
frozen, not too close to the
heat, for 5–7 minutes or until
the cheese has melted and
the bread is piping hot.

This is a great meal to make when there's not much left
in the fridge. Cheesy croutons don't need to be omitted
just because you're cutting back. You can use any hard,
full-flavoured cheese instead of the Gruyère but I think
its nuttiness complements the richness of the onions
particularly well.

Heat the oil in a large non-stick saucepan or flameproof
casserole. Add the onions, cover with a lid and cook over
a low heat for 20–25 minutes or until the onions are very
soft, stirring occasionally.

Remove the lid, increase the heat and cook for a further
15 minutes or until the onions have turned a rich golden brown
colour, stirring frequently and making sure that they do not
burn. Reduce the heat and stir in the thyme leaves and flour.

Pour the stock slowly over the onions, stirring continuously,
and bring to a simmer. Cook for 15 minutes or until the soup
thickens slightly. Season to taste with salt and pepper and
keep warm over a low heat.

Heat the grill to the hottest setting. Place the baguette slices
on a baking tray and toast close to the grill for 1 minute on each
side or until lightly browned.

Remove from under the grill and sprinkle a little of the grated
cheese on each slice of bread. Return to the grill and cook
until the cheese melts and begins to brown.

Ladle the hot soup into warm, deep bowls and top each one
with 2 pieces of the cheesy toast. Sprinkle with tiny sprigs
of thyme just before serving.

122
CALORIES
PER SERVING

cream of tomato soup

SERVES 4
PREP: 20 MINUTES
COOK: 25 MINUTES

1 tbsp sunflower oil
2 medium onions,
   roughly chopped
2 garlic cloves, chopped
2 x 400g cans chopped
   tomatoes
600ml cold water
½ tsp mixed dried herbs
2 tsp caster sugar
4 tbsp single cream
flaked sea salt
ground black pepper
snipped fresh chives,
   to serve (optional)
chive cream (see right),
   to serve

Freeze the cooled soup
(without the chive cream),
by dividing between
labelled zip-seal bags.
Seal and flat freeze. To
serve, warm through gently
in a large saucepan until
thawed then simmer until
piping hot throughout,
stirring regularly.

There is something intensely comforting about a rich
tomato soup and this one certainly hits the spot. You
might imagine that you'd need fresh tomatoes for the
classic flavour, but canned tomatoes work perfectly
well and are much more convenient.

Heat the oil in a large non-stick saucepan and fry the
onions and garlic over a medium heat for 4–5 minutes
or until beginning to soften, stirring frequently. Do not
allow the garlic to burn. Stir in the tomatoes and then
the water.

Add the herbs, sugar, a good pinch of salt and plenty
of black pepper. Bring to a gentle simmer and cook
for 20 minutes, stirring occasionally.

Remove the pan from the heat and blitz the soup with
a stick blender until it is as smooth as possible. Alternatively,
leave to cool for a few minutes, then blend in a food
processor and return to the saucepan.

Stir in the cream and adjust the seasoning to taste, adding
a little more sugar if necessary. Serve sprinkled with fresh
chives and an added swirl of chive cream if you like.

Chive cream: Mix 2 tablespoons of snipped fresh chives
and 3 tablespoons of soured cream in a small bowl.
Spoon onto the hot soup and swirl lightly. Serves 4.
Calories per serving: 23

chicken

212
CALORIES
PER SERVING

rosemary roasted chicken with lemon and tomatoes

SERVES 6

PREP: 25 MINUTES

COOK: 35 MINUTES

12 boneless, skinless chicken
   thighs (around 1kg)
3 fresh rosemary stalks,
   each around 15cm long
½ tsp paprika (not smoked)
½ tsp flaked sea salt, plus
   extra to taste
oil, for spraying or brushing
2 medium onions, each
   cut into 12 wedges
12 garlic cloves, unpeeled
   and left whole
1 lemon
275g cherry tomatoes
   on the vine
ground black pepper

A one-pan meal that makes a quick and delicious supper. The garlic cloves roast in their skins and become sweet and sticky. Squeeze out the soft garlic purée and smear onto the chicken for extra flavour as you eat.

Preheat the oven to 210°C/Fan 190°C/Gas 6½. Remove the visible fat from each of the chicken thighs – a good set of kitchen scissors works well. Put the chicken thighs on a board and carefully slash each thigh 2–3 times with a knife. Strip the rosemary leaves off 2 stalks and finely chop – you should end up with around 2 teaspoons of chopped rosemary. Mix the paprika, chopped rosemary, salt and a few twists of ground black pepper together in a bowl. Rub the herb seasoned salt into the thighs.

Spray or brush a medium roasting tin with oil. Put the onions and garlic in the tin and nestle the seasoned chicken pieces among them. Cut the lemon in half and squeeze the juice of half over the chicken. Chop the remaining lemon half into chunks and place the chunks around the chicken. Roughly remove the leaves from the remaining rosemary stalk and scatter them around the tin.

Bake in the oven for 25 minutes, then place the tomatoes on top and cook for a further 10 minutes or until the chicken is golden and cooked through.

Squeeze the garlic out of the skins as you eat and discard the skins. It should be deliciously soft and fragrant.

357
CALORIES
PER SERVING

chicken fajita bowls

SERVES 4

PREP: 15 MINUTES

COOK: 8 MINUTES

4 soft regular tortilla wraps
(each about 40g)
3 boneless, skinless
chicken breasts
1 tbsp fresh lime juice
1 tbsp sunflower oil
2 medium red onions,
each cut into 12 wedges
1 yellow pepper and
1 red pepper, deseeded
and sliced
1 tsp ground cumin
1 tsp ground coriander
½ tsp dried oregano
½ tsp hot chilli powder
2 little gem lettuces,
leaves separated
4 tbsp soured cream
lime wedges, for squeezing
(optional)
flaked sea salt
ground black pepper

TO SERVE
fresh tomato salsa
(see right)
4 tbsp soured cream
lime wedges, for squeezing
(optional)

I've found that baking soft tortillas into bowl shapes means you can pile them high with the low-fat chicken and pepper combination without needing to indulge in more than one wrap. Make sure you buy the regular flour tortillas rather than the large sandwich wraps.

Preheat the oven to 200°C/Fan 180°C/Gas 6. Place a flour tortilla inside 4 x 11cm mini spring-clip cake tins and place on a baking tray. Cook for 5 minutes until lightly browned, then leave to cool and crisp a little in the tins. If you don't have any 11cm tins, bake over balls of crumpled foil to make bowl shapes.

Cut the chicken into long thin strips, 1cm wide, and place in a bowl. Pour over the lime juice and season with salt and pepper.

Heat the oil in a large wok or non-stick frying pan over a high heat. Stir-fry the chicken, onions and peppers for 5 minutes or until lightly browned.

Mix the ground cumin, coriander, oregano and chilli powder in a small bowl and sprinkle over the chicken and vegetables. Stir-fry for a further 1–2 minutes or until the chicken is cooked through. You may need to open a window or use an extractor fan as the chilli may make you cough.

While the chicken is cooking, line the tortilla bowls with lettuce leaves. Pile the hot chicken and peppers on top, then spoon over the salsa if you like, and soured cream.

Fresh tomato salsa: Mix ½ thinly sliced small red onion or 4 spring onions, 2 roughly chopped ripe tomatoes, 15g of roughly chopped fresh coriander leaves and 1 finely chopped plump red or green chilli. Season with flaked sea salt and ground black pepper. Leave to stand for 10 minutes before serving. Serves 4. Calories per serving: 17

251

quick chicken kiev

SERVES 4

PREP: 15 MINUTES

COOK: 25 MINUTES

4 boneless, skinless chicken
    breasts (each about 175g)
5 tbsp light soft cheese
    with garlic and herbs
¼ tsp ground turmeric
¼ tsp paprika (not smoked)
40g dried coarse white
    breadcrumbs or
    panko breadcrumbs
oil, for spraying
flaked sea salt
ground black pepper

Open freeze the uncooked
but coated chicken, then
pack into a freezer-proof
container, interleaving the
breasts with baking
parchment. Seal and freeze
for up to 1 month. Thaw on
a covered baking tray in the
fridge overnight. Bake as
the recipe, and increase the
cooking time by 5–10 minutes
or until the chicken is cooked
and piping hot throughout.

I use light garlic and herb soft cheese as a filling and only
coat the chicken on one side to keep the calories low for this
Kiev. Serve the chicken with a large, mixed salad and a few
new potatoes, if you like.

Preheat the oven to 220°C/Fan 200°C/Gas 7. Line a baking
tray with non-stick baking parchment.

Put a chicken breast on a board and, using a sharp knife,
carefully cut horizontally through the breast from the curved
side almost all the way through to the other side and open
out like a book. Season with salt and pepper. Repeat with
the rest of the chicken breasts.

Spoon 1 tablespoon of the cheese down the centre of each
split breast, then fold over to enclose the filling. Place the
chicken breasts on the prepared tray and smear with the
remaining cheese.

Mix the turmeric and paprika into the breadcrumbs in a small
bowl. Divide the breadcrumb mixture between each chicken
breast and press down gently to ensure the breadcrumbs stick.
Spray all over with the oil.

Bake for 25 minutes or until golden brown and thoroughly
cooked. There should be no pinkness remaining in the chicken
meat when you cut it. If you do find some, just pop the chicken
back into the oven for a couple more minutes.

339
CALORIES
PER SERVING

chicken tetrazzini

SERVES 6

PREP: 20 MINUTES

COOK: 20–25 MINUTES

200g dried linguine
or spaghetti
oil, for spraying or brushing
25g butter
1 small onion, finely
chopped
1 celery stick, thinly sliced
2 garlic cloves, crushed
1 tbsp finely chopped
fresh thyme leaves
40g plain flour
100ml white wine
500ml chicken stock (made
with 1 chicken stock cube)
200g button mushrooms,
sliced
3 tbsp single cream
150g frozen peas
75ml semi-skimmed milk
300g skinless, cooked
chicken breast, cut
into 2.5cm chunks
20g dried coarse
breadcrumbs or
panko breadcrumbs
25g Parmesan cheese,
finely grated

Tetrazzini is an American-Italian hybrid, apparently created by first-generation Italian Americans to satisfy the tastes of people unused to rustic and bold Italian cooking. The result is creamy pasta with a satisfyingly crunchy topping.

Half fill a large saucepan with water and bring to the boil over a high heat. Cook the pasta in the boiling water for 10–12 minutes or until only just tender. Drain in a colander and spray with a little of the oil to stop it sticking, then return to the pan.

While the pasta is boiling, melt the butter in a large non-stick saucepan and gently cook the onion, celery, garlic and thyme for 5 minutes, or until the onion is well softened but not coloured, stirring regularly.

Sprinkle the flour over the sautéed onion and garlic and stir well. Slowly add the wine, then the stock, stirring continuously to avoid any lumps. Bring to a gentle simmer and cook for 5 minutes, stirring frequently.

Meanwhile, spray or brush a large non-stick frying pan or wok with oil and stir-fry the mushrooms for 3–4 minutes over a high heat until lightly browned.

Stir the mushrooms, cream, peas and milk and chicken into the sauce and cook for a further 2–3 minutes more, stirring until hot. Tip onto the drained pasta and toss well together. Transfer to a warmed, shallow flameproof lasagne dish.

Mix the breadcrumbs and Parmesan together and sprinkle over the top of the pasta. Cook under a preheated hot grill for 5–10 minutes or until golden brown.

347
CALORIES
PER SERVING

jambalaya

SERVES 6
PREP: 25 MINUTES
COOK: 25–30 MINUTES

oil, for spraying or brushing
2 medium onions, roughly
  chopped
3 celery sticks, sliced
2 small green peppers,
  deseeded and cut into
  2cm chunks
6 boneless, skinless chicken
  thighs (around 500g)
100g cooking chorizo
  sausage, cut into
  5mm slices
2 large garlic cloves,
  crushed
1 tbsp paprika (not smoked)
1 tsp hot smoked paprika
1 tbsp fresh thyme leaves
  or 1 tsp dried thyme
2 bay leaves
200g easy-cook long-
  grain rice
½ 400g can chopped
  tomatoes
400ml chicken stock (made
  with 1 chicken stock cube)
pinch of flaked sea salt
250g cooked and peeled
  king prawns, thawed
  if frozen
1 bunch of spring onions,
  sliced
ground black pepper

An American classic from the Deep South, this is an all-in-one dish that you can put on the table for everyone to help themselves. The dish typically contains andouille, a highly spiced, garlicky sausage, but soft cooking chorizo makes a great substitute, and is more readily available.

Spray or brush a large non-stick frying pan or sauté pan with the oil and place over a medium heat. Add the onions, celery and green peppers. Cook for 8–10 minutes over a low heat, or until well softened, stirring occasionally.

Trim the chicken of any visible fat and cut each thigh into 3 chunks.

Add the chicken and chorizo and cook for 2 minutes, stirring continuously. Add the garlic and sprinkle over the paprika, smoked paprika, thyme and bay leaves. Stir well together.

Add the rice and tomatoes, then pour over the chicken stock, season with a pinch of salt and lots of black pepper. Bring to a simmer and cook without covering for around 10 minutes or until the rice is just tender and most of the liquid has been absorbed. Stir frequently towards the end of the cooking time to prevent the rice sticking. If the rice isn't ready before the liquid has disappeared, add a splash more water and continue cooking.

Add the prawns and spring onions and cook for 2–3 minutes more, stirring regularly until the prawns are hot.

423

one-pot chicken

1 medium chicken
    (around 1.6kg)
oil, for spraying or brushing
20 shallots, peeled
300g baby carrots, peeled
450g baby parsnips, peeled
2 tbsp plain flour
150ml white wine
400ml chicken stock (made
    with 1 chicken stock cube)
8–10 fresh thyme sprigs,
    plus extra to garnish
flaked sea salt
ground black pepper

Tip: To make peeling easier,
soak the shallots in just-
boiled water for a couple
of minutes then drain.

A simple and generous all-in-one roast. Just braise all the ingredients in the same casserole and serve at the table. This amount of calories per serving is calculated with no skin on the chicken. If you are the only one watching your weight, simply slip the skin from your serving before eating.

Preheat the oven to 180°C/Fan 160°C/Gas 4. To remove the skin, untruss the chicken, slide your fingers between the flesh and skin and gently lift before pulling away. Use a pair of kitchen scissors to snip any difficult-to-reach areas and don't worry about the wing tips. Season the chicken with salt and plenty of black pepper.

Spray or brush a large frying pan with oil and place over a medium heat. Brown the chicken until golden all over, then transfer it to a large plate.

Fry the shallots, carrots and parsnips in the frying pan for around 10 minutes until lightly browned on all sides. Tip the vegetables into a flameproof casserole large enough to fit the chicken and vegetables. Add the flour and toss with the vegetables.

Pour the wine into the frying pan and stir to lift any flavoursome bits from the bottom. Place the chicken on top of the vegetables and sprinkle the thyme sprigs on top. Pour over the wine and stock and bring the liquid to a simmer. Cover with a tight-fitting lid and cook in the oven for 1½ hours or until the vegetables are tender and the chicken is cooked through.

299

chicken cacciatore

SERVES 6

PREP: 30 MINUTES

COOK: 65-70 MINUTES

150ml just-boiled water
15g dried, mixed wild
  mushrooms
6 boneless, skinless chicken
  breasts (each about 175g)
6 slices Parma ham
1 tbsp oil
2 medium onions,
  thinly sliced
200g small chestnut
  mushrooms, halved
2 garlic cloves, crushed
2 bay leaves
1 tsp fresh thyme leaves
1 tbsp plain flour
300ml chicken stock (made
  with 1 chicken stock cube)
150ml red wine
2 tbsp tomato purée
1 tbsp redcurrant jelly
flaked sea salt
ground black pepper
roughly chopped fresh
  flat-leaf parsley, to
  garnish (optional)

Freeze the cooked chicken
and sauce in labelled
zip-seal bags or shallow
freezer-proof containers
when cool. Label and freeze
for up to 3 months. Defrost
in the fridge overnight and
reheat in the microwave or
in a covered dish as the
recipe for 25-30 minutes or
until piping hot throughout.

This is a fab recipe for a dinner party. It's the classic Italian dish of chicken breasts wrapped in Parma ham and cooked in a rich red wine and mushroom sauce. If you don't need all six servings, freeze the leftover portions for another day.

Pour the just-boiled water over the dried mushrooms in a bowl and leave to soak for 20-30 minutes.

Wrap each chicken breast in a slice of Parma ham. Heat 1 teaspoon of the oil in a large non-stick frying pan and fry the chicken in batches for 2-3 minutes on each side or until nicely browned. Place the chicken in a single layer in a large, shallow ovenproof dish (a lasagne dish is ideal).

Preheat the oven to 190°C/Fan 170°C/Gas 5. Return the frying pan to the heat, add the remaining oil and fry the onions and fresh mushrooms over a medium-high heat for 5 minutes or until lightly browned, stirring regularly.

Drain the dried mushrooms, reserving the stock, roughly chop them and add to the pan with the onions and mushrooms. Stir in the garlic, bay leaves and thyme and fry for a further minute, while stirring.

Sprinkle over the flour and stir well. Slowly add the chicken stock and wine, stirring constantly. Strain the mushroom stock through a fine sieve into the pan and add the tomato purée and redcurrant jelly. Bring the sauce to a simmer and season with salt and pepper.

Pour the sauce over the chicken breasts, cover the dish with foil and bake in the centre of the oven for 40 minutes. Remove the foil and bake for a further 15-20 minutes or until the chicken is tender and cooked through. Divide the chicken between six warmed plates, give the sauce a quick stir and spoon over the top. Sprinkle with some roughly chopped parsley if you like.

259
CALORIES
PER SERVING

crispy chicken bites

SERVES 4

PREP: 15 MINUTES

COOK: 15–20 MINUTES

4 boneless, skinless
   chicken breasts
1 large egg
50g coarse dried white
   breadcrumbs or
   panko breadcrumbs
½ tsp paprika (not smoked)
good pinch of fine sea salt
oil, for spraying
ground black pepper
sticky barbecue sauce
   (see right), to serve

Open freeze the uncooked but coated chicken then pack into a freezer-proof container, interleaving the pieces with baking parchment. Seal and freeze for up to 1 month. Cook from frozen as above, but increase the cooking time by 8–10 minutes or until the chicken is cooked and piping hot throughout.

These home-made chicken nuggets are really easy to make using fresh chicken breasts and ready-prepared, coarse breadcrumbs. I always keep a pack of dried natural breadcrumbs in the cupboard and then add a little paprika for a richer colour. Japanese panko breadcrumbs can also be used for coatings.

Preheat the oven to 220°C/Fan 200°C/Gas 7. Line a baking tray with baking parchment.

Put the chicken breasts on a board and cut each breast into roughly 3cm chunks. Beat the egg in a bowl until smooth. Sprinkle half the breadcrumbs into a large bowl and season with half the paprika and a little salt.

Take the chicken breast pieces one at a time and dip them straight into the beaten egg, then coat in the breadcrumbs until evenly covered.

Put the pieces on the prepared baking tray while you make the rest of the chicken bites, adding the reserved breadcrumbs, paprika and salt to the large bowl, and stirring, after coating roughly half the pieces.

Spray the chicken pieces with oil and bake in the oven for 15–20 minutes or until crisp, golden brown and cooked through (there should be no pinkness remaining in the centre of the chicken). Serve with sticky barbecue sauce if you like.

Sticky barbecue sauce: Put 5 tablespoons tomato ketchup, ½ tablespoon Worcestershire sauce, ½ tablespoon light soft brown sugar and 1 tablespoon dark soy sauce in a small saucepan and heat gently. Bring to a simmer and cook for 1–2 minutes, stirring continuously, or until thick. Pour into a small bowl and leave to cool. Serves 4. Calories per serving: 29

chicken, ham
and leek filo pie

SERVES 4
PREP: 25 MINUTES
COOK: 40 MINUTES

oil, for spraying or brushing
1 slender leek, thinly sliced
2 boneless, skinless chicken
   breasts, cut into roughly
   2.5cm chunks
25g plain flour
250ml chicken stock (made
   with 1 chicken stock cube)
200ml semi-skimmed milk
3tbsp white wine (optional)
pinch of flaked sea salt,
   plus extra to taste
3–4 slices of lean smoked
   ham, cut into strips
   (about 100g)
3 filo pastry sheets
   (each about 45g)
ground black pepper

Open freeze the cooled,
unbaked pie for 1 hour, then
wrap with a double layer of
foil. Label and freeze for up
to 1 month. To serve, defrost
overnight in the fridge and
bake as the recipe, increasing
the cooking time by about
10 minutes, or until piping
hot throughout.

This chicken pie is probably one of the easiest you'll ever bake and is surprisingly low in calories, despite its rich-tasting filling. The filo pastry topping doesn't feel like a compromise and is very simple to prepare. Stirring white wine into the sauce will add 10 calories per tablespoon.

Preheat the oven to 200°C/Fan 180°C/Gas 6. Spray or brush a non-stick saucepan with oil and place over a medium heat. Add the leek and chicken and fry for 2 minutes, or until the chicken is lightly coloured, stirring regularly. Sprinkle over the flour and cook for a few seconds before gradually adding the stock and milk, just a little at a time. Adding the stock slowly should help prevent the sauce from becoming lumpy.

Bring the sauce to a simmer and season well with a pinch of salt and lots of black pepper. Cook for 4 minutes or until the sauce thickens, stirring constantly. Remove the pan from the heat and stir in the ham and wine, if using.

Transfer the pie filling to a roughly 1.75 litre pie dish. Spray each sheet of filo pastry with oil and cut into 4 wide strips. Working quickly, top the dish with strips of the filo, oiled-side up, crumpling and scrunching loosely as you go.

Bake in the centre of the oven for about 30 minutes or until the pastry is golden brown and the filling is hot and bubbling.

322

thai red chicken curry

SERVES 4

PREP: 20 MINUTES

COOK: 15 MINUTES

4 boneless, skinless
   chicken breasts
oil, for spraying or brushing
2 tbsp red Thai curry paste
1 tbsp cornflour
100ml cold water
150g baby sweetcorn,
   halved lengthways if large
1 red and 1 yellow pepper,
   deseeded and cut into
   3cm chunks
150g sugar snap peas
400g can of reduced-fat
   coconut milk, shaken well
1 tbsp Thai fish sauce
   (nam pla)
1 tbsp lemongrass paste
   (from a jar)
1 tbsp soft dark brown sugar
4 fresh, frozen or dried
   Kaffir lime leaves
fresh coriander and basil
   leaves (optional), to serve

Tip: Adding cornflour to
the curry sauce will help
stabilise the coconut milk
and make the curry taste
extra creamy and luxurious.

**Ready-made curry paste is a really useful store-cupboard
standby. Go for authentic Thai brands for the best flavour and
give a little extra lift with fresh or frozen Kaffir lime leaves and
lemongrass, or roughly chopped fresh coriander.**

Cut each chicken breast into thin strips. Spray a large, deep
non-stick frying pan or wok with oil, add the chicken and cook
over a medium heat for 2 minutes, stirring until the chicken is
lightly coloured on both sides. Stir in the curry paste and cook
for 1 minute more.

Mix the cornflour with 2 tablespoons of the cold water in
a small bowl. Add the vegetables to the pan with the chicken
and stir-fry for 1 minute. Stir in the coconut milk, the remaining
water and the cornflour mixture. Add the fish sauce,
lemongrass paste, lime leaves and sugar. Bring to a gentle
simmer and cook for 5 minutes or until the chicken and
vegetables are tender.

Ladle into deep bowls and serve scattered with fresh coriander
and basil if you like. (Don't eat the lime leaves.)

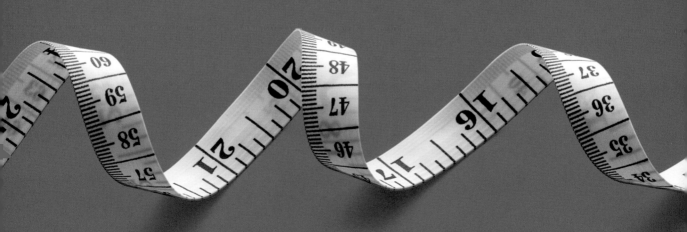

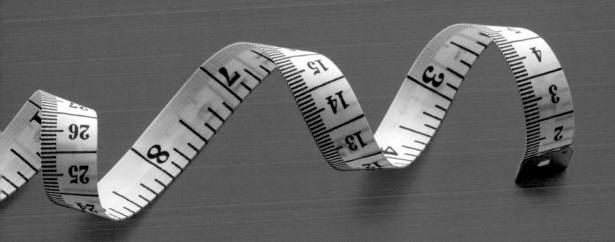

beef
and lamb

375

roast beef, yorkshire puddings and gravy

1.2kg lean beef topside, rolled and tied
2 tsp coarsely ground black pepper, plus extra to season
oil, for spraying or brushing
150ml red wine
1 beef stock cube
4 tsp cornflour
350ml water
2 tbsp cold water
flaked sea salt

FOR THE YORKSHIRE PUDDINGS
2 large eggs
115g plain flour
225ml semi-skimmed milk
½ tsp flaked sea salt

Topside of beef is a lean cut that roasts well as long as you serve it quite rare. Use a shallow bun tin to make the Yorkshire puddings and use only a minimal amount of oil to grease it. Add lots of vegetables but try to avoid roast potatoes – the Yorkshire puddings should be filling enough.

Preheat the oven to 200°C/Fan 180°C/Gas 6. Season the beef on both sides with salt and rub all over with the 2 teaspoons of ground black pepper. Spray or brush a large non-stick frying pan with oil and place over a medium-high heat. Brown the beef for 5 minutes, until well coloured all over.

Transfer the beef to a roasting tin and roast in the oven for 40 minutes for rare meat. Add 10–15 minutes to the cooking time for medium and 25 minutes for well-done beef.

While the beef is roasting, make the batter for the Yorkshire puddings. Put the eggs, flour, milk and salt in a food processor and blitz until smooth. Alternatively, beat the eggs with the flour, salt and half the milk in a bowl until smooth. Whisk in the remaining milk. Pour the batter into a jug, cover and chill in the fridge.

Remove the beef from the oven and transfer to a board. Loosely cover with foil and leave to rest for 15 minutes. Increase the oven temperature to 220°C/Fan 200°C/Gas 7. Spray or brush a shallow 12-hole bun tin with oil and put the tin in the oven to heat through for 5 minutes.

Carefully remove the hot tin from the oven and fill each of the 12 holes equally with the batter. Return to the oven for 15–18 minutes or until they are well-risen and golden brown.

To make the gravy, place the roasting tin on the hob, add the red wine, crumble over the beef stock cube and add 350ml of water. Bring to a simmer, stirring. Mix the cornflour with 2 tablespoons of water and stir into the tin.

Season to taste with salt and plenty of black pepper and return to a simmer. Strain the gravy through a fine sieve into a warmed jug. Carve the beef into thin slices and tip any of the carving and resting juices into the hot gravy.

377

CALORIES
PER SERVING

chilli con carne

SERVES 6
PREP: 20 MINUTES
COOK: 2–2¼ HOURS

oil, for spraying or brushing
1kg braising steak (ideally
    chuck steak)
2 medium onions, chopped
2 garlic cloves, finely chopped
2 tsp hot chilli powder
2 tsp smoked paprika (not
    hot smoked)
2 tsp ground cumin
2 tsp ground coriander
2 tbsp plain flour
150ml red wine or beef stock
600ml beef stock (made
    with 1 beef stock cube)
400g can chopped tomatoes
2 tsp caster sugar
1 tsp dried oregano
2 x 400g cans red kidney
    beans, drained and rinsed
2 tbsp fresh lime juice
flaked sea salt
ground black pepper

Freeze the cooled chilli
in labelled zip-seal bags
or freezer-proof containers
for up to 3 months. Defrost
in the fridge overnight and
reheat thoroughly in a large,
wide-based saucepan over
a medium heat, stirring
gently until piping hot.

My chilli is a little different because I use chunks of beef instead of mince. If you have never made it this way, give it a go – I think it makes the dish far more satisfying and it freezes brilliantly too. Don't forget to add extra calories if serving with rice. Garnish with roughly chopped tomato and red onion salsa and lots of fresh coriander.

Preheat the oven to 180°C/Fan 160°C/Gas 4. Spray or brush a large non-stick frying pan with oil.

Trim the beef of any hard fat, cut into roughly 3cm chunks and season with salt and pepper. Fry the beef in two batches over a fairly high heat until browned on all sides. Tip into a large flameproof casserole.

Return the frying pan to the heat, spray with a little more oil and add the onions to the pan. Cook for 5 minutes over a medium heat, until softened. Add the garlic, chilli powder and other spices and cook for 2–3 minutes more, stirring continuously. Sprinkle over the flour and stir well.

Gradually stir in the wine and half the beef stock. Bring to a simmer, while stirring. Pour the onions and liquid over the beef in the casserole and add the canned tomatoes, the remaining stock, the sugar and oregano. Season with salt and plenty of black pepper.

Bring the liquid to a simmer, then cover with a lid and transfer carefully to the oven. Cook for 1 hour, then remove from the oven and stir in the kidney beans. Return to the oven and cook for a further 45–60 minutes or until the beef is very tender and the sauce is thickened. Stir in the lime juice and season to taste.

64 BEEF AND LAMB

425
CALORIES
PER SERVING

beef and guinness stew with herby dumplings

SERVES 6

PREP: 25 MINUTES

COOK: 2¾ HOURS

1 tbsp sunflower oil
2 medium onions, sliced
1kg braising steak (such
 as chuck steak)
4 tbsp plain flour
1 tsp flaked sea salt
2 tbsp fresh thyme leaves
 or 1 tsp dried thyme
1 bay leaf
440ml can stout
 (such as Guinness)
250ml beef stock
 (made with 1 stock cube)
2 tbsp tomato purée
2 tsp caster sugar
3 carrots, peeled and cut
 into 3cm lengths
3 celery sticks, cut into
 3cm lengths
ground black pepper

FOR THE HERBY DUMPLINGS

100g self-raising flour,
 plus extra for dusting
25g butter, chilled
1 tbsp finely chopped fresh
 flat-leaf parsley
50ml cold water

Freeze the cooled stew
in shallow, freezer-proof
containers for up to 3 months.
Open freeze the uncooked
dumplings then place in a zip-
seal bag. Defrost the stew in
the fridge overnight and transfer
to a large saucepan with 300ml
water. Bring to a simmer,
stirring occasionally. Add the
frozen dumplings. Cover and
simmer for 15–20 minutes.

I've reduced the fat in these dumplings as much as possible while still keeping them light and fluffy. Use good-quality braising steak and not extra lean steak as a little bit of fat will keep the meat moist as it cooks and add flavour to the stew.

Preheat the oven to 180°C/Fan 160°C/Gas 4. Heat the oil in a large flameproof casserole. Fry the onions over a medium-high heat for about 5 minutes, stirring frequently, or until lightly browned. Remove from heat.

Trim any visible fat from the beef and cut into roughly 3cm chunks. Put the flour, salt and thyme in a large bowl. Season with lots of ground pepper and combine, then toss the meat in the flour until coated evenly all over. Tip the meat into the casserole dish with the onions.

Add the bay leaf, stout, stock, tomato purée and sugar. Stir well and bring to the boil. Cover and transfer to the oven for 1 hour or until the beef and vegetables are just tender. Take the casserole out of the oven and stir in the carrots and celery. Cover and return to the oven for 1 hour further, or until the beef and vegetables are just tender.

To make the dumplings, put the flour and butter in a medium bowl and rub the fat into the flour until it resembles fine breadcrumbs. Stir in the parsley, then add enough water to form a soft, spongy dough, mixing with a round-bladed table knife.

Form the dumpling mixture into a fat sausage shape on a lightly floured surface and cut into 12 even portions. Roll each portion into a small ball. Take the beef out of the oven and remove the lid. Stir the stew and drop the dumplings gently on top of the meat and vegetables. Cover with the lid and return to the oven for 20 minutes or until the dumplings are well risen, light and fluffy.

430

steak and mushroom pies

SERVES 6
PREP: 30 MINUTES
**COOK: 2¼ HOURS,
PLUS COOLING TIME**

800g braising steak
   (ideally chuck steak)
oil, for spraying or brushing
2 medium onions, sliced
2 garlic cloves, crushed
3 tbsp plain flour, plus
   extra for dusting
500ml beef stock (made
   with 1 beef stock cube)
100ml red wine
1 tbsp tomato purée
2 bay leaves
1 tsp dried thyme
400g small button
   mushrooms, halved
320g ready-rolled light
   puff pastry
beaten egg, to glaze
flaked sea salt
ground black pepper

Open freeze the cooled,
assembled pies, without
baking, until solid. Cover
with a double layer of foil.
Label and freeze for up to
3 months. Defrost overnight
in the fridge and cook as
above, adding an extra 5–10
minutes to the cooking time
and ensuring the filling is
piping hot throughout.

I've become a huge fan of ready-made lower-fat puff pastry.
It works just as well as the regular type and means you can
serve a traditional pie while still keeping a close eye on the
calories. If you prefer to make one large pie, increase the
cooking time by about 10 minutes. If you use full-fat puff
pastry, you'll need to add an extra 26 calories per serving.

Preheat the oven to 180°C/Fan 160°C/Gas 4. Trim any visible
fat from the beef and cut into roughly 2.5cm chunks.

Spray or brush a medium flameproof casserole with oil and
place over a medium heat. Fry the onions for 4–5 minutes,
or until softened and lightly coloured, stirring occasionally.
Add the garlic and cook for 1 minute more.

Add the beef and flour to the casserole, season well and toss
together. Stir in the beef stock, wine, tomato purée, bay leaves
and thyme. Bring the liquid to a simmer, cover with a lid and
cook in the oven for 1½ hours.

Remove the casserole from the oven and stir in the mushrooms.
Simmer on the hob for 15 minutes or until the sauce has
thickened, stirring regularly. Spoon into individual 300ml
ovenproof pots or pie dishes and leave to cool for 30 minutes.

Preheat the oven to 200°C/Fan 180°C/Gas 6. Roll out the
pastry on a lightly floured surface until large enough for you
to cut out 6 squares to fit the pots or pie dishes. Cut 6 squares
that are just big enough to overhang the pots or dishes.
Depending on the shape of your pie dishes, you may need
to cut your pastry into strips to be able to cover all the dishes.
(You can lay the strips 1cm apart, in a lattice pattern, to make
the pastry go further.) Lightly score the pastry.

Brush the rim of the pie dishes with a little egg and place the
pastry on top, pressing down around the edges to secure.
Brush the pastry with egg and season the tops with pepper.

Bake the pies on a baking tray for 25–30 minutes or until the
pastry is well risen and golden and the filling is hot throughout.

352

CALORIES
PER SERVING

beef goulash

SERVES 6

PREP: 20 MINUTES

COOK: 2¼ HOURS

1.2kg braising steak
(ideally chuck steak)
1 tbsp sunflower oil
2 medium onions, each
cut into 12 wedges
2 tsp hot smoked paprika
1 tbsp paprika (not smoked)
1 beef stock cube
2 x 400g cans chopped
tomatoes
2 tbsp tomato purée
1 large red and 1 large yellow
pepper, deseeded and cut
into roughly 2.5cm chunks
flaked sea salt
ground black pepper
roughly chopped flat-leaf
parsley, to garnish
(optional)

Freeze the cooled goulash
in labelled zip-seal bags or
freezer-proof containers for
up to 3 months. Defrost in
the fridge overnight and
reheat thoroughly in a large,
wide-based saucepan, stirring
gently until piping hot.
Alternatively, reheat from
frozen with an extra 200ml
water over a medium-low
heat until thawed. Bring to
a simmer, stirring gently
until piping hot throughout.

This is the perfect dish to make ahead and cook from frozen. Flat frozen in zip-seal bags, it can be reheated straight from the freezer and ready in under 20 minutes. Serve with extra vegetables or a small portion of rice and a spoonful of soured cream.

Preheat the oven to 170°C/Fan 150°C/Gas 3. Trim any hard fat from the beef and cut the meat into roughly 3cm chunks. Season well with salt and black pepper.

Heat the oil in a large flameproof casserole. Add the steak and fry over a high heat until lightly coloured, turning every now and then. Tip the onions into the pan and cook with the beef for a few seconds

Sprinkle both paprikas over the meat and crumble the beef stock cube on top. Add the tomatoes and tomato purée. Season with salt and pepper, stir well and bring to a simmer. Cover with a tight-fitting lid and transfer to the oven. Cook for 1 hour.

Carefully remove the casserole from the oven. Stir in the peppers, replace the lid and cook for a further hour or until the beef is tender. Garnish with parsley before serving, if you like.

302
CALORIES
PER SERVING

no-fuss cottage pie

SERVES 6

PREP: 25 MINUTES

COOK: 1½ HOURS

500g lean minced beef
2 medium onions, chopped
2 celery sticks, thinly sliced
3 medium carrots, peeled
    and diced
400g can chopped
    tomatoes with herbs
3 tbsp tomato purée
500ml beef stock
    (made with 1 stock cube)
1 tbsp Worcestershire sauce
flaked sea salt
ground black pepper

FOR THE LEEKY MASH
700g potatoes, peeled
    and cut into roughly
    4cm chunks
1 large leek, cut into 1cm
    slices
2 tbsp fat-free fromage frais
100ml semi-skimmed milk
flaked sea salt
ground black pepper

Freeze the cooled and
assembled pie without
baking. Cover with a lid
or a double layer of foil.
Label and freeze for up
to 3 months. Defrost in the
fridge overnight and cook
as above, adding an extra
10-15 minutes to the baking
time or until golden brown
and piping hot throughout.

The leeky mash topping for this pie makes the smaller amount of potatoes feel much more luxurious. You don't need to be too neat about it; just drop spoonfuls of the mash on top of the meat and bung it in the oven.

Place a large non-stick saucepan over a medium heat and cook the mince with the onions, celery and carrots for 10 minutes, stirring regularly, breaking up the meat as it cooks.

Stir in the canned tomatoes, tomato purée, beef stock and Worcestershire sauce. Season with a good pinch of salt and plenty of black pepper. Bring to a simmer, then reduce the heat, cover loosely and simmer gently for about 45 minutes, stirring occasionally, or until the mince is tender and sauce is thick.

Roughly 20 minutes before the beef is ready, make the leeky mash. Put the potatoes in a large saucepan and cover with cold water. Bring to the boil, then reduce the heat slightly and simmer for 15–18 minutes or until the potatoes are very tender.

Cook the sliced leek for 2–3 minutes in a small pan of boiling water until just softened. Preheat the oven to 220°C/Fan 200°C/Gas 7. Drain the potatoes, then return them to the pan and mash with the fromage frais and seasoning to taste, until smooth. Stir in the milk and leeks.

Spoon the beef mixture into a shallow ovenproof dish. Using a large spoon, top the beef with the leeky mash.

Bake for 25–30 minutes or until the topping is golden and the filling is bubbling.

324
CALORIES
PER SERVING

swedish meatballs in gravy

SERVES 4
PREP: 25 MINUTES
COOK: 40 MINUTES

250g lean minced beef
250g minced pork
½ medium onion,
  roughly chopped
2 garlic cloves, roughly
  chopped
15g fresh dill, finely
  chopped, plus extra
  to garnish
15g fresh flat-leaf parsley,
  leaves finely chopped
50g fresh white
  breadcrumbs
1 tsp flaked sea salt
oil, for spraying or brushing
ground black pepper
4 tbsp lingonberry or
  cranberry sauce, to serve

FOR THE GRAVY
oil, for spraying or brushing
½ medium onion, very
  finely chopped
2 tbsp plain flour
750ml beef stock (made
  with 1 beef stock cube)
2 tsp tomato purée
1 tbsp single cream
flaked sea salt
ground black pepper

Freeze the cooled gravy-
coated meatballs in labelled
zip-seal bags or freezer-
proof containers for up to
3 months. Defrost in the
fridge overnight and reheat
thoroughly in a large, wide-
based saucepan, stirring
gently until piping hot.

This familiar Swedish dish can be terrifically high in calories
due to the creamy gravy. I've made this version as lean as
possible, but it still has all the traditional flavours. Garnish with
fresh dill and serve with a little cranberry sauce if you like.

To make the meatballs, place the beef and pork mince into
the bowl of a food processor with the onion, garlic, herbs,
breadcrumbs and salt. Blend until a thick paste is formed,
similar to sausage meat. Divide the mixture into 20 portions
and roll into small, neat balls.

Spray or brush a large, deep non-stick frying pan with the oil
and fry the meatballs for 6–8 minutes, or until nicely browned.
Roll and turn the meatballs around in the pan as they brown
to prevent them becoming flattened on the side. Transfer them
to a medium saucepan or sauté pan using a slotted spoon.

To make the gravy, spray or brush a little oil in the same pan
used to fry the meatballs. Fry the onion over a low heat for
3 minutes, or until softened and lightly browned, stirring
regularly. Sprinkle the flour into the pan and stir well.

Slowly stir in the stock, then add the tomato purée and bring
to a simmer, stirring continuously. The gravy may have become
a little lumpy, but keep stirring (using a silicone whisk preferably),
and it should come together. Cook for 4 minutes, stirring
continuously. Season and strain the gravy through a sieve
into the pan with the meatballs.

Bring the sauce to a gentle simmer. Cover loosely and cook for
20 minutes, or until the meatballs are tender, stirring occasionally.
Add a little extra stock or water if the sauce has reduced too
much. Remove the lid, stir in the cream and increase the heat
under the pan.

Simmer the gravy for a further 2–3 minutes or until thickened
enough to lightly coat the meatballs. Adjust the seasoning to
taste and serve.

74 BEEF AND LAMB

374
CALORIES
PER SERVING

throw-it-together beef lasagne

SERVES 6

PREP: 20 MINUTES

COOK: 2¼ HOURS

400g lean minced beef

2 medium onions, chopped

2 garlic cloves, finely chopped

200g small mushrooms, sliced

1 tbsp plain flour

150ml Martini Rosso or red wine

400g can chopped tomatoes

2 tbsp tomato purée

500ml beef stock (made with 1 beef stock cube)

1 tsp caster sugar

1 heaped tsp dried oregano

2 bay leaves

good pinch of flaked sea salt, plus extra to taste

2 medium courgettes, thinly sliced lengthways

3 large tomatoes, sliced

250g ricotta, drained

3 sheets of fresh lasagne (around 125g)

125g reduced-fat mozzarella

20g Parmesan cheese, finely grated

handful of fresh basil leaves

freshly ground black pepper

Tip: Dip the pasta sheets in a bowl of warm water as you use them and they will soften more quickly in the lasagne.

Lasagne usually involves a laborious process of layering cheese sauce, mince and pasta. For this one, I've used mozzarella and ricotta cheese, so once the meat mixture is ready, the dish can be put together very quickly. The pasta quantity is quite low but no-one will notice as I've added long strips of courgette, which have a similar texture.

Place a large saucepan or flameproof casserole over a medium heat and cook the mince with the onion and garlic for 10 minutes or until lightly browned, breaking up the meat as it cooks. Add the mushrooms and cook for 3 minutes more.

Stir in the flour followed by the Martini, tomatoes, tomato purée, beef stock, sugar, oregano and bay leaves. Season with a good pinch of salt and plenty of black pepper.

Bring to the boil, then reduce the heat and simmer gently for 40 minutes, or until the mince is tender and the sauce has thickened, stirring occasionally. Season with a little more salt and pepper to taste.

Preheat the oven to 200°C/Fan 180°C/Gas 6. As this is a relaxed lasagne, there is no need to carefully layer all the ingredients. Simply arrange the mince, courgettes, tomatoes, ricotta (leaving one-third for the topping) and lasagne sheets loosely in a shallow ovenproof dish. Tear the mozzarella and scatter over the remaining ricotta, then sprinkle the Parmesan over the top.

Bake in the centre of the oven for about 25 minutes or until the top is golden and the filling is bubbling. Garnish with a few basil leaves just before serving.

333
CALORIES
PER SERVING

pot roast beef

SERVES 6
PREP: 15 MINUTES
COOK: 2³/₄- 3¹/₄ HOURS

1.2kg lean beef topside, rolled and tied
1 tsp flaked sea salt, plus extra to season
1 tbsp sunflower oil
3 medium onions, each cut into 8 wedges
3 fresh bushy thyme sprigs
1 large bay leaf
2 tbsp tomato purée
200ml red wine
400ml hot beef stock (made with 1 beef stock cube)
500g medium carrots (about 6), each cut into roughly 4cm lengths
6 celery sticks, cut into roughly 4cm lengths
ground black pepper
roughly chopped flat-leaf parsley, to garnish (optional)

This is an easy way to cut the calories in your usual Sunday roast and it is one of those all-in-one dishes you can bung in the oven and almost forget about for a few hours. Serve with freshly cooked green beans or shredded savoy cabbage.

Season the beef all over with the salt and lots of black pepper. Heat the oil in a large non-stick frying pan and brown the beef over a fairly high heat for about 10 minutes, turning every couple of minutes. Preheat the oven to 170°C/Fan 150°C/Gas 3.

Transfer the beef to a casserole and put it to one side. Add an onion to the frying pan and fry over a medium heat for 5 minutes, or until nicely browned, stirring regularly. Stir in the thyme and bay leaf and cook for a few seconds more, then add to the casserole and tuck around the beef.

Stir the tomato purée and wine into the hot beef stock and pour around the beef. Cover the pan with a lid and cook in the oven for 1 hour.

Remove the dish from the oven and take off the lid. Turn the beef over and nestle all the remaining vegetables around it. Cover with the lid again and return to the oven for a further 1¹/₂ –2 hours or until the beef is very tender and yields completely to the pressure of a spoon.

Lift the beef out of the dish with a couple of forks and place it on a board or serving platter. If you prefer a thicker gravy, reduce the sauce on the hob at this point. Cut the string away from the beef and carve it into slices. Serve with the poached vegetables and the rich cooking liquor for gravy. Garnish with parsley, if using.

295

samosa pie

SERVES 6

**PREP: 20 MINUTES,
PLUS COOLING TIME**

COOK: 50 MINUTES

½ tsp cumin seeds
½ tsp coriander seeds
450g lean minced beef
2 large onions,
    finely chopped
2 garlic cloves, finely
    chopped
¼ tsp ground turmeric
¼ tsp cayenne pepper
1 tbsp medium curry
    powder
finely grated zest
    of ½ lemon
2 bay leaves
1 tbsp plain flour
2 tbsp mango chutney
1 tbsp Worcestershire sauce
300g potatoes (ideally
    Maris Piper), peeled and
    cut into 1cm dice
400ml lamb stock (made
    with 1 lamb stock cube)
100g frozen peas
3 sheets of filo pastry
    (each about 45g)
oil, for spraying or brushing
¼ tsp poppy seeds, to
    garnish (optional)

Freeze the cooled and
assembled pie without
baking. Cover with a double
layer of foil. Label and
freeze for up to 1 month.
Thaw overnight in the fridge
and cook as the recipe,
adding an extra 10 minutes
and ensuring the filling is
piping hot throughout.

**This dish incorporates many of the ingredients used in
a traditional Indian samosa and bakes them together
in a mildly curried pie. It's a real favourite in my family
and the filo pastry topping means it's very easy to make.**

Fry the whole spices in a dry, large non-stick saucepan for 1–2
minutes or until you start to smell the aromas. Add the mince,
onions, garlic, ground spices, lemon zest and bay leaves.

Fry over a medium heat for 5–6 minutes, breaking up the
mince as it cooks. Stir the flour into the mince, mixing well
before adding the mango chutney and Worcestershire sauce.
Add the potatoes and the stock to the pan and bring to
a simmer. Cook for 15 minutes or until the potatoes are just
tender, adding the peas for the final 5 minutes, stirring
regularly so nothing sticks.

Pour the mince into a small roasting tin or shallow ovenproof
dish and leave to cool for at least 30 minutes. Preheat the
oven to 200°C/Fan 180°C/Gas 6.

Spray or brush a filo pastry sheet lightly with oil, then carefully
place it over the mince. Repeat with the remaining pastry,
misting each lightly with oil before adding. Score the pastry
lightly with a knife. Sprinkle with poppy seeds, if using. Bake
in the oven for 25–30 minutes or until the pastry is crisp and
golden and the filling is bubbling.

345
CALORIES
PER SERVING

lazy lamb tagine

SERVES 6

PREP: 25 MINUTES

COOK: 1½ HOURS

800g lean lamb leg steaks
   (or lean lamb meat)
2 medium onions, halved
   and sliced
4 garlic cloves, peeled and
   thinly sliced
1 tbsp ras-el-hanout mix
oil, for spraying or brushing
2 tbsp plain flour
400ml hot lamb stock (made
   with 1 lamb stock cube)
2 x 400g cans chopped
   tomatoes
4 tsp harissa paste
2 tbsp clear honey
1 preserved lemon, drained
   and cut into thin strips
400g can chickpeas, rinsed
   and drained
175g green beans, cut in half
flaked sea salt
ground black pepper
chopped fresh flat-leaf
   parsley or coriander,
   to garnish

Freeze the cooled tagine in
labelled zip-seal bags or foil
containers for up to 4 months.
Thaw in the fridge overnight.
Reheat thoroughly in a large,
wide-based saucepan, stirring
gently until piping hot.

Tip: If you don't have ras-
el-hanout, mix 2 tsp ground
coriander, 1 tsp ground
ginger and ½ tsp ground
cinnamon instead.

**Tender chunks of lamb in a lightly spiced tomato and
chickpea sauce. If you can't get hold of preserved lemons
in a jar, add the grated zest of half a large lemon instead.
Serve with couscous or rice.**

Preheat the oven to 200°C/Fan 180°C/Gas 6. Trim any excess
fat from the lamb, cut it into 3–4cm chunks and season all over
with salt and pepper. Toss the lamb with the onions, garlic
and ras-el-hanout in a bowl.

Spray or brush a large non-stick frying pan with the oil and
fry the meat in 2 batches over a medium-high heat until lightly
browned, turning every now and then. Tip the meat into
a flameproof casserole and toss with the flour.

Deglaze the frying pan with 150ml of the stock, stirring to lift
any flavoursome bits, and pour it over the lamb. Add the rest
of the stock, canned tomatoes, harissa, honey and lemon.
Bring to a gentle simmer.

Cover and cook in the oven for 1 hour or until the lamb is
just tender. Remove from the oven and stir in the chickpeas
and green beans. Cover and return to the oven for a further
20–30 minutes or until the beans are tender.

359

moussaka

450g lean minced lamb
1 large onion, finely
    chopped
1 tbsp plain flour
1½ tsp dried mint
2 bay leaves
½ tsp ground cinnamon
150ml red wine
450ml lamb stock (made
    with 1 lamb stock cube)
400g can chopped
    tomatoes with herbs
3 tbsp tomato purée
2 aubergines (each about
    300g)
oil, for spraying or brushing
flaked sea salt
ground black pepper

FOR THE WHITE SAUCE
40g cornflour
550ml semi-skimmed milk
2 large eggs, well beaten
100g feta cheese, drained
flaked sea salt
ground black pepper

This lamb bake can be made in one large dish or six smaller dishes. I like the small dishes best as it's easy to keep an eye on portion sizes. Serve with a small mixed salad.

Put the lamb and onion in a large non-stick saucepan and cook over a medium high heat for 10 minutes, stirring and breaking up the meat as it cooks.

Stir in the flour, mint, bay leaves and cinnamon. Season with salt and plenty of black pepper. Pour over the wine and add the lamb stock, tomatoes and tomato purée. Bring to a simmer, then cook for 30 minutes, or until the lamb is tender and the sauce is thick, stirring occasionally.

Meanwhile, prepare the aubergines. Preheat the grill to its hottest setting. Cut the aubergines into 1cm slices, discarding the ends. In two batches, arrange the aubergines in a single layer on a lightly oiled large baking tray. Spray or brush with a little oil.

Place the tray under the grill and cook for about 5 minutes or until lightly browned. Turn over, spray or brush with a little more oil and cook on the other side for a further 5 minutes. Repeat with the second batch of aubergine slices.

Preheat the oven to 200°C/Fan 180°C/Gas 6. Just before the mince is ready, make the white sauce. Mix the cornflour with 50ml of the milk until smooth. Pour into a saucepan, stir in the rest of the milk and heat until just below boiling, stirring continuously. Remove from the heat and whisk in the eggs. Season with salt and black pepper.

Gently stir the aubergines into the meat sauce. Spoon into either a shallow ovenproof dish or individual dishes. Pour over the white sauce, dot with crumbled feta, then bake for 20–25 minutes or until the filling is hot and the topping has set.

332
CALORIES
PER SERVING

lamb and lentil curry

SERVES 6
PREP: 25 MINUTES
COOK: 1½–2 HOURS

800g lean lamb leg steaks
(or lean lamb meat)
oil, for spraying or brushing
3 medium-large onions,
roughly chopped
4 large garlic cloves,
roughly chopped
25g chunk fresh root ginger,
peeled and roughly
chopped
1 red chilli, roughly chopped
(deseed first if you like)
4 tbsp medium curry paste
100g red split lentils, rinsed
and drained
400g can chopped
tomatoes
600ml water
2 bay leaves
1 tsp flaked sea salt,
plus extra to season
1 tsp caster sugar
100g bag young spinach
leaves (optional)
ground black pepper
cucumber raita (see
page 140), to serve

Freeze the cooled curry
in labelled zip-seal bags
or foil containers for up
to 4 months. Thaw in the
fridge overnight. Reheat
thoroughly in a large, wide-
based saucepan, stirring
gently until piping hot.

Adding lentils to a curry is a great way of making it feel more filling without adding too many extra calories. I like to stir in some baby spinach towards the end of the cooking time and serve with a generous spoonful of cooling cucumber raita (see page 140).

Trim the lamb of any hard fat, cut into roughly 3cm pieces and season well. Spray or brush a large non-stick frying pan with oil and fry the lamb in batches until lightly coloured on all sides. Transfer the lamb to a flameproof casserole as each batch is browned.

Spray the frying pan with more oil. Add the onions to the pan and cook over a medium heat for 6–8 minutes, or until lightly browned, stirring continuously. Reduce the heat, add the garlic, ginger and chilli and cook for 5 minutes, while stirring. Tip the mixture into a food processor and leave to cool for 5 minutes.

Preheat the oven to 180°C/Fan 160°C/Gas 4. Blend the onion mixture into as fine a paste as you can. You may need to remove the lid and push the mixture down a couple of times until the right consistency is reached.

Add the onion mixture and curry paste to the lamb. Place over a medium heat and cook together for 2–3 minutes. Add the lentils, tomatoes, water, bay leaves, salt and sugar.

Bring to a gentle simmer, then reduce the heat. Cover the pan loosely with a lid and cook in the oven for 1½–2 hours or until the lamb is very tender. Adjust the seasoning and stir in the spinach, if using, replace the lid and leave to stand for 5 minutes to wilt the spinach. Stir well and serve.

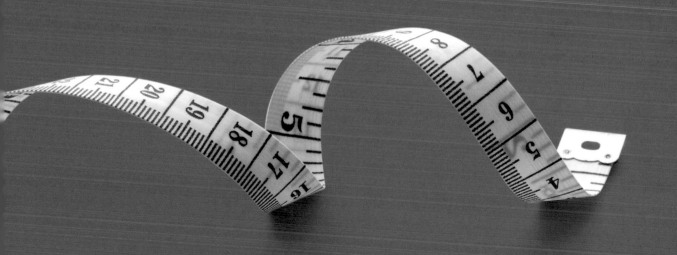

pork
and ham

329

CALORIES
PER SERVING

roast loin of pork
with braised fennel

SERVES 6
PREP: 20 MINUTES
COOK: 1¼–1½ HOURS

1 tsp fennel seeds
1 tsp flaked sea salt,
    plus extra to taste
1 tsp black peppercorns
1 tbsp finely chopped fresh
    rosemary, plus 2 extra
    stalks
1.3kg lean rindless loin
    of pork, rolled and tied
oil, for spraying or brushing
2 large fennel bulbs (each
    about 250g), cut into
    thick wedges lengthways
200ml white wine
250ml pork stock (made
    with 1 pork stock cube)
3 eating apples
2 tbsp double cream
ground black pepper

**I think the aniseed flavour of fennel complements pork really
well, especially when it is roasted and lightly caramelised.
Cooked in one pan with the apples, this simple dish is delicious
served with small portions of mashed potatoes and green beans.**

Preheat the oven to 200°C/Fan 180°C/Gas 6. Bash the fennel
seeds, salt, peppercorns and chopped rosemary together in
a pestle and mortar, leaving the mixture fairly coarse. Rub
the herb mix over the pork, covering all sides.

Heat a large wide-based, fairly shallow flameproof casserole
and spray or brush with oil. Fry the pork for 5 minutes or until
browned on all sides. Transfer to a plate and add the fennel
bulbs to the pan. Cook for 3 minutes or until lightly browned
on all sides, turning every now and then.

Return the pork to the pan and place it on top of the fennel.
Add the remaining rosemary, picked off the stems in small
sprigs, followed by the wine and stock. Allow the liquid to
bubble for 30 seconds or so and give the pan a good stir to
remove any meaty bits from the bottom. Transfer the dish
to the oven and cook for 40 minutes. Meanwhile, quarter
and core the apples and cut each into eight wedges.

Remove the dish from the oven and place the apple pieces
around the pork. Cook for a further 20–30 minutes or until
the pork is cooked through.

Transfer the pork to a board to rest for around 5 minutes and
put the fennel and apple into a warmed serving dish to serve.
Return the casserole to the hob. Stir in the cream and season
well. Simmer for a few seconds then carefully strain into
a jug. Serve with the pork.

454

tex mex toad-in-the-hole

SERVES 4
PREP: 15 MINUTES
COOK: 45 MINUTES

6 good-quality spicy pork
   sausages
1 tsp sunflower oil
1 medium red onion,
   cut into 12 wedges
1 red pepper and 1 yellow
   pepper, deseeded and
   cut into roughly 3cm
   chunks
75g jalapeño peppers
   (from a jar), drained
15g coriander, leaves
   roughly chopped

FOR THE BATTER
2 large eggs
115g plain flour
225ml semi-skimmed milk
½ tsp flaked sea salt
ground black pepper

This toad-in-the-hole uses just six sausages, but when they are cut in half and tossed with lots of vegetables, the serving size looks very generous. Make sure the tin is very hot when you add the batter or it won't rise.

Preheat the oven to 220°C/Fan 200°C/Gas 7. Place the sausages in a small shallow roasting tin. Pour over the oil and roll the sausages around until lightly coated. Add the onions and peppers, dotting them around the sausages. Bake in the oven for 10 minutes, turning once. Take the tin out of the oven and slice the sausages in half. Scatter over the jalapeño peppers and coriander and toss lightly. Return the tin to the oven for 10 minutes more or until very hot.

To make the batter, beat the eggs in a large bowl using a large metal whisk. Add the flour, half the milk, the salt and lots of black pepper. Whisk the mixture until smooth, then whisk in the remaining milk until there are no lumps remaining.

Take the hot tin out of the oven and pour the batter over the sausages and vegetables. Carefully return to the oven and bake for 25 minutes or until the batter is well risen and golden brown.

412
CALORIES
PER SERVING

smoky sausage and beans

SERVES 4
PREP: 10 MINUTES
COOK: 25 MINUTES

oil, for spraying or brushing
12 good-quality pork
    chipolatas
2 medium red onions, sliced
1–2 tsp hot smoked paprika
    (depending on how
    much heat you like)
1 tsp ground cumin
1 tsp ground coriander
400g can chopped
    tomatoes with herbs
415g can baked beans
400g can red kidney beans,
    drained and rinsed
flaked sea salt
ground black pepper
roughly chopped fresh
    flat-leaf parsley, to
    garnish (optional)

Freeze the cooled casserole
in labelled zip-seal bags
or freezer-proof containers
for up to 3 months. Defrost
in the fridge overnight.
Reheat thoroughly in a
large, wide-based saucepan,
stirring gently until piping
hot throughout.

Using chipolata sausages will make each serving of this
family-friendly casserole feel more generous and allows
you to serve between four and six people more easily.
Smoked paprika adds a lovely smoky barbecue flavour
and some chilli heat. Go for sweet smoked rather than
hot smoked if you don't like your food too spicy.

Spray or brush a large, deep non-stick frying pan or sauté
pan with oil and fry the chipolatas over a medium heat for
6–8 minutes or until browned on all sides. Transfer to a plate.

Add the onions to the pan and cook over a medium heat for
5 minutes, or until they begin to soften, stirring frequently.
Sprinkle over the paprika, cumin and coriander and cook
for a few seconds more, stirring continuously.

Add the tomatoes, half fill the can with water and pour this
into the pan. Stir in the baked beans and kidney beans, and
bring to a gentle simmer. Return the sausages to the pan.
Cook for 10 minutes, stirring regularly. Season to taste with
salt and pepper and garnish with parsley, if using.

239
CALORIES
PER SERVING

braised peas with lettuce and bacon

SERVES 2
PREP: 5 MINUTES
COOK: 8-10 MINUTES

4 rashers smoked
   back bacon
15g butter
½ small onion, finely
   chopped
300g frozen peas
175ml chicken stock
   (made with ½ chicken
   stock cube)
2 baby gem lettuces
freshly ground black pepper

This dish makes a lovely alternative lunch when you fancy something light but more filling than soup. Serve with thin slices of French bread or ciabatta if you like. It's also perfect to serve with plain grilled chicken and will stretch to four as an accompaniment.

Trim all visible fat off the bacon and cut it into 2cm pieces. Melt the butter in a large frying pan over a low heat and fry the bacon and onion for 5 minutes until lightly coloured, stirring regularly.

Tip the peas into the pan, add the chicken stock and bring to a simmer. Cook for a couple of minutes or until the peas are tender and hot, stirring occasionally.

While the peas are cooking, trim the lettuces and remove any damaged leaves. Thickly slice the lettuces and separate the leaves.

Add the lettuce to the peas and cook for just a few seconds until the lettuce is softened but maintains its colour. Season with black pepper and serve hot.

327
CALORIES
PER SERVING

sticky pork steaks with coleslaw

SERVES 4
PREP: 15 MINUTES
COOK: 10 MINUTES

4 lean pork loin steaks
(each about 150g)
oil, for spraying or brushing
6 tbsp ketchup
2 tbsp clear honey
2 tbsp Worcestershire sauce
flaked sea salt
ground black pepper

FOR THE COLESLAW
150g celeriac
1 large carrot
6 spring onions
75g light mayonnaise
100g fat-free natural
yoghurt
ground black pepper

Cut most of the excess fat from a pork chop and the meat that is left will be succulent and lean. I always fry my chops so I can keep a close eye on the temperature and to make sure they don't dry out. You need only a tiny amount of oil as well as a good non-stick frying pan. Serve with oven-baked chips (see below).

To prepare the coleslaw, peel the celeriac and cut it into very thin slices. Pile up the slices and cut through the stack to make long thin matchsticks. Put the matchsticks in a large bowl.

Peel and coarsely grate the carrot and thinly slice the spring onions. Add the carrot and spring onions to the celeriac. Spoon the mayonnaise and yoghurt on top, season with lots of black pepper and mix well together. Set aside.

Trim any visible fat from the pork steaks and season them with salt and pepper. Spray or brush a large non-stick frying pan with oil and place it over a medium heat. Cook the steaks for 5–8 minutes, depending on their thickness (turning to cook both sides evenly).

Mix the ketchup, honey and Worcestershire sauce in a bowl. Pour over the pork and continue cooking for a further 1–2 minutes on each side or until well coated in the sauce and sticky. Serve the pork with the coleslaw and oven-baked chips.

Oven-baked chips: Preheat the oven to 240°C/Fan 220°C/Gas 9. Half fill a large saucepan with water and bring it to the boil. Peel 600g medium potatoes and cut them into chips. Carefully add the chips to the water and return to the boil. Parboil the chips for 4 minutes then drain well in a colander. While still in the colander, spray with oil and toss a few times until lightly coated. Scatter over a large baking tray and season with salt and black pepper. Bake for 20 minutes, then turn them with a spatula. Spray with more oil and return to the oven for a further 10 minutes or until golden and crisp. Serves 4. Calories per serving: 119

217
CALORIES
PER SERVING

chorizo with butter beans

SERVES 2
PREP: 10 MINUTES
COOK: 15-18 MINUTES

oil, for spraying or brushing
1 medium onion, halved
    and thinly sliced
50g cooking chorizo,
    cut into very thin slices
2 garlic cloves, very thinly
    sliced
200g can chopped
    tomatoes
300ml cold water
400g can butter beans,
    drained and rinsed
flaked sea salt
ground black pepper
roughly chopped fresh flat-
    leaf parsley, to garnish

Freeze the cooled dish
in labelled zip-seal bags
or foil containers for up
to 1 month. Defrost in the
fridge overnight. Reheat
thoroughly in a large wide-
based saucepan, stirring
gently until piping hot.

Use soft cooking chorizo sausage for this recipe as the hard version can become a little dry. If you can only get hold of hard chorizo, peel off the skin before using and add it at the same time as the garlic.

Spray or brush a large non-stick frying pan with oil and place it over a medium heat. Add the onion and cook for 3–5 minutes, or until lightly coloured, stirring constantly.

Add the chorizo and cook with the onion for a further 2–3 minutes or until it releases its oil and begins to lightly brown. Don't let it get too brown. Stir in the garlic and cook for a few seconds more, stirring constantly.

Tip the tomatoes into the pan, add the cold water and butter beans and bring to a gentle simmer. Cook for 10 minutes or until the sauce is well reduced, stirring regularly. Season to taste and scatter with parsley.

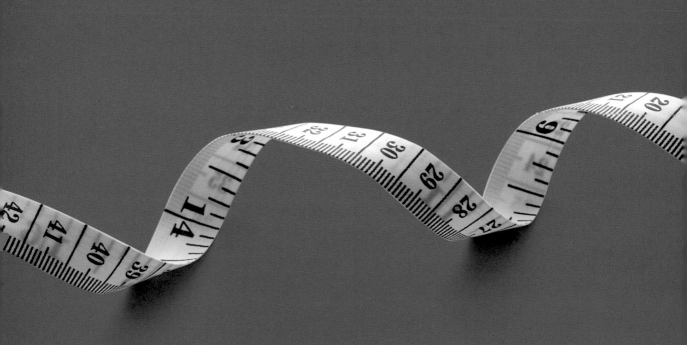

fish and
seafood

313
CALORIES
PER SERVING

creamy scallops
with bacon

SERVES 2
PREP: 10 MINUTES
COOK: 18-20 MINUTES

1 litre water
½ chicken stock cube
1 small cauliflower (about
    700g), cut into small
    florets
200g large roeless scallops,
    thawed if frozen
3 rashers (about 95g)
    smoked back bacon
oil, for spraying or brushing
3 tbsp double cream
flaked sea salt
ground black pepper
fresh finely chopped
    parsley, to garnish
    (optional)

Tip: If you cut the scallops
in half horizontally and cook
for just 1 minute on each
side, this dish will serve
four as a light starter.

This clever dish might look and taste creamy, but I've made
the sauce with puréed cauliflower rather than cream. It may
sound a bit odd, but it works beautifully and complements
the flavour of the soft scallops and salty bacon. Serve as
a main meal with green vegetables.

Pour the water into a medium saucepan, add the stock cube
and cauliflower florets and bring to the boil. Cook for about
10 minutes, stirring occasionally until the cauliflower is very
tender. Drain the cauliflower in a colander, reserving the liquid,
then tip the cauliflower back into the pan.

Use a stick blender to blitz the cauliflower into a purée, adding
a little of the reserved stock to help blend it. Alternatively,
place the cauliflower in a food processor and leave to cool for
5 minutes before blending. Add 150–200ml of the stock and
blend again until as smooth as possible and is the consistency
of double cream. Set aside.

Pat the scallops dry on kitchen paper. Trim all visible fat off
the bacon and cut into 1.5cm strips. Spray or brush a non-stick
frying pan with oil and place over a medium-high heat. Fry the
bacon for 2 minutes or until lightly browned; transfer to a plate.

Season the scallops on both sides with salt and pepper. Place
them in the hot pan and cook for 1–1½ minutes on each side or
until well browned and just cooked through. Put the scallops
on the same plate as the bacon.

Return the pan to the heat, add the cauliflower sauce and
double cream. Bring to a simmer, stirring well. Season with
salt and pepper and return the bacon and scallops to the pan.
Warm through for a few seconds then sprinkle with parsley,
if using, and serve.

188
CALORIES
PER SERVING

tuna fishcakes

SERVES 6

**PREP: 30 MINUTES,
PLUS COOLING TIME**

COOK: 1¼ HOURS

3 medium-large potatoes
(each about 250g)
1 tbsp light mayonnaise
185g can tuna steak in
spring water, drained
3 spring onions, thinly sliced
2 tbsp baby capers, drained
50g cornichons (baby
gherkins), drained
and thinly sliced
¼ tsp paprika (not smoked)
65g dried fine breadcrumbs
1 egg, beaten
oil, for spraying
flaked sea salt
ground black pepper
lemon wedges, for
squeezing

Open freeze the coated
(but not cooked) fishcakes
until solid. Place them
into a rigid freezer-proof
container and freeze for up
to 3 months. Defrost in the
fridge overnight and cook
as the recipe, adding 1–2
minutes on each side.

These fishcakes are made with store cupboard ingredients
and are really easy. If you don't fancy the capers and gherkins,
swap them for canned sweetcorn, but don't forget to add the
extra calories. Serve with a lightly dressed mixed salad.

Preheat the oven to 200°C/Fan 180°C/Gas 6. Bake the
potatoes on a tray for 1 hour until completely soft inside.
When cool enough to handle, halve the potatoes and scoop
the insides into a large bowl, discarding the skins. Mash
lightly with a fork and leave to cool.

Add the mayonnaise, tuna, spring onions, capers and cornichons
to the potato and mix together, taking care not to break up
the chunks of tuna too much. Season well with salt and black
pepper and lightly mix together. Use clean wet hands to form
into six balls, then flatten into 2cm-thick fishcakes.

Mix the paprika into the breadcrumbs. Put the beaten egg
in a shallow bowl and scatter half the breadcrumbs on a plate.
Dip each fishcake into the egg and then the crumbs and press
gently all over to lightly coat. Make sure to roll the sides in the
crumbs too. Add the rest of the crumbs to the plate after the
first three fishcakes have been coated.

Line a large baking tray with baking parchment and spray
or brush lightly with oil. Place all the fishcakes on the tray
and spray lightly with a little more oil. Bake for 25–30 minutes,
or until golden brown, turning after 15 minutes. Serve with
lemon wedges for squeezing.

258
CALORIES
PER SERVING

tuna and sweetcorn pasta

SERVES 6
PREP: 10 MINUTES
COOK: 15-20 MINUTES

100g dried pasta shapes,
   such as fusilli or penne
150g small broccoli florets
25g butter
40g plain flour
500ml semi-skimmed milk
198g can sweetcorn, drained
185g can tuna in water
   or brine, drained
75g ready-grated
   mozzarella
flaked sea salt
ground black pepper

Tip: Cut any large florets
in half or quarters as they
need to cook quickly for
this dish.

Lots of broccoli makes this easy dish more substantial and
by making the sauce using an all-in-one method, you can
get away with less fat. Make sure your whisk is covered with
heatproof silicone if you use a non-stick pan to make the
sauce, otherwise you could damage the coating of the pan.

Half fill a large saucepan with water and bring to the boil.
Add the pasta, return to the boil and cook for 10–12 minutes, or
according to the packet instructions, stirring occasionally until
tender. Add the broccoli florets and cook for 1 minute more.

While the pasta is cooking, prepare the sauce. Put the butter,
flour and milk in a non-stick saucepan and bring to a gentle
simmer, whisking continuously with a silicone whisk.

Cook for 3 minutes or until the sauce is thickened and smooth,
stirring continuously. Add half the cheese and season with salt
and black pepper. Cook for 1–2 minutes more, stirring until the
cheese has melted. Preheat the grill to its hottest setting.

Drain the pasta and broccoli in a large colander and return
to the pan. Gently stir in the hot cheese sauce and sweetcorn
until thoroughly combined. Flake the tuna into the saucepan
and stir lightly so it doesn't break up too much.

Tip the tuna mixture into a warmed ovenproof dish (a lasagne
dish is ideal) or six individual pie dishes. Place on a baking tray
and sprinkle with the remaining cheese. Grill for 1–2 minutes
or until lightly browned.

299
CALORIES
PER SERVING

sticky mango roasted salmon

SERVES 2
PREP: 5 MINUTES
COOK: 10–12 MINUTES

oil, for spraying or brushing
2 x 150g skinless
    salmon fillets
2 tsp mango chutney
½ tsp cumin seeds
100g cherry tomatoes,
    halved
ground black pepper
lime wedges, for squeezing

Open freeze the salmon
once it is topped with
mango and cumin. Transfer
to a rigid container, cover,
label and freeze for up to
1 month. Bake from frozen
on a lined baking tray in a
preheated oven as the
recipe, adding 5–10 minutes
to the cooking time.

The combination of mango chutney and cumin seeds really gives plain salmon an exotic lift. You could try it on any thick fish fillet or even skinless chicken breasts. It's lovely served with lightly curried vegetable rice.

Preheat the oven to 200°C/Fan 180°C/Gas 6. Spray or brush a small roasting tin with a little oil. Place the salmon fillets in the tin and spread them with the mango chutney. Sprinkle with cumin seeds and season with black pepper, then bake for 5 minutes.

Take the tin out of the oven and add the tomatoes. Return to the oven for a further 5–7 minutes or until the salmon is just cooked and the tomatoes are softened but holding their shape.

376
CALORIES
PER SERVING

beer battered fish

SERVES 4
PREP: 20 MINUTES
COOK: 25 MINUTES

1.5–2 litres sunflower oil
2 tbsp plain flour
½ tsp fine sea salt
4 x 200g skinless white fish
  fillets, such as haddock,
  cod or hake

FOR THE BATTER
40g cornflour
100g plain flour
1 tsp paprika (not smoked)
½ tsp fine sea salt
100ml real ale, chilled
50ml fizzy water, chilled
1 tbsp white wine vinegar

Tip: If you don't want to
use ale, swap for extra
fizzy water instead.

Battered and deep-fried fish is usually a complete no-no when you are following a low-calorie diet, but I've come up with a special batter that should absorb less fat than usual. This fish is also baked after quickly pre-frying in hot oil so you still get the crispy texture. Team with oven-baked chips (see page 98).

To make the batter, mix the cornflour, flour, paprika and salt together in a large bowl. Make a well in the centre and stir in the ale, fizzy water and vinegar. Beat with a large metal whisk to make a smooth batter with the consistency of double cream.

Fill a large, deep saucepan a third full with sunflower oil and heat to 190°C. It's important to use a cooking thermometer and check the temperature regularly. Do not allow the oil to overheat or leave hot oil unattended. (Alternatively, use an electric deep-fat fryer heated to 190°C.) Preheat the oven to 220°C/Fan 200°C/Gas 7.

Put the flour in a wide dish and season with the salt. Add the fish fillets, one at a time, and turn to coat them in the seasoned flour.

When the oil has reached the right temperature, stir the batter well. Take a floured fish fillet and dip it in the batter to thoroughly coat it. Lift it out with two forks and gently shake off the excess batter. Lower the fish gently into the hot oil. Watch out for splashes as the oil will be extremely hot. Cook for 1½ minutes then lift out with tongs and place on a rack over a baking tray.

Pre-fry the other fish fillets in the same way. Bake all the fish together for 15 minutes or until golden, crisp and cooked through. Serve with a small portion of oven-baked chips (see page 98) and some tartare sauce if you like (but remember to add the extra calories).

398
CALORIES
PER SERVING

fish soup with rouille

SERVES 4
PREP: 30 MINUTES
COOK: 40–45 MINUTES

1 tbsp olive oil
1 large onion, thinly sliced
½ large fennel bulb,
    very thinly sliced
2 large garlic cloves,
    thinly sliced
1 heaped tsp coriander
    seeds, lightly crushed
1 tsp fennel seeds,
    lightly crushed
good pinch saffron threads
2 bay leaves
good pinch of flaked sea
    salt, plus extra to taste
150ml white wine
400g can chopped
    tomatoes
1 tbsp tomato purée
400g potatoes (ideally
    Maris Piper), peeled and
    cut into 1.5cm chunks
700ml cold water
1 tsp caster sugar
400g skinless white fish,
    such as cod, haddock
    or pollack, cut into
    3cm chunks
4 x 100g sea bass or bream
    fillets, skin scored lightly
    with a knife and cut in half
ground black pepper
roughly chopped fresh
    flat-leaf parsley, to serve
    (optional)

ROUILLE
4 tbsp light mayonnaise
1 small garlic clove, crushed
good pinch cayenne pepper

This fish soup is blended so it's very smooth, but topped with a grilled fish fillet, it makes a really delicious light lunch or supper. Serve with garlicky rouille-style mayonnaise and thin slices of toast rather than hunks of bread and you'll be able to keep the calories low. For an extra lift, sprinkle with a little freshly grated Gruyère cheese. You'll need to add an extra 40 calories for each 10g you use.

To make the rouille, mix the ingredients together thoroughly in a small bowl until needed.

Heat the oil in a large flameproof casserole or saucepan and gently fry the onion and fennel for 10 minutes or until well softened, stirring occasionally, and adding the garlic for the last 2 minutes of the cooking time. Stir in the coriander and fennel seeds, saffron and bay leaves. Cook for a couple of minutes, stirring occasionally. Season with a good pinch of salt and plenty of black pepper.

Pour over the wine and bubble for a few seconds before adding the tomatoes, tomato purée, potatoes, water and sugar. Bring to a gentle simmer and cook for 20 minutes, or until the potatoes are very soft, stirring occasionally.

Drop the fish pieces on top of the hot liquid and cover with a lid. Poach over a medium heat for 5 minutes or until the fish is just cooked (it should be firm but not dry), stirring occasionally.

Remove the dish from the heat, then take out the bay leaves and blitz with a stick blender until smooth. Alternatively, allow to cool for a few minutes then blend it in a food processor and return to the saucepan. Place the fish fillets on a lightly oiled baking tray and cook, skin-side up, in a preheated hot grill for 2 minutes or until cooked and lightly browned.

Adjust the seasoning to taste and warm until gently bubbling. Ladle the soup into deep, warmed bowls and top with rouille and cheese, if using, and fish fillet in the centre of each one. Scatter with roughly chopped parsley and a spoonful of rouille.

212

pan-fried salt and pepper squid with lime chilli mayo

SERVES 2

PREP: 10 MINUTES

COOK: 2 MINUTES

1 tsp Szechuan peppercorns (Sichuan pepper) or black peppercorns

1 tsp black peppercorns

½ tsp flaked sea salt

200g whole prepared squid cones, cleaned and patted dry

2 tsp sunflower oil

20g dried coarse white breadcrumbs (or panko breadcrumbs)

1 red chilli, finely chopped, or 1 tsp dried chilli flakes

10g fresh coriander, leaves finely chopped

lime wedge, for squeezing

FOR THE LIME CHILLI MAYO

2 tbsp light mayonnaise

2 tbsp fat-free natural yoghurt

1 tbsp sweet chilli dipping sauce

finely grated zest of 1 lime

My take on salt and pepper squid doesn't have a greasy batter but does have loads of flavour. The Szechuan peppercorns give it a lip-tingling spiciness, but crushed black or multi-coloured peppercorns will work well too. Use uncoated squid rings if you can't get hold of prepared squid cones. You can serve this as a starter for four, which will take the calories per serving down to 106.

To make the lime mayo, mix together all the ingredients in a small bowl and set aside.

Pound the peppercorns and salt with a pestle and mortar until finely crushed but not powdery. Tip into a medium bowl.

Put the squid on a board and cut into 1.5cm rings. Toss with the crushed peppercorns and salt mix and set aside.

Place a large non-stick frying pan or wok over a medium heat and add the oil. When very hot, add the squid and fry for 1 minute. Add the breadcrumbs and fry for 30 more seconds. Don't overcook the squid or it will become rubbery. Remove the pan from the heat and stir in the chilli and coriander. Serve with the lime chilli mayo for dipping and lime wedges for squeezing.

287

baked sea bass with peppers and pine nuts

SERVES 4
PREP: 20 MINUTES
COOK: 15 MINUTES

4 sea bass fillets
   (each about 150g)
2 tbsp fresh lemon juice
2 tsp extra virgin olive oil
ground black pepper

FOR THE STUFFING
25g pine nuts
6 spring onions, thinly sliced
1 garlic clove, thinly sliced
20 basil leaves (roughly
   10g), shredded
finely grated zest
   of ½ lemon
50g dried coarse white
   breadcrumbs
   (or panko breadcrumbs)
170g roasted peppers in oil
   (from a jar), drained well
   in a sieve
pinch of flaked sea salt
ground black pepper

You should be able to find sea bass fillets in any supermarket or fish shop. They make a lovely low-calorie meal and only take a few minutes to cook. If you feel a bit nervous about cooking fish, this is a great recipe to start with as everything is chucked on a tray and baked in the oven, so there are no tricky methods or timings.

To make the stuffing, first toast the pine nuts in a large non-stick frying pan for 3–4 minutes, turning regularly, or until lightly browned. Tip them into a large bowl and add the spring onions, garlic, basil, lemon zest and breadcrumbs.

Put the peppers on a board and chop them into roughly 2cm pieces, if not already chopped. Add to the pine nut mixture, season with a pinch of salt and lots of black pepper and stir well. Preheat the oven to 220°C/Fan 200°C/Gas 7.

Slash each fish fillet 3–4 times with a knife through the skin. Spoon the pepper mixture onto a large baking tray in four piles and spread until roughly the size of a sea bass fillet.

Place a fish fillet on top of each pile of stuffing and tuck any loose bits of stuffing underneath so it doesn't burn. Drizzle the fish with the lemon juice and the olive oil. Season with black pepper and bake for 15 minutes or until the fish is lightly browned and cooked through and the stuffing is hot. The fish is cooked if the flesh feels soft when pressed with your finger towards the head – the thickest part.

263
CALORIES
PER SERVING

creamy fish gratin

SERVES 4
PREP: 20 MINUTES
COOK: 25–30 MINUTES

2 slender leeks, cut
  into 1.5cm slices
200g skinless cod fillet
200g skinless smoked
  haddock fillet
400ml semi-skimmed milk
4 tbsp cornflour
4 tbsp cold water
200g peeled cooked
  prawns, thawed if frozen
25g dried coarse white
  breadcrumbs
  (or panko breadcrumbs)
20g Parmesan cheese,
  finely grated
flaked sea salt
ground black pepper

Tip: Use a silicone whisk to
mix the sauce and it should
remain lump-free.

A very quick way to make a fish pie. Buy your fish ready
prepared and stir it into the hot sauce. Using a light gratin
topping rather than mashed potatoes cuts out calories
and makes the dish easier to prepare.

Preheat the oven to 220°C/Fan 200°C/Gas 7. Half fill a medium
saucepan with water and bring it to the boil. Add the leeks and
simmer for 3 minutes, or until almost tender. Drain them in a
sieve, rinse under cold water and place to one side.

Cut the fish into 3cm chunks and set to one side. Pour the milk
into a large non-stick saucepan and bring to a gentle simmer.
Mix the cornflour and water together until smooth, then pour
it into the warm milk. Return to a simmer and cook over a low
heat for 4–5 minutes, stirring constantly until the sauce is
smooth and very thick. Season well. Preheat the grill to its
hottest setting.

Add the fish pieces to the sauce and cook for 3–4 minutes,
stirring gently so the fish doesn't break up too much. Add the
leeks and prawns and stir gently to coat them in the sauce.
Pour the mixture into a warmed, shallow flameproof dish.

Make the topping by tossing the breadcrumbs and Parmesan
together with a generous pinch of pepper in a small bowl and
sprinkle over the fish mixture. Grill for 2–3 minutes or until the
topping is golden brown and crisp.

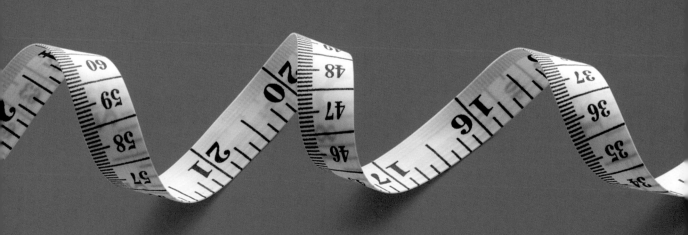

salads

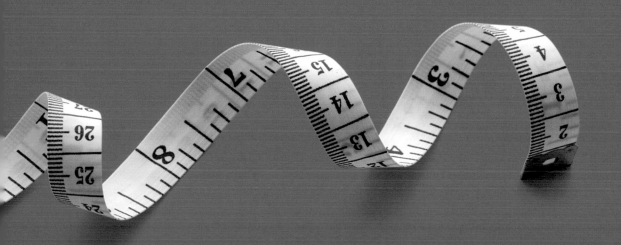

234
CALORIES
PER SERVING

chicken caesar salad

PREP: 20 MINUTES
COOK: 6-8 MINUTES

2 boneless, skinless chicken
   breasts (each about 175g)
1 tsp sunflower oil
2 romaine lettuce hearts
4 ciabatta bread slices, each
   around 1½cm (15g a slice)
15g Parmesan cheese
   shavings, to serve
flaked sea salt
ground black pepper

FOR THE DRESSING
2 anchovy fillets in oil (from
   a can or jar), drained and
   roughly chopped
1 garlic clove, roughly
   chopped
4 tbsp light mayonnaise
1 tsp fresh lemon juice
15g Parmesan cheese,
   finely grated
5 tbsp cold water

Adding lean, protein-rich foods such as chicken or prawns to a salad will make it much more filling and will keep the calories low. I've tweaked the dressing to make my own creamy version, but if time is short use a ready-made light Caesar salad dressing instead.

To make the dressing, put the anchovy fillets in a mortar, add the chopped garlic and pound together with a pestle to form a paste. Add the mayonnaise, lemon juice, Parmesan and water and stir well to make a pourable dressing.

Put the chicken breasts onto a chopping board and carefully slice in half horizontally. Season the chicken breast pieces on both sides with a little salt and plenty of black pepper.

Brush the oil over the base of a large non-stick frying pan or griddle pan and place over a medium heat. Cook the chicken in the pan for 3 minutes. Turn over and cook for a further 3 minutes on the other side or until nicely browned and cooked through. Remove from the heat and leave in the warm pan. This will give the chicken a chance to rest.

While the chicken is cooking, make the salad. Separate the lettuce leaves, then wash and drain them well. Use a clean tea towel to soak up any excess water if you like. Arrange the lettuce in a large serving dish. Toast the ciabatta and tear or cut it into bite-sized pieces.

Put the cooked chicken breasts onto a board and cut them into thick strips. Scatter the chicken over the lettuce and toss together lightly. Spoon over half the dressing and the croutons and Parmesan shavings and serve while the chicken is warm with the remaining dressing for drizzling.

124 SALADS

347

cobb salad

SERVES 2

PREP: 15 MINUTES

COOK: 12 MINUTES

2 fridge-cold eggs
2 smoked back bacon
  rashers
1 romaine lettuce heart,
  leaves separated
½ large avocado, stoned,
  peeled and sliced
2 ripe tomatoes, cut
  into wedges
1 cooked boneless, skinless
  chicken breast, torn into
  thin strips
½ small red onion, thinly
  sliced
2 cooked beetroot (about
  125g), drained if in
  vinegar, cut into chunks
blue cheese dressing
  (see right), to serve

The cobb is a classic American main meal salad containing lots of different ingredients. To help you remember what's in it, think 'Eat Cobb' – Egg, Avocado, Tomato, Chicken, Onion, Bacon and Beetroot. This recipe has got the lot – but in the right quantities to help you lose weight too.

Half fill a medium saucepan with water and bring to the boil. Carefully add the eggs and boil for 7 minutes. When cooked, drain, then plunge the eggs straight into cold water. Leave for 5 minutes before peeling.

Meanwhile, heat a small non-stick frying pan over a medium heat and add the bacon. Cook for about 2 minutes on each side until lightly crisp. Remove and drain on kitchen paper. Cut into small pieces.

Roughly tear the lettuce and scatter over a serving platter. Top with the eggs (cut into quarters), bacon, avocado, tomatoes, chicken, onion and beetroot. Serve with blue cheese dressing or a drizzle of thick balsamic vinegar.

Blue cheese dressing: Mix together 1 tablespoon light mayonnaise, 3 tablespoons buttermilk or fat-free natural yoghurt and ½ teaspoon white wine vinegar in a small bowl until well combined. Crumble 20g Roquefort cheese into the dressing, season with a little flaked sea salt and ground black pepper and combine until almost smooth. Serves 2. Calories per serving: 65

258

smoked mackerel, fennel and orange salad

SERVES 4
PREP: 15 MINUTES

1 small fennel bulb
   (about 200g), trimmed
1 chicory bulb (about 125g)
2 large oranges
4 cooked beetroot (about
   250g), drained if in
   vinegar, cut into wedges
50g bunch or bag of
   watercress (or lamb's
   lettuce), trimmed
3 smoked mackerel fillets
   (about 175g), skinned

**FOR THE HONEY
CITRUS DRESSING**
2 tsp harissa paste
1 tbsp clear honey
2 tbsp orange juice
flaked sea salt
freshly ground black pepper

This is a colourful salad with big flavours – the citrus cuts through the oiliness of the fish very well. Make sure to slice the fennel as thinly as possible, using a mandolin if you have one, or the aniseed flavour could overpower the other ingredients.

Prepare the vegetables and fruit. Cut the fennel bulb into wafer-thin slices lengthways. Trim the chicory bulb and separate the leaves.

Slice the ends off the oranges and place them on a chopping board, cut-side down. Using a small sharp knife, cut off the peel and pith, working your way around the orange. Do the same to the second orange. Next, slice the oranges and put the slices in a salad bowl, but do not add any juice from your board. This can be added to the dressing.

To make the dressing, whisk all the ingredients together in a small bowl.

Arrange the fennel, chicory, orange, beetroot and leaves on a platter. Tear the mackerel into large flakes and scatter on top. Drizzle with the dressing just before serving.

243
CALORIES
PER SERVING

argentinian roast beef salad

SERVES 6

PREP: 20 MINUTES

COOK: 45-75 MINUTES, PLUS RESTING TIME

1 tbsp black peppercorns
1 tsp flaked sea salt
1kg beef topside, rolled and tied
1 small red onion, thinly sliced and separated into rings
2 tbsp red wine vinegar
85g bunch or bag of watercress
2 little gem lettuces, leaves separated
4 large ripe tomatoes, cut into wedges

FOR THE HERB DRESSING
15g fresh flat-leaf parsley, leaves finely chopped
1 tsp dried oregano or 1 tbsp finely chopped fresh oregano
1 plump red chilli, deseeded and finely chopped
1 small garlic clove, crushed
1 tsp Dijon mustard
2 tbsp red wine vinegar
1 tbsp extra virgin olive oil
2 tbsp cold water
pinch of flaked sea salt
ground black pepper

Tip: Freshly boiled new potatoes go very well with this salad. A 150g portion contains 112 calories.

A great salad for a summer party. Use really lean beef and cook it rare. The dressing is based on the Argentinian chimichurri sauce but with a lot less oil. Any leftover meat can be wrapped in foil and kept in the fridge for a couple of days, and can be used later for salads or open topped sandwiches.

Preheat the oven to 200°C/Fan 180°C/Gas 6. Crush the peppercorns with a pestle and mortar, stir in the salt and sprinkle everything onto a board. Roll the beef in the spices and place it in a small roasting tin.

Roast for 45 minutes for rare meat, about 60 minutes for medium and 1¼ hours for well-done beef. Leave to rest in the tin for at least 30 minutes before slicing.

Put the sliced red onion in a bowl and stir in the vinegar. Leave to stand for 10 minutes, then drain. (This will brighten the colour and add flavour.)

To make the dressing, put the parsley, oregano, chilli, garlic, mustard, vinegar, oil and water in a small jam jar. Add a pinch of salt and a few twists of black pepper. Cover with a tight-fitting lid and shake vigorously until well combined. Adjust seasoning to taste.

Put the beef on a board and snip off the string. Carve the beef into thin slices. Arrange the beef, watercress, lettuce and tomatoes on a large platter. Scatter over the lightly pickled red onions, drizzle with the herb dressing and serve.

155 CALORIES PER SERVING

skinny potato salad

400g small new potatoes, well scrubbed
4 tbsp light mayonnaise
6 tbsp fat-free natural yoghurt
1 garlic clove, crushed
2 eating apples, quartered, cored and sliced
4 celery sticks, sliced
6 spring onions, thinly sliced, including lots of green
flaked sea salt
ground black pepper

Tip: This salad is extra delicious and crunchy with a few broken pieces of walnut halves. Add an extra 128 calories for each 20g.

I love potato salad but it can be very high in calories. My version uses less mayonnaise and bulks out the potatoes with crunchy celery and apples to really fill you up.

Half fill a medium saucepan with water and bring to the boil. Carefully add the potatoes and return to the boil. Cook for 18–20 minutes or until just tender. Drain the potatoes, then put into a bowl of cold water and leave to cool.

Mix the mayonnaise, yoghurt and garlic. Cut each of the potatoes in half or quarters, depending on their size, and put in a large bowl. Add the apples, celery and spring onions. Toss lightly and season with salt and pepper to taste. Scatter gently over a large platter. Spoon over the dressing and mix just before serving.

260
CALORIES
PER SERVING

roasted pepper, mozzarella and bean salad

SERVES 4
PREP: 25 MINUTES, PLUS COOLING TIME
COOK: 12–18 MINUTES

4 large peppers
  (assorted colours)
20g pine nuts
400g can cannellini beans,
  drained and rinsed
75g pitted Kalamata olives
  (or black olives), drained
125g reduced-fat
  mozzarella, drained
large handful of fresh
  basil leaves
ground black pepper

FOR THE REDUCED-FAT FRENCH DRESSING
1 large egg yolk
1 tsp Dijon mustard
½ small garlic clove, crushed
½ tsp caster sugar
good pinch of flaked sea
  salt, plus extra to taste
2 tsp white wine vinegar
1 tbsp olive oil
ground black pepper

Note: This recipe contains raw egg.

The bold Mediterranean flavours of this salad are well suited to the garlicky dressing. Grilling the peppers is a bit of a bore but you can get on with other things while they are toasting – use peppers from a jar if you prefer, but make sure they aren't swimming in oil.

Preheat the grill to its hottest setting. Place the peppers on a rack above a grill pan and grill for 10–15 minutes, turning them every few minutes until the skins are well blistered and burnt in places. This will loosen them ready for peeling.

Transfer the peppers to a large bowl using tongs and cover tightly with cling film. Leave for 20 minutes or until cool enough to peel.

Meanwhile, make the French dressing. Put the egg yolk, mustard, garlic, sugar, salt and vinegar in a small bowl and whisk with a metal whisk until very light and thick. Slowly add the oil, whisking constantly. Season to taste.

Scatter the pine nuts into a small frying pan and toast over a medium heat for 2–3 minutes, turning regularly until lightly browned.

Put the peppers on a board and carefully strip off all the skin. Remove the stalks and cut the peppers into quarters.

Arrange the peppers on a large platter and add the beans and olives. Squeeze each olive as you place it on the salad to lightly crush it. Tear the mozzarella into pieces and scatter it over the salad, sprinkle with the pine nuts and tear the basil leaves roughly on top.

Toss the salad lightly and season with ground black pepper. Drizzle with the French dressing and serve.

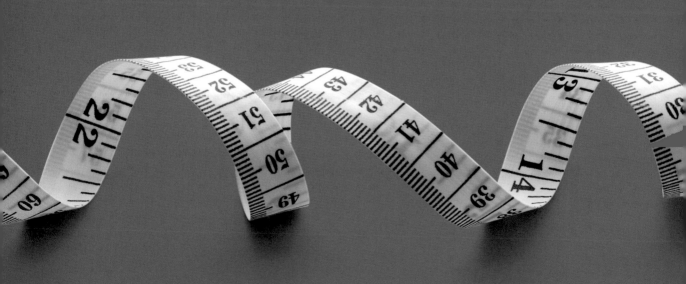

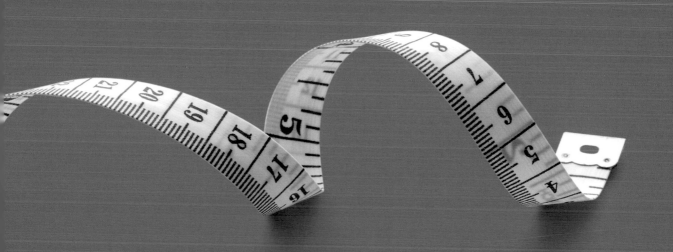

meat-free

438

CALORIES
PER SERVING

roasted squash, tomato and spinach lasagne

SERVES 4

PREP: 20 MINUTES

COOK: 1½ HOURS

1 small butternut squash
(about 700g), peeled,
deseeded and cut into
roughly 3cm chunks

2 tsp olive oil

1 tsp dried chilli flakes

2 medium onions,
cut into wedges

6 large ripe tomatoes,
halved

100g dried lasagne sheets
(about 6)

100g mature spinach leaves,
tough stalks removed

2 tsp thick balsamic vinegar

ground black pepper

FOR THE SAUCE

25g butter

50g plain flour

600ml semi-skimmed milk

50g half-fat mature Cheddar
cheese, coarsely grated

15g Parmesan cheese,
finely grated

flaked sea salt

ground black pepper

Freeze the unbaked lasagne
by leaving to cool completely.
Cover with foil, label and
freeze for up to 2 months.
Defrost in the fridge
overnight and bake as the
recipe, adding an extra
15 minutes or until piping
hot throughout.

This is a great veggie lasagne that's really simple to make. Keeping the layers loose means you can get away with using less pasta and sauce, while upping the quantity of colourful veg.

Preheat the oven to 220°C/Fan 200°C/Gas 7. Place the squash on a large baking tray. Toss with 2 teaspoons of the oil and season with the dried chilli flakes and lots of black pepper. Bake for 20 minutes.

Take the tray out of the oven and turn the squash. Scatter the onions and tomatoes and return to the oven for a further 20–25 minutes or until the vegetables are tender and lightly charred.

Meanwhile, prepare the sauce. Put the butter, flour and milk in a large non-stick saucepan and bring to a gentle simmer, whisking continuously with a silicone whisk.

Cook for 3 minutes or until the sauce is thickened and smooth, stirring continuously. Add all the cheese and season with salt and black pepper. Cook for 2 minutes more, stirring until the cheese is melted. Take off the heat and cover the sauce carefully with a piece of cling film to prevent a skin forming. (Remember the pan will be hot!)

Fill a large saucepan about a third full with water and bring to the boil. Add the lasagne, return to the boil and cook for 6–8 minutes or until just tender, turning with tongs. (It's important to precook the lasagne as the baking time is fairly short.)

Add the spinach leaves to the hot water and as soon as they are wilted, remove the pan from the heat and drain the pasta and spinach in a large colander. Rinse quickly in cold water until the pasta is cool enough to handle.

Arrange the roasted vegetables, lasagne and spinach leaves loosely in a lasagne dish or small roasting tin. Sprinkle over the balsamic vinegar, pour on the cheese sauce and season with black pepper. Bake for 20–25 minutes or until the sauce is lightly browned and bubbling.

371
CALORIES
PER SERVING

golden split pea dhal with spiced onions

SERVES 2
PREP: 20 MINUTES
COOK: 1¼ HOURS

200g yellow split peas,
  rinsed and drained
1.1 litres water
½ large onion, thinly sliced
3 garlic cloves, crushed
20g chunk fresh root ginger,
  peeled and finely grated
2 green chillies, finely
  chopped (deseed first
  if you like)
¼ tsp ground turmeric
½ tsp fine sea salt
1–2 tbsp fresh lemon juice
cucumber raita (see right),
  to serve

FOR THE TOPPING
oil, for spraying or brushing
½ large onion, very
  thinly sliced
½ tsp black mustard seeds
½ tsp cumin seeds

Freeze the cooled dhal by
dividing between labelled
zip-seal bags. Seal and
flat freeze. To serve, warm
through gently in a large
saucepan with 200ml extra
water until thawed, then
simmer until piping hot,
stirring regularly.

An inexpensive and comforting dish that's very simple to prepare. I like to add the spiced onions for extra flavour and serve with a few spoonfuls of cooling yoghurt. Older split peas will take longer to cook; if you know you have an older pack, soak them overnight in cold water in the fridge before serving.

Tip the split peas into a large, heavy-based saucepan or flameproof casserole and cover with the water. Bring to the boil over a high heat. Skim off any foam that rises to surface. Stir in the onion, garlic, ginger, chillies and turmeric.

Reduce the heat to low. Cover loosely with a lid and leave to simmer gently for 60 minutes, stirring occasionally. Remove the lid and continue to cook for a further 5–10 minutes or until the peas are very tender and thick. They should have the texture of a thick soup. Stir regularly and especially towards the end as the dhal thickens. If the split peas aren't tender, add a little extra water and cook for longer.

When the dhal is ready, remove the saucepan from the heat and season with the salt and lemon juice to taste. Pour the hot dhal into a warmed serving dish. Cover and keep warm.

To make the topping, spray or brush a small frying pan with oil and place over a medium-high heat. Fry the onion for 3–5 minutes or until it is golden brown, stirring continuously. Do not allow the onion to burn.

Stir the mustard and cumin seeds into the frying pan with the onion and cook for just a few seconds until the mustard seeds begin to pop. Scatter over the dhal. Stir gently just before serving. Serve with cucumber raita.

Cucumber raita: Cut ½ deseeded cucumber into quarters lengthways and then slice into small chunks. Put in a bowl and season with ¼ teaspoon flaked sea salt. Stir in 150g fat-free natural yoghurt, then loosely fold in 1 thinly sliced long red chilli and 3 tablespoons roughly chopped mint leaves. Serves 4. Calories per serving: 28

394
CALORIES
PER SERVING

macaroni cheese in a hurry

SERVES 4
PREP: 10 MINUTES
COOK: 15–20 MINUTES

200g dried macaroni
25g butter, plus extra
  for greasing
50g plain flour
600ml semi-skimmed milk
75g half-fat mature Cheddar
  cheese, finely grated
3 tomatoes, sliced
flaked sea salt
ground black pepper

Freeze the cooled and
assembled macaroni cheese
in individual microwave and
freezer-proof containers for
up to 2 months. Defrost in
the fridge overnight. Reheat
in the microwave until
piping hot throughout.

**My cheese sauce contains less butter than usual and is very
simple to make. Grilling rather than baking the macaroni
cheese saves time but you'll need to warm the dish before
you add the pasta.**

Half fill a large saucepan with water and bring to the boil.
Add the macaroni, return to the boil and cook for 10–12 minutes,
or according to the packet instructions, stirring occasionally
until tender.

Meanwhile, prepare the sauce. Put the butter, flour and milk
in a non-stick saucepan and bring to a gentle simmer, whisking
continuously with a silicone whisk.

Cook for 3 minutes or until the sauce is thickened and smooth,
stirring continuously. Add roughly two-thirds of the cheese and
season with salt and black pepper. Cook for 2–3 minutes more,
while stirring, and add a little more seasoning if necessary.
Preheat the grill to its hottest setting.

Drain the pasta in a colander and return to the pan. Gently
stir in the hot cheese sauce until thoroughly combined. Tip the
macaroni cheese mixture into a warmed shallow flameproof
dish (a lasagne dish is ideal) and spread to all the corners.

Arrange the sliced tomatoes on top. Sprinkle with the rest of
the cheese and add a couple of twists of ground black pepper.
Cook under the hot grill for 3–5 minutes or until the tomatoes
are hot and the cheese is lightly browned.

369
CALORIES
PER SERVING

primavera risotto

SERVES 4
PREP: 15 MINUTES
COOK: 25 MINUTES

oil, for spraying or brushing
1 medium onion, finely
    chopped
2 garlic cloves, crushed
1 bay leaf
long strip of lemon rind
300g risotto rice
100ml white wine
1.4 litres hot vegetable or
    chicken stock (made with
    1 stock cube), kept warm
    in a pan on the hob
150g long-stemmed
    broccoli, trimmed
100g fresh or frozen peas
100g slender young
    asparagus, trimmed
    and cut in half
25g Parmesan cheese,
    finely grated
10g Parmesan cheese
    shavings
flaked sea salt
ground black pepper

Using lots of vegetables in this risotto means I can cut the quantity of rice but still serve generous portions. Grate your own block of Parmesan rather than using the ready-grated kind as it has a much more distinct flavour.

Spray or brush a large non-stick saucepan with oil and fry the onion very gently for 5 minutes or until softened but not coloured. Add the garlic and cook for 1 more minute. Spray with a little more oil and stir in the bay leaf, lemon rind and risotto rice. Cook for a few seconds more or until the rice is glistening.

Slowly add the wine, then start gradually adding the stock, just a ladleful at a time, stirring well between each addition. Simmer for 1–2 minutes or until the liquid has almost all been absorbed before adding more.

Cook for 15–20 minutes or so until the rice is tender and looking thick. It is important to stir regularly while the rice is cooking so it can release its starch into the liquid.

Half fill a large pan with water and bring to the boil. Add the broccoli, peas and asparagus and return to the boil. Cook for 3 minutes, then drain in a colander.

When you have just a couple of ladles of stock left to add, discard the bay leaf, stir in the vegetables with all the remaining stock and cook for 1–2 minutes until hot. Remove from the heat.

Stir in the grated Parmesan and season with salt and pepper. The risotto should look fairly moist but the rice should be tender. Cover with a lid and leave to stand for 3 minutes. Give the risotto a good stir and spoon into warm, deep plates, top with the Parmesan shavings and a good grind of black pepper.

290
CALORIES
PER SERVING

arrabbiata pasta

SERVES 6
PREP: 10 MINUTES
COOK: 35 MINUTES

oil, for spraying or brushing
1 medium onion,
    thinly sliced
1 large red pepper and
    1 large yellow pepper,
    deseeded and sliced
2 large garlic cloves,
    thinly sliced
1 heaped tsp dried
    chilli flakes
2 x 400g cans chopped
    tomatoes
1 tbsp clear honey
100ml red wine or water
300g dried penne pasta
    or pasta spirals
200g bag baby spinach
    leaves
75g reduced-fat mature
    Cheddar cheese,
    coarsely grated
flaked sea salt
ground black pepper

Freeze the cooled
assembled pasta in
individual microwave and
freezer-proof containers for
up to 1 month. Defrost in the
fridge overnight. Reheat in
the microwave until piping
hot throughout.

A simple pasta dish with a bit of a kick. Cooking the vegetables gently at the beginning will help bring out their natural sweetness and make the bake taste richer and even more delicious. Serve with a large salad.

Spray or brush a large non-stick saucepan with oil and cook the onion and peppers over a medium heat for 5 minutes, stirring regularly. Add the garlic and chilli and cook for 1 minute more, while stirring.

Pour the tomatoes, honey and wine or water into the pan and bring to a gentle simmer. Cover loosely with a lid and cook for 25 minutes, or until rich and thick, stirring regularly.

Meanwhile, half fill a large pan with water and bring it to the boil. Add the pasta, return the pan to the boil and cook for 10–12 minutes until tender, stirring occasionally.

Drain the pasta in a colander and return it to the pan. Stir in the tomato sauce and spinach leaves and cook for 1 minute, stirring until the spinach wilts. Season with salt and pepper.

Preheat the grill to its hottest setting. Spoon the pasta mixture into a warmed, shallow flameproof dish (a lasagne dish is ideal) and sprinkle over the cheese. Place the dish on a baking tray and cook under the hot grill for 5 minutes or until the cheese is melted and beginning to brown.

271

vietnamese aubergine, sweet potato and green bean curry

SERVES 4
PREP: 15 MINUTES
COOK: 45 MINUTES

oil, for spraying or brushing
2 medium onions, chopped
3 tbsp medium curry paste
1 tbsp galangal paste
    (from a jar) or 20g fresh
    galangal, peeled and
    finely grated
2 tsp lemongrass paste
    (from a jar)
500ml cold water
2 sweet potatoes
    (each about 200g),
    peeled and cut into
    3cm chunks
5–6 fresh, frozen or dried
    Kaffir lime leaves
200g green beans, trimmed
1 tbsp soft light brown sugar
1 small aubergine (about
    300g), cut into 3cm
    chunks
200ml coconut milk
fresh coriander, to garnish
    (optional)
flaked sea salt
ground black pepper

An intensely spicy and fragrant veggie curry based on flavours used in Vietnamese cooking. You can serve it with a small portion of basmati rice but I don't think this curry needs it.

Spray or brush a large non-stick saucepan or flameproof casserole with oil and add the chopped onions. Stir well then cover with a lid and cook over a medium-low heat for 15 minutes or until the onions are softened. Remove the lid and stir the onions occasionally so they don't burn. Stir in the curry paste, galangal and lemongrass. Cook for a further 3 minutes, stirring constantly.

Take the pan off the heat and leave to cool for a few minutes then transfer to a food processor and blitz to a fine paste. You will need to remove the lid and push the mixture down a couple of times with a rubber spatula until the right texture is reached.

Return the paste to the pan and stir in the water, sweet potato chunks and lime leaves. Bring to a gentle simmer and cook for 15 minutes, stirring occasionally. Add the green beans and brown sugar and cook for 10 minutes more or until the beans are just tender, stirring regularly.

While the potatoes and beans are cooking, heat a non-stick frying pan or wok and spray or brush with oil. Add the aubergine and stir fry over a high heat for 4–5 minutes or until lightly browned.

Pour the coconut milk into the pan with the sweet potatoes and add the aubergine pieces. Stir well and season with salt and pepper. Bring to a simmer and cook for 5 minutes, stirring occasionally. Garnish with fresh coriander. (Don't eat the lime leaves.)

385

CALORIES
PER SERVING

roasted vegetable tart

oil, for spraying or brushing
2 small courgettes,
    cut into 1.5cm slices
1 red and 1 yellow pepper,
    deseeded and cut into
    2cm chunks
1 medium red onion,
    cut into 12 wedges
320g ready-rolled,
    reduced-fat puff pastry
beaten egg, for glazing
75g soft goat's cheese
flaked sea salt
ground black pepper

If you can't get hold of lower-fat puff pastry for this tart, use four sheets of filo pastry instead, spraying or brushing lightly with oil between each layer. Serving the tart as a starter or light lunch for six will reduce your calories to 256 per serving.

Preheat the oven to 220°C/Fan 200°C/Gas 7. Heat a large frying pan or wok over a high heat and spray or brush lightly with oil. Add the vegetables to the pan and stir-fry for around 6–8 minutes or until they have softened slightly and are nicely coloured. Season with salt and pepper and tip into a large bowl.

Line a large baking tray with baking parchment and place the pastry sheet on top. Trim the edges neatly with a sharp knife to encourage a good rise. Leaving a 2cm gap around the edge, scatter the cooked vegetables over the pastry. Brush the beaten egg around the border of the pastry and bake in the oven for 20 minutes.

Remove the tray from the oven and scatter small chunks of the goat's cheese over the tart. Return it to the oven and bake for a further 10 minutes or until the pastry is golden and crisp.

225

aubergine parmigiana

SERVES 4
PREP: 20 MINUTES
COOK: 1–1¼ HOURS

3 aubergines (each
   about 250g)
½ tbsp sunflower oil
100g ready-grated
   mozzarella
15g Parmesan cheese,
   finely grated
2 tbsp dried coarse
   breadcrumbs
   (or panko breadcrumbs)

FOR THE SAUCE
1 tsp sunflower oil
1 large onion,
   finely chopped
2 large garlic cloves,
   crushed
2 x 400g cans chopped
   tomatoes
150ml red wine
100ml water
½ tsp dried chilli flakes
1 tsp dried oregano
flaked sea salt
ground black pepper

Freeze individual cooled
portions in oven and
freezer-proof containers for
up to 3 months. Defrost in
the fridge overnight. Reheat
in the oven as the recipe.

These aubergines are grilled rather than fried so need far less
oil than usual. Teamed with a rich tomato sauce and grated
cheese, they make a really filling supper.

To make the sauce, heat the oil in a medium non-stick pan and
add the onion and garlic. Cover the pan with a lid and fry gently
for 6–8 minutes, or until soft and light golden brown, stirring
occasionally.

Tip the tomatoes into the pan, add the wine and water, stir
in the chilli flakes and oregano. Bring to a gentle simmer
and cook for 30–40 minutes, or until rich and thick, stirring
regularly. Season with salt and pepper.

While the sauce is simmering, reheat the grill to its hottest
setting. Trim and slice the aubergines lengthways into 1cm
slices. Place the slices on a baking sheet and brush both sides
with the oil.

Cook under the hot grill for 5–7 minutes or until the aubergine
is golden and starting to soften. Carefully turn each slice over
and grill for a further 5 minutes. Preheat the oven to 220°C/
Fan 200°C/Gas 7.

Arrange the aubergine slices, the sauce and grated mozzarella
in loose layers in a shallow ovenproof dish (a lasagne dish is
ideal), making sure you finish with mozzarella on top. Mix the
Parmesan with the breadcrumbs and sprinkle over the top.

Bake for 25–30 minutes or until the topping is crisp and
golden and the filling is bubbling.

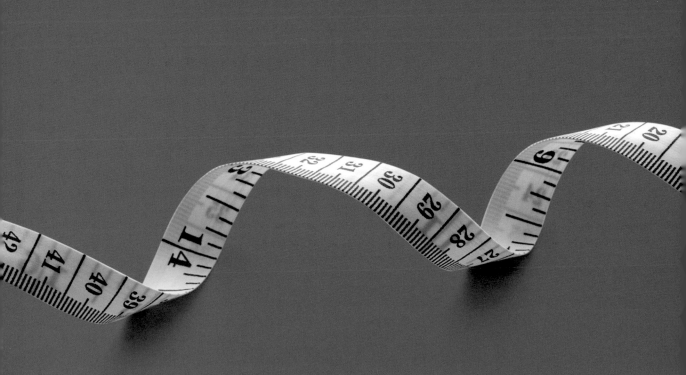

sweet
things

226
CALORIES
PER SERVING

cappuccino chocolate pots

SERVES 6

PREP: 10 MINUTES, PLUS COOLING AND CHILLING TIME

COOK: 5 MINUTES

2 tsp instant coffee granules
2 tbsp just-boiled water
500g ready-made, low-fat custard
50g plain, dark chocolate (about 70% cocoa solids)
150ml whipping cream
¼ tsp cocoa powder

Ready-made, low-fat custard makes a great base for these chocolate dessert pots. It's one of the few ready-made sauces I use, but it's really handy for quick puddings.

Put the coffee in a cup and stir in the just-boiled water until dissolved. Set aside.

Pour the custard into a saucepan, break the plain chocolate into pieces and drop on top. Stir in the coffee solution. Heat very gently for about 2 minutes, or until the chocolate melts, stirring regularly. Do not allow to simmer.

Pour the mixture into six small coffee cups or glasses. Put the cups on a tray, cover with cling film and chill for at least 1 hour.

Whip the cream until thick and light. Spoon a good dollop into each cup. Sift a little cocoa powder over the top and serve.

258
CALORIES
PER SERVING

tropical eton mess

SERVES 5
PREP: 20 MINUTES

425g can mango slices
   in syrup, drained
100ml double cream
100g fat-free Greek yoghurt
227g can pineapple slices
   in juice, drained and cut
   into small chunks
2 kiwi fruit, peeled and
   cut into small chunks
1 large banana, peeled
   and sliced
finely grated zest of ½ lime
3 x 15g meringue nests,
   roughly broken
1 large passion fruit, halved

Eton mess doesn't have to be all about berries. This one uses lightly broken ready-made meringues combined with mango purée and tropical fruits. There is no disguising that it's high in sugar, so keep for an occasional treat.

Blitz the mango slices with a stick blender or in a food processor until smooth. Whip the double cream until thick and stir in the Greek yoghurt. Pour the mango purée on top and fold through once to roughly marble.

Put the pineapple, kiwis and bananas in a large dish and toss lightly with the grated lime zest. Spoon half the broken meringues into a glass bowl and top with the fruit and then the mango cream.

Repeat the layers ending in the mango cream. Spoon over the passion fruit pulp and serve immediately.

296

CALORIES
PER SERVING

bakewell pudding

SERVES 6
PREP: 20 MINUTES
COOK: 30 MINUTES

butter, for greasing
4 large eggs
75g soft light brown sugar
½ tsp almond extract
100g ground almonds
4 tbsp self-raising flour
150g fresh raspberries
4 ripe but firm nectarines,
    stoned and quartered
10g flaked almonds

This lovely pudding has all the traditional ingredients you'd find in a Bakewell tart, but I've cut down on sugar and fat and baked it without the pastry to save around 200 calories per serving.

Preheat the oven to 200°C/Fan 180°C/Gas 6. Lightly grease a 26cm ceramic flan or shallow pie dish. Using an electric whisk, beat the eggs, sugar and almond essence for 5–8 minutes or until very thick, pale and fluffy.

Mix the ground almonds with the flour in a bowl and gently fold into the egg mixture using a large metal spoon. Don't worry too much about any lumps.

Pour the mixture into the prepared dish and dot with the raspberries and nectarine quarters. Scatter the flaked almonds over the top.

Bake for 30 minutes or until the filling is firm and nicely risen. Serve warm with lower-fat custard (see page 166) if you like.

155

CALORIES
PER SERVING

mississippi mud pie

SERVES 6
PREP: 20 MINUTES
COOK: 25 MINUTES

BASE
50g butter
1 tbsp golden syrup
25g cocoa powder
25g caster sugar
100g plain flour
1 tsp cold water

FILLING
100g plain dark chocolate
   (70% cocoa solids),
   broken into pieces
400g can chickpeas,
   drained and rinsed
25g butter
50g caster sugar
2 large eggs, separated

TOPPING
150ml whipping cream
¼ tsp cocoa powder, to dust

This is very rich and chocolatey, but contains canned chickpeas instead of heaps of butter and sugar. A very surprising ingredient but one that works really well here, adding just the right amount of texture.

To make the base, melt the butter and syrup in a small non-stick saucepan and stir in the cocoa powder until smooth. Remove the pan from the heat and add the sugar and flour. Sprinkle over 1 teaspoon of cold water and stir until the mixture forms a stiff dough, adding a little extra water if necessary.

Tip the dough into a lined 20cm metal pie dish with sloping sides, and press it into shape with your fingers. Chill in the fridge while you make the filling.

Place the chocolate in a heatproof bowl over a pan of gently simmering water until almost melted. Carefully take the bowl off the pan and stir the chocolate until smooth. Leave to cool for 20 minutes. Preheat the oven to 200°C/Fan 180°C/Gas 6.

Put the chickpeas, butter and sugar in a food processor and blend until the mixture is as smooth as possible. You may need to remove the lid and push the mixture down a few times with a rubber spatula until the right consistency is reached.

While the processor is running, add the egg yolks and when combined add the cooled melted chocolate and blend until smooth. Scrape the chocolate mixture into a large bowl.

Whisk the egg whites with an electric whisk in a clean bowl until stiff but not dry. Loosen the chocolate mixture with a small spoonful of the egg whites before folding in the rest. Gently spoon the chocolate mixture onto the base and bake for 15 minutes until just set. Remove the dish from the oven and cool at room temperature.

Whip the cream until soft peaks form and spoon onto the cooled pie. Dust with a little sifted cocoa powder and cut into wedges to serve.

155
CALORIES
PER SERVING

panna cotta

SERVES 6

PREP: 15 MINUTES, PLUS CHILLING TIME

COOK: 5 MINUTES

3 leaf gelatine sheets
1 vanilla pod
75ml double cream
250ml semi-skimmed milk
50g caster sugar
300g fat-free Greek yoghurt
100g fresh raspberries
75g fresh blueberries

Tip: Use 1 teaspoon vanilla bean paste instead of the vanilla pod if you prefer.

Panna cotta is traditionally made with lots of double cream, but I've created these with semi-skimmed milk and fat-free Greek yoghurt, lightly set with gelatine. Top with either fresh berries or a luscious rhubarb compote (see below).

Put the gelatine sheets in a bowl of cold water and leave to soak for 5 minutes. Split the vanilla pod in half lengthways and scrape out the seeds.

Put the double cream, milk, scraped vanilla seeds and sugar into a saucepan and heat though very gently, stirring occasionally, until the sugar dissolves. Remove from the heat.

Take the softened gelatine sheets in one hand and squeeze any excess water back into the bowl. Drop the gelatine into the warm cream and stir until dissolved. Pour the mixture into a large jug and whisk in the Greek yoghurt.

Working quickly, pour the cream mixture into six separate 175ml ramekins or little dishes and place them on a tray. Dot with fresh raspberries and blueberries. Cover with cling film and chill for 4 hours or until set.

Rhubarb compote: Cut 150g of slender pink rhubarb into 2.5cm lengths and put the pieces in a wide saucepan, large enough for the rhubarb to cover the base in a single layer. Sprinkle with 2 tablespoons caster sugar and 1 tablespoon cornflour and toss lightly. Pour over 4 tablespoons cold water and swish about the pan for a few seconds until the cornflour dissolves. Cover and place over a gentle heat. Cook for 4–5 minutes or until the rhubarb is tender but still holding its shape. Don't stir, but lift the pan and swirl the rhubarb occasionally as it cooks. Serve warm or cold. Serves 6 as a topping or 3 as a dessert. Calories per serving: 17 to serve 6; 33 to serve 3

220

orchard crumble

SERVES 6
PREP: 25 MINUTES
COOK: 50–60 MINUTES

450g Bramley cooking
apples, peeled, cored
and thickly sliced
4 plums (around 300g),
stoned and cut into
quarters
6 Conference pears, peeled,
quartered, cored and
thickly sliced
10g cornflour
25g demerara sugar
1 tsp grated lemon zest
(around ½ lemon)
½ tsp ground cinnamon
100ml unsweetened
apple juice

FOR THE CRUMBLE
1 egg white
100g porridge oats
(not jumbo)
50g white bread with
crust removed, torn
into small pieces
25g demerara sugar

Freeze the assembled
pudding in a freezer-
proof baking dish double
wrapped in foil, for up to
3 months. To serve, bake
from frozen as the recipe,
adding an extra 20 minutes
to the cooking time or until
the fruit is soft and the
topping golden. Cover with
foil if necessary to prevent
overbrowning.

This crumble has a bread-based topping rather than the
more traditional high-fat version. It still has plenty of crunch
but far fewer calories. It makes a lovely breakfast, as well as
a pudding, served with spoonfuls of fat-free natural yoghurt
or lower-fat custard (see below) and a drizzle of honey.

Preheat the oven to 200°C/Fan 180°C/Gas 6. To make the
filling, place the fruit, cornflour, sugar, lemon zest and cinnamon
in a bowl and toss together. Tip the mixture into a shallow
ovenproof dish and set aside.

To make the crumble topping, whisk the egg white with a metal
whisk until frothy and add the oats and bread pieces. Stir
gently to coat in the egg white.

Pour the apple juice over the fruit before scattering the
crumble topping over the top. Sprinkle the remaining sugar
over the top of the crumble and bake for 50–60 minutes or
until the topping is golden and the fruit is soft.

Lower-fat vanilla custard: Pour 350ml semi-skimmed milk
into a medium non-stick saucepan. Split a vanilla pod in half
lengthways and scrape the seeds into the pan. (Or add 1
teaspoon vanilla bean paste.) Bring to a gentle simmer, stirring
occasionally. Remove from the heat. Put 4 large egg yolks,
25g caster sugar and 1 tablespoon cornflour in a bowl and
beat with a metal whisk until mixed. Pour the warm milk over
the egg mixture, whisking until smooth. Return to the saucepan
and cook over a low heat for 4-5 minutes, stirring constantly
until the custard is thickened. Do not allow to overheat.
Serves 6. Calories per serving: 89

176
CALORIES
PER SERVING

vanilla cheesecake
with berries

SERVES 12

**PREP: 20 MINUTES,
PLUS COOLING AND
CHILLING TIME**

COOK: 40–50 MINUTES

oil, for spraying or brushing
750g ricotta cheese
75g caster sugar
2 tbsp cornflour
4 large eggs
2 large egg yolks
finely grated zest of 1 lemon
1 tsp vanilla extract
    (or vanilla bean paste)

TO SERVE
15g (about 2) Amaretti
    biscuits, lightly broken
    (optional)
100g raspberries
fresh mint leaves
½ tsp icing sugar

Shop-bought cheesecake can contain a massive number
of calories per serving. I've employed some smart tricks
here to reduce the calorie content to something much more
acceptable. Be sure to wrap the cake tin really well in foil
to stop any water seeping in.

Preheat the oven to 170°C/Fan 150°C/Gas 3½. Grease the sides
of a 23cm spring-clip cake tin and line with baking parchment.
Cover the outside of the tin with large pieces of foil to prevent
water getting in. Place the cake tin in a deep roasting tin.

Drain the ricotta cheese and put it in a mixing bowl. Mix the
sugar with the cornflour, then add the mixture to the ricotta.
Using an electric whisk, beat until well combined. Gradually
add the eggs and yolks, one at a time, whisking well in between
each addition. Stir in the lemon zest and vanilla. The mixture
will be very soft and light.

Pour the cheese mixture slowly into the prepared tin. Fill the
roasting tin with just-boiled water halfway up the cheesecake
tin. Carefully transfer the tin to the centre of the oven and bake
for 45–50 minutes. Do not allow the cheesecake to brown.
If it does start to brown while it is still very wobbly, cover the
tin loosely with a large piece of foil.

When the cheesecake is ready, turn the oven off and open
the door slightly. Wedge a folded tea towel or wooden spoon
in the door to keep it ajar and leave the cheesecake to cool
completely. This will take 3–4 hours and should prevent the
top from cracking. When the cake is completely cool, transfer
it to the fridge and chill for at least 2 hours before removing
it from the tin.

Slide a knife around the top of the cheesecake, cover with
a serving plate and turn over carefully onto the plate. Loosen
the sides and gently left the tin off. Remove the base and slowly
strip off the lining paper. Top with broken Amaretti biscuits,
raspberries, mint leaves and a light dusting of icing sugar.

186
CALORIES
PER SERVING

eve's pudding

SERVES 6

PREP: 20 MINUTES

COOK: 35 MINUTES

750g Bramley cooking
apples, peeled, cored
and cut into roughly
2–3cm chunks
250g fresh blackberries
100g caster sugar
½ tsp ground cinnamon
2 tbsp fresh lemon juice
finely grated zest of 1 lemon
2 large eggs
½ tsp vanilla extract
75g plain flour

There is something very comforting about sponge puddings
but they are usually a complete no-no when you are counting
calories. This one is a bit different as I've cut out all the fat and
kept the sugar to a minimum. Serve hot with a little cream or
my lower-fat vanilla custard (see page 166).

Preheat the oven to 200°C/Fan 180°C/Gas 6. Put the apples,
all but eight blackberries (for decoration), 50g of the sugar, the
cinnamon, lemon juice and zest in a saucepan. Stir to combine
the ingredients then cover and cook over a medium heat for 6–8
minutes, or until the fruit is soft but still holding its shape. Spoon
everything into a 1.5 litre ovenproof dish and leave to cool.

Put the eggs, the remaining sugar and vanilla extract in
a heatproof bowl and place over a pan of gently simmering
water. Using an electric whisk, whisk until the mixture is
pale, creamy and thick enough to leave a trail when you
lift the whisk.

Remove the bowl from the heat and sift over half the flour.
Gently fold it in using a large metal spoon. Sift over the
remaining flour and fold it in, being careful not to release any
air out of the mixture. Pour the sponge mixture over the fruit
and dot the reserved blackberries on top.

Bake in the centre of the oven for about 25 minutes or until the
sponge is well risen, golden and firm. Sprinkle with a little icing
sugar if you like (but don't forget to add the extra calories).
Serve warm with custard or cream.

324

chocolate bread and butter pudding

SERVES 6
PREP: 20 MINUTES, PLUS STANDING TIME
COOK: 40 MINUTES

400ml semi-skimmed milk
25g golden caster sugar, plus 1 heaped tsp for sprinkling
1 tsp finely grated orange zest
1 tsp vanilla extract (or vanilla bean paste)
220g chocolate chip brioche rolls (about 6), sliced in half lengthways
4 large egg yolks
2 large eggs
75ml double cream

This luscious pudding is great served after a weekend lunch. The chocolate brioche stays soft and silky inside while the top crisps beautifully. Although it contains far fewer calories than the traditional version, watch your serving size and don't be tempted to overindulge.

Pour the milk into a medium non-stick saucepan. Stir in the sugar, orange zest and vanilla extract. Bring to a gentle simmer, stirring occasionally, then remove the pan from the heat.

Arrange the brioche slices in a roughly 1.6 litre, shallow ovenproof dish, slightly upright but leaning against each other.

Whisk the egg yolks, whole eggs and cream together in a large jug or bowl until smooth. Strain the infused milk through a fine sieve onto the egg mixture and stir well to combine.

Pour the creamy liquid slowly over the brioche. The bread will float, so press it down gently with a spatula for a few seconds to help it absorb the custard. Leave to stand for 15 minutes. Preheat the oven to 180°C/Fan 160°C/Gas 4.

Put the dish in the centre of a roasting tin and sprinkle with the teaspoon of sugar. Pour enough just-boiled water around the outside of the dish to come halfway up the sides of the tin.

Bake for 30–35 minutes or until the custard is just set, but still just a little creamy in the centre, and the brioche is golden brown and crisp on top. Remove from the oven and, using an oven cloth, carefully lift the dish out of the water bath.

136
CALORIES
PER SERVING

rice pudding

SERVES 6
PREP: 5 MINUTES
COOK: 16–18 MINUTES

150g pudding rice
600ml semi-skimmed milk
500ml cold water
¼ whole nutmeg, finely
    grated, or ½ tsp ground
    nutmeg (optional)
1 tsp caster sugar

Rice pudding made with semi-skimmed milk and with just enough sugar to fool your taste buds. You can serve it warm with a spoonful of reduced sugar jam or cold with my juicy berry compote (see page 10).

Put the rice, milk, water and nutmeg if using in a large non-stick saucepan and bring to a gentle simmer over a medium heat. Cook for 16–18 minutes, stirring regularly, or until the rice is tender and the sauce is creamy – don't forget that it will continue to thicken as it cools. Stir frequently towards the end of the cooking time as it thickens.

Sweeten with a little caster sugar and serve warm. Alternatively, leave to cool, spoon into tumblers or dessert dishes and top with juicy berry compote for a refreshing, chilled dessert.

a few notes on the recipes

INGREDIENTS

Where possible, choose free-range chicken, meat and eggs. Eggs used in the recipes are medium unless otherwise stated.

All poultry and meat has been trimmed of as much hard or visible fat as possible, although there may be some marbling within the meat. Boneless, skinless chicken breasts weigh around 175g. Fish has been scaled, gutted and pin-boned, and large prawns are deveined. You'll be able to buy most fish and seafood ready prepared but ask your fishmonger if not and they will be happy to help.

PREPARATION

Do as much preparation as possible before you start to cook. Discard any damaged bits, and wipe or wash fresh produce before preparation unless it's going to be peeled.

Onions, garlic and shallots are peeled unless otherwise stated, and vegetables are trimmed. Lemons, limes and oranges should be well washed before the zest is grated. Weigh fresh herbs in a bunch, then trim off the stalks before chopping the leaves. I've used medium-sized vegetables unless stated. As a rule of thumb, a medium-sized onion and potato (such as Maris Piper) weighs around 150g.

All chopped and sliced meat, poultry, fish and vegetable sizes are approximate. Don't worry if your pieces are a bit larger or smaller than indicated, but try to keep to roughly the size so the cooking times are accurate. Even-sized pieces will cook at the same rate, which is especially important for meat and fish.

I love using fresh herbs in my recipes, but you can substitute frozen herbs in most cases. Dried herbs will give a different, more intense flavour, so use them sparingly.

The recipes have been tested using sunflower oil, but you can substitute vegetable, groundnut or mild olive oil. I use dark soy sauce in the test kitchen but it's fine to use light instead – it'll give a milder flavour.

CALORIE COUNTS

Nutritional information does not include the optional serving suggestions. When shopping, you may see calories described as kilocalories on food labels; they are the same thing.

HOW TO FREEZE

Freezing food will save you time and money, and lots of the dishes in this book freeze extremely well. If you don't need all the servings at the same time, freeze the rest for another day. Where there are no instructions for freezing a dish, freezing won't give the best results once reheated.

When freezing food, it's important to cool it rapidly after cooking. Separate what you want to freeze from what you're going to serve and place it in a shallow, freezer-proof container. The shallower the container, the quicker the food will cool (putting it in the freezer while it's still warm will raise the freezer temperature and could affect other foods). Cover loosely, then freeze as soon as it's cool.

If you're freezing a lot of food at once, for example after a bulk cooking session or a big shop, flip the fast freeze button on at least two hours before adding the new dishes and leave it on for twenty-four hours afterwards. This will reduce the temperature of your freezer and help ensure that food is frozen as rapidly as possible.

When freezing food, expel as much air as possible by wrapping it tightly in a freezer bag or foil to help prevent icy patches, freezer burn and discolouration, or flavour transfer between dishes. Liquids expand when frozen, so leave a 4–5cm gap at the top of containers.

If you have a small freezer and need to save space, flat-freeze thick soups, sauces and casseroles in strong zip-seal freezer bags. Fill the bag halfway, then turn it over and flatten it until it is around 1–2cm thick, pressing out as much air as possible and sealing firmly.

Place delicate foods such as breaded chicken or fish fillets and burgers on a tray lined with baking parchment, and freeze in a single layer until solid before placing in containers or freezer bags. This method is called open freezing and helps stop foods sticking together in a block, so you can grab what you need easily.

Label everything clearly, and add the date so you know when to eat it at its best. I aim to use food from the freezer within about four months.

DEFROSTING

For the best results, most foods should be defrosted slowly in the fridge for several hours or overnight. For safety's sake, do not thaw dishes at room temperature.

Flat-frozen foods (see above) will thaw and begin to reheat at almost the same time. Just rinse the bag under hot water and break the mixture into a wide-based pan. Add a dash of water and warm over a low heat until thawed. Increase the heat, adding a little more water if necessary, and simmer until piping hot throughout.

Ensure that any foods that have been frozen are thoroughly cooked or reheated before serving.

HOW TO GET THE BEST RESULTS

Measuring with spoons

Spoon measurements are level unless otherwise stated. Use a set of measuring spoons for the best results; they're endlessly useful, especially if you're watching your sugar, salt or fat intake.

1 tsp (1 teaspoon) = 5ml
1 dsp (1 dessertspoon) = 10ml
1 tbsp (1 tablespoon) = 15ml

A scant measure is just below level and a heaped measure is just above. An Australian tablespoon holds 20ml, so Australian cooks should use three level teaspoon measures instead.

CONVERSION CHARTS

Oven temperature guide

	Electricity °C	Electricity °F	Electricity (fan) °C	Gas Mark
Very cool	110	225	90	1/4
	120	250	100	1/2
Cool	140	275	120	1
	150	300	130	2
Moderate	160	325	140	3
	170	350	160	4
Moderately hot	190	375	170	5
	200	400	180	6
Hot	220	425	200	7
	230	450	210	8
Very hot	240	475	220	9

Liquid measurements

Metric	Imperial	Australian	US
25ml	1fl oz		
60ml	2fl oz	1/4 cup	1/4 cup
75ml	3fl oz		
100ml	3 1/2fl oz		
120ml	4fl oz	1/2 cup	1/2 cup
150ml	5fl oz		
180ml	6fl oz	3/4 cup	3/4 cup
200ml	7fl oz		
250ml	9fl oz	1 cup	1 cup
300ml	10 1/2fl oz	1 1/4 cups	1 1/4 cups
350ml	12 1/2fl oz	1 1/2 cups	1 1/2 cups
400ml	14fl oz	1 3/4 cups	1 3/2 cups
450ml	16fl oz	2 cups	2 cups
600ml	1 pint	2 1/2 cups	2 1/2 cups
750ml	1 1/4 pints	3 cups	3 cups
900ml	1 1/2 pints	3 1/2 cups	3 1/2 cups
1 litre	1 3/4 pints	1 quart or 4 cups	1 quart or 4 cups
1.2 litres	2 pints		
1.4 litres	2 1/2 pints		
1.5 litres	2 3/4 pints		
1.7 litres	3 pints		
2 litres	3 1/2 pints		

essential extras

Here's my list of suggested 50–150 calorie foods that you can use to supplement the 123 Plan. All calories listed in this list are approximate; a few wayward calories here and there won't make a difference to your allowance. See page 6 for more information on essential extras and how they fit into the plan. I've also listed some 'free' vegetable ideas, of which you can eat as much as you like! Make sure your plate is half filled with vegetables or salad, or serve them in a large bowl on the side. Eating more greens will help fill you up and provide lots of extra nutrients in your diet. Your skin will look better and the weight should drop off.

50 CALORIES PER SERVING

30g (about 5) ready-to-eat dried apricots
15g (1 tbsp) light mayo
30g (2 tbsp) hummus
40g drained artichoke antipasti in oil
60g whole olives

4 fresh apricots
200g fresh blackberries
200g fresh blackcurrants
100g fresh cherries
2 clementines or satsumas
100g fresh figs
½ grapefruit
85g grapes
2 kiwis
100g fresh mango
200g melon
1 medium nectarine
1 medium orange
1 medium peach
1 medium pear
125g fresh pineapple
100g canned pineapple in juice
2 plums
200g papaya
100g pomegranate seeds
200g raspberries
200g strawberries

100g fresh tomato salsa
50g tzatziki
1 level tbsp orange marmalade
1 level tbsp mango chutney
1 level tsp taramasalata
1 level tbsp honey

2cm slice (about 20g) ciabatta
1 x 10g rye crispbread, such as Ryvita
50g cooked puy lentils, green lentils
1 x measure (25ml) spirits (light or dark, e.g. rum, vodka)

1 tbsp single cream
1 tbsp half-fat crème fraiche
10g Parmesan
30g soft French goat's cheese
25g (1½ tbsp) light soft cheese
150ml orange juice (not from concentrate)
100ml regular soy milk
100g low-fat natural yoghurt
50g (about 3 wafer thin slices) of ham, turkey or chicken

75 CALORIES PER SERVING

150ml semi-skimmed milk
100g low-fat cottage cheese
25g (small wedge) Camembert
1 tbsp double cream
1 tbsp crème fraiche
50g ricotta cheese
¼ 125g ball of fresh mozzarella

¼ average avocado (35g)
50g smoked salmon
1 rasher back bacon, grilled or dry-fried
50g cooked, skinless chicken breast
100g cooked jumbo prawns (about 9)

1 medium apple
100g blueberries
25g dried mango

2 cream crackers
20g rice cakes (2 or 3)
20g plain breadsticks (about 4)
½ English muffin
1 slice medium white or brown bread
15g shop-bought (not takeaway) prawn crackers
1 oatcake

½ 160g tin tuna in brine, drained
40g sun-dried (or sun-blush) tomatoes in oil, drained
30g (2 tbsp) raisins
1 medium egg, boiled

100 CALORIES PER SERVING

1 large egg
40g feta cheese
100g plain cottage cheese
50g (2½ tbsp) soured cream
25g blue cheese
100ml fresh custard
25g cooking chorizo
30g ready-to-eat chorizo
    (about 5 thin slices)
25g salami (about 5 thin
    slices)
1 heaped tbsp pesto

45g Parma ham
    (about 3 slices)
30g smoked mackerel fillet
1 medium banana

1 level tbsp peanut butter
1 tbsp extra virgin olive oil
30g popping corn kernels
20g unsalted plain cashews
20g tortilla chips
25g wasabi peas

20g plain crisps

1 slice of thick cut bread
½ plain bagel
1 x 45g soft white bread roll
½ regular pitta bread
1 slice German style rye bread
1 crumpet
120g baked beans
45g dried couscous
30g dried wholewheat pasta
25g dried soba noodles
30g dried quinoa

125ml wine (white, red, rose)
125ml sparkling wine/
    Champagne
½ pint lager
½ pint bitter
½ pint dry cider

150 CALORIES PER SERVING

35g Cheddar cheese
100g skinless chicken breast,
    baked or grilled

100g cooked brown rice
115g cooked easy-cook white
    rice
40g dried basmati rice
1 potato, baked, boiled or
    mashed without fat
    (195g raw weight)
130g baked sweet potato
    (about ½ large potato)
40g dried rice noodles
50g dried egg noodles
100g cooked pasta
40g porridge oats
50g shop-bought naan bread
    (about ½)

25g unsalted almonds
175ml wine (not sparkling)

'FREE' SAUCES

Brown sauce, in moderation;
    each tbsp is 24 calories
Fish sauce (nam pla)
Ketchup, in moderation;
    each tbsp is 20 calories
Horseradish sauce
Hot sauce (Tabasco)
Mint sauce (not jelly)
Mustard, any variety (English,
    Dijon, wholegrain,
    American)
Soy sauce
Vinegars (balsamic, white
    wine, malt, etc.)
Worcestershire sauce

Any herbs or spices

'FREE' VEGETABLES

Artichokes, including tinned
    hearts (but not in oil)
Asparagus
Aubergine
Baby sweetcorn
Beans, any green (not baked)
    (French, runner, etc.)
Bean sprouts
Beetroot, fresh, cooked
    or pickled
Broccoli
Brussels sprouts
Butternut squash
Cabbage, all kinds
    (savoy, red, white)
Carrots
Cauliflower
Celeriac
Celery
Chicory
Chillies, including pickled
    jalapeños
Cornichons
Courgettes
Cucumber
Fennel
Garlic
Kale
Leeks
Lemons
Limes
Lettuce and salad greens
    (watercress, baby
    spinach, romaine)
Mangetout
Marrow
Mushrooms
Onions
Peppers
Pickled onions
Radishes
Shallots
Spring onions
Sugar snap peas
Swede
Tomatoes, including tinned
    (but not sun-dried)
Turnips

nutritional information
per serving

page 10 / serves 4
overnight porridge

212 energy (kcal)
897 energy (kJ)
9.0 protein (g)
32.4 carbohydrate (g)
4.9 fat (g)
1.8 saturated fat (g)
4.9 fibre (g)
15.2 sugars (g)

page 12 / serves 4
bircher muesli

188 energy (kcal)
793 energy (kJ)
7.4 protein (g)
26.9 carbohydrate (g)
5.8 fat (g)
0.9 saturated fat (g)
4.4 fibre (g)
16.3 sugars (g)

page 14 / serves 4
fluffy fruit pancakes

247 energy (kcal)
1049 energy (kJ)
8.8 protein (g)
51.0 carbohydrate (g)
2.2 fat (g)
0.9 saturated fat (g)
4.1 fibre (g)
19.0 sugars (g)

page 16 / makes 12
banana and blueberry muffins

145 energy (kcal)
612 energy (kJ)
4.2 protein (g)
22.6 carbohydrate (g)
4.8 fat (g)
1.0 saturated fat (g)
1.0 fibre (g)
6.5 sugars (g)

page 18 / serves 2
all-in-one breakfast

148 energy (kcal)
617 energy (kJ)
13.4 protein (g)
2.5 carbohydrate (g)
9.4 fat (g)
2.6 saturated fat (g)
2.1 fibre (g)
2.4 sugars (g)

page 20 / serves 2
scrambled eggs with smoked salmon

385 energy (kcal)
1607 energy (kJ)
29.5 protein (g)
18.4 carbohydrate (g)
20.7 fat (g)
7.3 saturated fat (g)
3.2 fibre (g)
2.2 sugars (g)

page 22 / serves 4
eggs benedict

320 energy (kcal)
1339 energy (kJ)
20.3 protein (g)
20.6 carbohydrate (g)
17.7 fat (g)
6.7 saturated fat (g)
0.9 fibre (g)
3.9 sugars (g)

page 26 / serves 4
smoked haddock chowder

266 energy (kcal)
1126 energy (kJ)
20.7 protein (g)
31.9 carbohydrate (g)
7.1 fat (g)
3.3 saturated fat (g)
3.6 fibre (g)
7.2 sugars (g)

page 28 / serves 4
minted pea soup with feta

145 energy (kcal)
605 energy (kJ)
9.1 protein (g)
9.8 carbohydrate (g)
7.9 fat (g)
4.8 saturated fat (g)
6.4 fibre (g)
3.7 sugars (g)

page 30 / serves 6
chunky minestrone

103 energy (kcal)
432 energy (kJ)
5.1 protein (g)
16.4 carbohydrate (g)
2.3 fat (g)
0.3 saturated fat (g)
5.3 fibre (g)
8.1 sugars (g)

page 32 / serves 4
chicken noodle soup

160 energy (kcal)
671 energy (kJ)
18.4 protein (g)
15.9 carbohydrate (g)
2.5 fat (g)
0.7 saturated fat (g)
1.8 fibre (g)
2.3 sugars (g)
*fresh chicken stock

page 34 / serves 6
french onion soup

188 energy (kcal)
791 energy (kJ)
7.4 protein (g)
31.4 carbohydrate (g)
4.9 fat (g)
2.0 saturated fat (g)
3.9 fibre (g)
9.3 sugars (g)

page 36 / serves 4
cream of tomato soup

122/23* energy (kcal)
510/97* energy (kJ)
3.5/0.4* protein (g)
14.5/0.5* carbohydrate (g)
6.0/2.2* fat (g)
2.2/1.4* saturated fat (g)
3.3/ fibre (g)
12.2/0.5* sugars (g)
*chive cream

page 40 / serves 6
rosemary roasted chicken

212 energy (kcal)
892 energy (kJ)
36.0 protein (g)
5.6 carbohydrate (g)
5.2 fat (g)
1.4 saturated fat (g)
1.6 fibre (g)
4.1 sugars (g)

page 42 / serves 4
chicken fajita bowls

357/17* energy (kcal)
1507/70* energy (kJ)
37.1/0.7* protein (g)
35.9/3.2* carb (g)
8.3/0.2* fat (g)
2.8/0.1* saturated fat (g)
5.1/1.0 fibre (g)
10.6/2.8* sugars (g)
*fresh tomato salsa

page 44 / serves 4
quick chicken kiev

251 energy (kcal)
1064 energy (kJ)
45.8 protein (g)
8.5 carbohydrate (g)
4.0 fat (g)
1.6 saturated fat (g)
0 fibre (g)
1.2 sugars (g)

page 46 / serves 6
chicken tetrazzini

339 energy (kcal)
1430 energy (kJ)
24.8 protein (g)
38.2 carbohydrate (g)
9.6 fat (g)
4.7 saturated fat (g)
4.4 fibre (g)
4.5 sugars (g)

page 48 / serves 6
jambalaya

347 energy (kcal)
1465 energy (kJ)
34.1 protein (g)
36.1 carbohydrate (g)
8.4 fat (g)
2.8 saturated fat (g)
3.0 fibre (g)
5.9 sugars (g)

page 50 / serves 4
one-pot chicken

423 energy (kcal)
1780 energy (kJ)
45.0 protein (g)
26.0 carbohydrate (g)
13.6 fat (g)
3.4 saturated fat (g)
11.4 fibre (g)
14.2 sugars (g)

page 52 / serves 6
chicken cacciatore

299 energy (kcal)
1260 energy (kJ)
48.3 protein (g)
9.1 carbohydrate (g)
6.0 fat (g)
1.4 saturated fat (g)
1.8 fibre (g)
5.3 sugars (g)

page 54 / serves 4
crispy chicken bites

259/29* energy (kcal)
1094/123* energy (kJ)
45.5/0.4* protein (g)
9.8//.2* carbohydrate (g)
4.5/0* fat (g)
1.1/0* saturated fat (g)
0/0.2* fibre (g)
0.6/7.0* sugars (g)
*sticky barbecue sauce

page 56 / serves 4
chicken, ham and leek filo pie

275 energy (kcal)
1163 energy (kJ)
31.2 protein (g)
27.9 carbohydrate (g)
4.2 fat (g)
1.3 saturated fat (g)
1.3 fibre (g)
3.5 sugars (g)

page 58 / serves 4
thai red chicken curry

322 energy (kcal)
1357 energy (kJ)
45.6 protein (g)
15.6 carbohydrate (g)
8.9 fat (g)
6.1 saturated fat (g)
3.7 fibre (g)
10.4 sugars (g)

page 62 / serves 6
roast beef, yorkshire puddings and gravy

375 energy (kcal)
1585 energy (kJ)
51.9 protein (g)
18.5 carbohydrate (g)
9.1 fat (g)
3.4 saturated fat (g)
0.8 fibre (g)
2.1 sugars (g)

page 64 / serves 6
chilli con carne

377 energy (kcal)
1585 energy (kJ)
43.5 protein (g)
24.4 carbohydrate (g)
10.4 fat (g)
4.1 saturated fat (g)
8.3 fibre (g)
9.1 sugars (g)

page 66 / serves 6
beef and guinness stew with dumplings

425 energy (kcal)
1783 energy (kJ)
40.2 protein (g)
29.0 carbohydrate (g)
15.5 fat (g)
6.5 saturated fat (g)
3.7 fibre (g)
9.8 sugars (g)

page 68 / serves 6
steak and mushroom pies

430 energy (kcal)
1800 energy (kJ)
35.7 protein (g)
30.0 carbohydrate (g)
17.8 fat (g)
7.9 saturated fat (g)
2.2 fibre (g)
3.4 sugars (g)

page 70 / serves 6
beef goulash

352 energy (kcal)
1477 energy (kJ)
46.3 protein (g)
11.3 carbohydrate (g)
13.6 fat (g)
5.0 saturated fat (g)
3.5 fibre (g)
10.0 sugars (g)

page 72 / serves 6
no-fuss cottage pie

302 energy (kcal)
1272 energy (kJ)
24.1 protein (g)
33.2 carbohydrate (g)
9.0 fat (g)
3.8 saturated fat (g)
6.4 fibre (g)
11.9 sugars (g)

page 74 / serves 4
swedish meatballs in gravy

324 energy (kcal)
1361 energy (kJ)
28.6 protein (g)
23.2 carbohydrate (g)
13.6 fat (g)
5.4 saturated fat (g)
1.8 fibre (g)
9.0 sugars (g)

page 76 / serves 6
**thow-it-together
beef lasagne**

374 energy (kcal)
1567 energy (kJ)
30.2 protein (g)
24.4 carbohydrate (g)
15.8 fat (g)
8.4 saturated fat (g)
4.4 fibre (g)
10.2 sugars (g)

page 78 / serves 6
pot roast beef

333 energy (kcal)
1403 energy (kJ)
47.8 protein (g)
13.6 carbohydrate (g)
7.7 fat (g)
2.5 saturated fat (g)
4.7 fibre (g)
11.4 sugars (g)

page 80 / serves 6
samosa pie

295 energy (kcal)
1241 energy (kJ)
21.5 protein (g)
34.5 carbohydrate (g)
8.3 fat (g)
3.3 saturated fat (g)
3.6 fibre (g)
8.7 sugars (g)

page 82 / serves 6
lazy lamb tagine

345 energy (kcal)
1450 energy (kJ)
33.2 protein (g)
25.6 carbohydrate (g)
12.9 fat (g)
4.8 saturated fat (g)
6.1 fibre (g)
14.4 sugars (g)

page 84 / serves 6
moussaka

359 energy (kcal)
1505 energy (kJ)
25.5 protein (g)
20.5 carbohydrate (g)
18.3 fat (g)
8.8 saturated fat (g)
4.4 fibre (g)
11.8 sugars (g)

page 86 / serves 6
lamb and lentil curry

332 energy (kcal)
1391 energy (kJ)
33.2 protein (g)
20.8 carbohydrate (g)
13.4 fat (g)
4.9 saturated fat (g)
3.3 fibre (g)
8.5 sugars (g)

page 90 / serves 6
**roast loin of pork with
braised fennel**

329 energy (kcal)
1389 energy (kJ)
48.2 protein (g)
8.9 carbohydrate (g)
9.2 fat (g)
3.1 saturated fat (g)
3.9 fibre (g)
7.5 sugars (g)

page 92 / serves 4
**tex mex
toad-in-the hole**

454 energy (kcal)
1902 energy (kJ)
24.9 protein (g)
38.4 carbohydrate (g)
23.1 fat (g)
8.5 saturated fat (g)
5.7 fibre (g)
14.6 sugars (g)

page 94 / serves 4
**smoky sausage and
beans**

412 energy (kcal)
1729 energy (kJ)
31.6 protein (g)
37.0 carbohydrate (g)
15.9 fat (g)
5.4 saturated fat (g)
14.0 fibre (g)
15.6 sugars (g)

page 96 / serves 2
**braised peas with
lettuce and bacon**

239 energy (kcal)
1000 energy (kJ)
18.2 protein (g)
17.3 carbohydrate (g)
11.2 fat (g)
5.5 saturated fat (g)
12.0 fibre (g)
6.9 sugars (g)

page 98 / serves 4
**sticky pork steaks
with coleslaw**

327/119* energy (kcal)
1378/505* energy (kJ)
36.6/3.0* protein (g)
21.1/25* carb (g)
11.2/1.0* fat (g)
2.7/0.1* sat fat (g)
3.6/2.6* fibre (g)
19.8/0.9* sugars (g)
*oven baked chips

page 100 / serves 2
**chorizo with
butter beans**

217 energy (kcal)
912 energy (kJ)
13.6 protein (g)
25.7 carbohydrate (g)
7.4 fat (g)
2.6 saturated fat (g)
9.8 fibre (g)
9.1 sugars (g)

page 104 / serves 2
**creamy scallops
with bacon**

313 energy (kcal)
1307 energy (kJ)
30.6 protein (g)
8.4 carbohydrate (g)
17.5 fat (g)
9.1 saturated fat (g)
5.3 fibre (g)
5.5 sugars (g)

page 106 / serves 6
tuna fishcakes

188 energy (kcal)
793 energy (kJ)
9.6 protein (g)
31.6 carb (g)
3.4 fat (g)
0.6 saturated fat (g)
2.6 fibre (g)
1.8 sugars (g)

page 108 / serves 6
**tuna and sweetcorn
pasta**

258 energy (kcal)
1089 energy (kJ)
16.9 protein (g)
29.7 carbohydrate (g)
8.5 fat (g)
4.9 saturated fat (g)
2.2 fibre (g)
7.3 sugars (g)

page 110 / serves 2
sticky mango salmon

299 energy (kcal)
1246 energy (kJ)
30.7 protein (g)
4.8 carbohydrate (g)
17.5 fat (g)
3.0 saturated fat (g)
0.7 fibre (g)
4.5 sugars (g)

page 112 / serves 4
beer battered fish

376 energy (kcal)
1583 energy (kJ)
39.5 protein (g)
30.9 carbohydrate (g)
10.1 fat (g)
1.3 saturated fat (g)
1.2 fibre (g)
1.3 sugars (g)

page 114 / serves 4
fish soup with rouille

398 energy (kcal)
1671 energy (kJ)
42.1 protein (g)
29.0 carbohydrate (g)
10.7 fat (g)
1.5 saturated fat (g)
5.2 fibre (g)
9.9 sugars (g)

page 116 / serves 2
pan-fried pepper squid & lime chilli mayo

212 energy (kcal)
893 energy (kJ)
17.6 protein (g)
15.7 carbohydrate (g)
9.2 fat (g)
1.4 saturated fat (g)
0 fibre (g)
2.7 sugars (g)

page 118 / serves 4
baked seabass with peppers and pine nuts

287 energy (kcal)
1205 energy (kJ)
31.8 protein (g)
13.4 carbohydrate (g)
12.1 fat (g)
1.5 saturated fat (g)
1.3 fibre (g)
3.8 sugars (g)

page 120 / serves 4
creamy fish gratin

263 energy (kcal)
1111 energy (kJ)
37.0 protein (g)
19.0 carbohydrate (g)
4.8 fat (g)
2.3 saturated fat (g)
2.1 fibre (g)
6.6 sugars (g)

page 124 / serves 4
chicken caesar salad

234 energy (kcal)
980 energy (kJ)
26.8 protein (g)
10.9 carbohydrate (g)
9.5 fat (g)
2.6 saturated fat (g)
2.1 fibre (g)
3.0 sugars (g)

page 126 / serves 2
cobb salad

347/65* energy (kcal)
1448/269* energy (kJ)
30.4/2.6* protein (g)
11.5/1.4* carbohydrate (g)
20.3/5.5* fat (g)
5.1/2.4* saturated fat (g)
6.5 fibre (g)
9.8/1.1* sugars (g)
*blue cheese dressing

page 128 / serves 4
smoked mackerel, fennel and orange salad

258 energy (kcal)
1078 energy (kJ)
12.2 protein (g)
21.8 carbohydrate (g)
14.4 fat (g)
2.9 saturated fat (g)
6.5 fibre (g)
20.3 sugars (g)

page 130 / serves 6
argentinian roast beef salad

243 energy (kcal)
1027 energy (kJ)
40.1 protein (g)
4.9 carbohydrate (g)
7.1 fat (g)
2.3 saturated fat (g)
2.5 fibre (g)
4.7 sugars (g)

page 132 / serves 4
skinny potato salad

155 energy (kcal)
654 energy (kJ)
3.8 protein (g)
25.9 carbohydrate (g)
4.8 fat (g)
0.8 saturated fat (g)
3.3 fibre (g)
10.3 sugars (g)

page 134 / serves 4
roasted pepper, mozzarella and bean salad

260 energy (kcal)
1082 energy (kJ)
14.8 protein (g)
18.4 carbohydrate (g)
14.4 fat (g)
4.1 saturated fat (g)
4.3 fibre (g)
8.1 sugars (g)

page 138 / serves 4
roasted squash, tomato and spinach lasagne

438 energy (kcal)
1847 energy (kJ)
19.2 protein (g)
60.4 carbohydrate (g)
15.1 fat (g)
7.4 saturated fat (g)
9.1 fibre (g)
24.6 sugars (g)

page 140 / serves 2
golden split pea dahl

371/28* energy (kcal)
1573/117* energy (kJ)
23.6/2.6* protein (g)
65.5/4.2* carb (g)
3.4/0.2* fat (g)
0.5 saturated fat (g)
9.9/0.4* fibre (g)
6.7/3.8* sugars (g)
*minted yoghurt

page 142 / serves 4
macaroni cheese in a hurry

394 energy (kcal)
1667 energy (kJ)
18.9 protein (g)
56.7 carbohydrate (g)
11.9 fat (g)
7.0 saturated fat (g)
3.4 fibre (g)
10.4 sugars (g)

page 144 / serves 4
primavera risotto

369 energy (kcal)
1561 energy (kJ)
12.6 protein (g)
66.1 carbohydrate (g)
4.4 fat (g)
2.0 saturated fat (g)
4.7 fibre (g)
4.1 sugars (g)

page 146 / serves 6
arrabbiatta pasta

290 energy (kcal)
1229 energy (kJ)
13.4 protein (g)
49.1 carbohydrate (g)
3.5 fat (g)
1.3 saturated fat (g)
4.0 fibre (g)
10.9 sugars (g)

page 148 / serves 4
vietnamese aubergine, sweet potato and green bean curry

271 energy (kcal)
1136 energy (kJ)
4.8 protein (g)
37.0 carbohydrate (g)
12.5 fat (g)
8.2 saturated fat (g)
8.1 fibre (g)
16.0 sugars (g)

page 150 / serves 4
roasted vegetable tart

385 energy (kcal)
1607 energy (kJ)
12.2 protein (g)
40.6 carbohydrate (g)
19.8 fat (g)
10.3 saturated fat (g)
3.0 fibre (g)
7.3 sugars (g)

page 152 / serves 4
aubergine parmigiana

225 energy (kcal)
946 energy (kJ)
12.6 protein (g)
17.6 carbohydrate (g)
9.4 fat (g)
4.4 saturated fat (g)
7.6 fibre (g)
11.8 sugars (g)

page 156 / serves 6
cappuccino chocolate pots

226 energy (kcal)
941 energy (kJ)
3.9 protein (g)
20.3 carbohydrate (g)
14.5 fat (g)
8.6 saturated fat (g)
0.3 fibre (g)
16.9 sugars (g)

page 158 / serves 5
tropical eton mess

258 energy (kcal)
1087 energy (kJ)
3.9 protein (g)
38.4 carbohydrate (g)
10.9 fat (g)
6.7 saturated fat (g)
2.2 fibre (g)
37.8 sugars (g)

page 160 / serves 6
bakewell pudding

296 energy (kcal)
1241 energy (kJ)
11.7 protein (g)
28.1 carbohydrate (g)
16.2 fat (g)
2.7 saturated fat (g)
2.6 fibre (g)
22.7 sugars (g)

page 162 / serves 6
missippi mud pie

155 energy (kcal)
656 energy (kJ)
7.7 protein (g)
15.1 carbohydrate (g)
7.5 fat (g)
4.6 saturated fat (g)
0.6 fibre (g)
14.6 sugars (g)

page 164 / serves 6
panna cotta

155/17* energy (kcal)
656/72* energy (kJ)
7.7/0.2* protein (g)
15.1/4.2* carbohydrate (g)
7.5/0* fat (g)
4.6/0* saturated fat (g)
0.6/0.7* fibre (g)
14.6/3.7* sugars (g)
*rhubarb compote

page 166 / serves 6
orchard crumble

220/89* energy (kcal)
932/372* energy (kJ)
3.6/3.9* protein (g)
48.6/8.3* carb (g)
2.0/4.7* fat (g)
0.3/1.7* sat fat (g)
6.7/0* fibre (g)
33.4/7.1* sugars (g)
*lower-fat vanilla custard

page 168 / serves 12
vanilla cheesecake with berries

176 energy (kcal)
734 energy (kJ)
9.4 protein (g)
10.6 carbohydrate (g)
10.9 fat (g)
5.6 saturated fat (g)
0.3 fibre (g)
8.3 sugars (g)

page 170 / serves 6
eve's pudding

186 energy (kcal)
785 energy (kJ)
4.6 protein (g)
37.4 carbohydrate (g)
2.9 fat (g)
0.7 sat fat (g)
4.1 fibre (g)
27.9 sugars (g)

page 172 / serves 6
chocolate bread and butter pudding

324 energy (kcal)
1353 energy (kJ)
10.7 protein (g)
27.2 carbohydrate (g)
19.2 fat (g)
8.2 saturated fat (g)
1.0 fibre (g)
14.3 sugars (g)

page 174 / serves 6
rice pudding

136 energy (kcal)
575 energy (kJ)
5.0 protein (g)
25.0 carbohydrate (g)
1.8 fat (g)
1.1 saturated fat (g)
0.4 fibre (g)
5.4 sugars (g)

index

First published in Great Britain in 2015
by Orion Publishing Group Ltd
Orion House, 5 Upper St Martin's Lane
London WC2H 9EA
An Hachette UK Company

10 9 8 7 6 5 4 3 2 1

Text © Justine Pattison 2015
Design and layout © Orion 2015

A CIP catalogue record for this book is available
from the British Library.
ISBN: 978 1 4091 5469 3

Designer: Smith & Gilmour
Photographer: Cristian Barnett
Props stylist: Claire Bignell
Creative director: Justine Pattison
Nutritional analysis calculated by: Lauren Brignell
Recipe assistants: Kirsty Thomas, Vanessa Graham
Kitchen assistants: Jess Blain, Emily PB
Project editor: Jillian Young
Copy editor: Elise See Tai
Proofreader: Mary-Jane Wilkins
Indexer: Rosemary Dear

Printed and bound in China

*Every effort has been made to ensure that the
information in this book is accurate. The information
will be relevant to the majority of people but may not
be applicable in each individual case, so it is advised
that professional medical advice is obtained for
specific health matters. Neither the publisher nor
author accept any legal responsibility for any personal
injury or other damage or loss arising from the use or
misuse of the information in this book. Anyone making
a change in their diet should consult their GP,
especially if pregnant, infirm, elderly or under 16.*

The Orion Publishing Group's policy is to use
papers that are natural, renewable and recyclable
products and made from wood grown in sustainable
forests. The logging and manufacturing processes
are expected to conform to the environmental
regulations of the country of origin.

www.orionbooks.co.uk

Acknowledgements

Firstly, huge thanks to everyone who enjoys my
recipes and the way I cook. You have given me such
fantastic feedback; I hope you like these dishes just
as much.

I'm truly grateful to the very talented photographer
Cristian Barnett for wonderful photographs that really
make my food come to life. And the brilliant Claire
Bignell for her superb creative skills, selecting the
perfect props and helping make the recipes look
both beautiful and achievable.

Massive thanks to Lauren Brignell for all her invaluable
nutritional support and the hundreds of recipes she has
analysed over the past few months. Also, thanks to the
extremely hard-working Kirsty Thomas and Vanessa
Graham for carefully testing the recipes and assisting
on shoot days. Your skill and input has been invaluable.

At Orion, I would like to thank Amanda Harris for
believing in this project right from the beginning and
for trusting me to get on and develop the series. Also
thank you to Jillian Young, my fantastic editor, for her
guidance and professionalism and Helen Ewing for
her design support.

A big thank you to everyone at Smith & Gilmour for
making the books look eye-catching, practical and
readable. I'm also grateful to my agent, Zoe King, at
The Blair Partnership, for her constant encouragement
and enthusiasm.

And, a final thank you to my family and friends:
Angela, Ann, Angie, Bella, Charlotte, Clare, Emma,
Michelle, Rachel, Sarah and Tamsin for their
unwavering support.

Thank you to Kitchen Aid for kindly lending me
their brilliant mixers, blenders and food processors
for recipe testing.